# The Software Industry in Emerging Markets

# The Software Industry in Emerging Markets

*Edited by*

Simon Commander

**Edward Elgar**
Cheltenham, UK • Northampton, MA, USA

Published by
Edward Elgar Publishing Limited
Glensanda House
Montpellier Parade
Cheltenham
Glos GL50 1UA
UK

Edward Elgar Publishing, Inc.
136 West Street
Suite 202
Northampton
Massachusetts 01060
USA

A catalogue record for this book
is available from the British Library

ISBN 1 84542 247 3

Printed and bound in Great Britain by MPG Books Ltd, Bodmin, Cornwall

# Contents

# Figures

# Tables

# Boxes

# Contributors

**Alfredo Behrens** works in the area of technology and technology transfer and is based in São Paulo, Brazil. He holds a PhD from Cambridge University and he has held positions at Princeton University and Florida State University. He worked at the World Bank in Washington DC and currently advises public officials, shareholders and board members of banks and large corporations and clients in both the private and public sector in the Americas, East and Western Europe and Southern Africa.

**Simon Commander** is Director of the Centre for New and Emerging Markets (CNEM) at London Business School and Adviser, European Bank of Reconstruction and Development. He holds a BA from Oxford University and a PhD from Cambridge University. He previously worked at the World Bank, and at EBRD he is one of the editors of the Annual Transition Report. He has published widely in both research journals and in books.

**Ashok V. Desai** is Consultant Editor of the Calcutta daily, *The Telegraph*, and writes in the *Business World* magazine on economic events in India. Previously he was Consultant Editor of *Business Standard,* a financial daily. He served as Chief Consultant in the Finance Ministry of India from 1991 to 1993, and helped design the early Indian economic reforms, especially in taxation, trade policy and regulation of financial markets. In the 1970s, he taught and researched at Sussex University as well as at the University of the South Pacific in Fiji. He also worked at the National Council of Applied Economic Research in Delhi. His recent books are *The Price of Onions* (Penguin 2000), and *My Economic Affair* (Wiley Eastern 1994).

**Susanna Khavul** is an assistant professor at the London Business School. Her research programme focuses on explaining the innovative performance of high-technology firms operating in a global economy. She is the winner of the Academy of Management's 2001 Heizer Award for 'Outstanding Research in the Field of New Enterprise Development' and the Taylor & Francis Publisher's 2002 Award for 'Best Research on

Venture Capital'. She was previously a member of a venture capital and investment banking boutique that specialised in high-technology finance, as well as working for a time with George Soros. She has a BA in Economics from the University of California, Berkeley and a PhD in Strategic Management from Boston University.

**Xiaohong (Iris) Quan** is currently a PhD candidate at the University of California, Berkeley. Her research interests are in technology and innovation management, multinational corporations' research and development activities, competitive strategy, and urban and regional economic development. Her recent research projects and publications have revolved around high-tech industries. She holds a Master's Degree in Economics.

**AnnaLee Saxenian** is Dean of the School of Information Management and Systems (SIMS) and Professor in the Department of City and Regional Planning at the University of California, Berkeley. She holds a PhD in Political Science from MIT, a Master's in Regional Planning from the University of California, Berkeley, and a BA in Economics from Williams College in Massachusetts. She is an expert in regional economic development and information technology, and has published extensively on the social and economic organization of production in technology regions like Silicon Valley. Her current research explores how immigrant engineers and scientists are transferring technology entrepreneurship to regions in Asia. Her publications include *Regional Advantage: Culture and Competition in Silicon Valley and Route 128* (Harvard University Press, 1994), *Silicon Valley's New Immigrant Entrepreneurs* (Public Policy Institute of California, 1999), and *Local and Global Networks of Immigrant Professionals in Silicon Valley* (Public Policy Institute of California, 2002).

# Acknowledgements

This research has been supported by the Centre for New and Emerging Markets at London Business School. The editor would like to thank Kerrie Quirk and Anna Malaczynska, at CNEM, for wonderful support throughout the project. Kerrie Quirk and Leann Player have had the unenviable task of putting the entire manuscript into camera-ready-copy, and have done a superb job. Thanks also to Paul Ellis for editorial assistance. For financial support we thank the UK Department for International Development who supported the work under DfID/DRC project no. R7844.

Susanna Khavul would like to thank Herve Andre Durand, Jacob Greenblatt, Emily Ng, Roy Wetzberger, and CongCong Zheng for their contributions at different stages.

Alfredo Behrens would like to thank Circe Monteiro, of UFPe, Jose Cavalcanti of FUNDEPE, Claudio Marinho of SECTMA and Softex for support. Also, Joaquim Celestino Jr. of INSOFT, Paulo Tosta da Silva of FINEP and Carlos Castelo Branco of BNDES. Dr. Kaizô Beltrão's help was key in providing access to IBGE and the Ministry of Labour's data. Thanks also to Mr. Descartes Teixeira of CITS, Eliane D'Ippolito, whose research assistance was essential. Maria de Lourdes Delgado also provided excellent research assistance.

Anna-Lee Saxenian would like to thank Tang Huihao, former post doc at UC Berkeley, who provided extensive insight into the Chinese software industry and economy.

The UK Department for International Development (DFID) supports policies, programmes and projects to promote international development. DFID provided funds for this study as part of that objective but the views and opinions expressed here are those of the authors alone.

# Abbreviations

| | |
|---|---|
| APTECH | Company name |
| ASSESSPRO | Brazilian Association of Software Developers |
| BNDES | Banco Nacional de Desenvolvimento Economico e Social |
| CDAC | Centre for Development of Advanced Computing (India |
| CMM | Carnegie Mellow Capability Maturity Model |
| DSP | Digital signal processing |
| EDI | Electronic data interchange |
| EFY | EFY Enterprises |
| EIT | Enterprise income tax |
| ERT | Enterprise resource planning |
| FINEP | Financiadora de Estodos e Projetos |
| GAAP | The USA auditing standard |
| ICT | Information and communications technology |
| IDC | International Data Corporation (China) |
| IPO | Initial public offer (of shares by a company) |
| IPR | Intellectual property rights |
| ITES | Information technology-enabled services |
| MIS | Management Information Systems |
| MOU | Memorandum of Understanding |
| NASSCOM | National Association of Software and Service Companies (India) |
| NGO | Non-governmental organisation |
| NIIT | Company name |
| NPL | Non-performing loans |
| OECD | Organisation for Economic Co-operation and Development |
| PPB | Portuguese abbreviation for Basic Production Process |
| SEBRAE | Brazil's small and medium-sized enterprise support organization |
| SGKI | Subject Group on Knowledge-based Industries (India) |
| SOC | System-on-a-chip |
| SOE | State-owned enterprises |
| STP | Software technology park |
| STPI | Software technology parks of India (government company set up to run software technology parks) |
| TASE | Tel Aviv Stock Exchange |

| VAR | Value added reseller |
| VC | Venture capital |
| VSAT | Very small aperture terminal (a device for long-distance wireless communication and data transmission) |
| WTO | World Trade Organisation |

# 1. What Explains the Growth of a Software Industry in Some Emerging Markets?

## Simon Commander

### INTRODUCTION

The last twenty-five years have seen an explosive growth in the software industry. From a rudimentary base in the 1970s, the global software market now exceeds $370 billion. Annual growth in the global software industry has been above 15 per cent since the early 1990s and remains on a rising trend, particularly in some emerging market economies. In the USA, which has remained the leading country, their software sector accounts for nearly half of global sales, with Western Europe accounting for roughly a third. Despite setbacks associated with the post-2000 fallout from the collapse in equity values, particularly in the technology sector, software remains among the most rapidly growing industries in the OECD. Both packaged software and software services have likewise seen a growth in their share of aggregate IT sales.

One striking and, as yet, only partially acknowledged phenomenon has been that the software industry has developed and expanded dramatically in a number of countries outside the core of the advanced economies of North America, Europe and Japan. The share of developing countries in the global software market has risen and now accounts for around 5 per cent of sales.[1] A small number of developing countries have successfully developed their own software industries and have, in some cases, continued to strengthen the sector even post-2000. This growth in software activity has in part been attributable to the relatively low entry barriers operating in the industry, relatively high local human capital and strong cost advantages favouring developing countries. Software also has relatively low physical capital requirements – being mainly labour intensive – a feature that obviously plays to the advantage of developing countries. Even so, this has occurred despite the fact that the bulk of the developing economies that have seen strong software growth remain relatively rich in unskilled labour and at fairly low levels of aggregate development.

Clearly countries that may be poorly endowed with physical capital but have a significant stock of educated labour may choose to specialise in skill-intensive activity, rather than in the labour-intensive production associated with abundant unskilled labour. However, for that to happen may also require supportive government policy to ensure that the high-skill activity can get off the ground. For example, in the context of East Asia, Rodrik (1994) has argued that public interventions that raised educational levels and improved coordination supported, rather than replaced, the market and may have been key in allowing the shift toward higher-skill activity. In the case of software the combination of efficient communications and information flows and investment in human capital, primarily financed by the public sector have played major roles.

Possibly the most striking case among developing countries has been India, where the growth of a skilled labour-intensive software sector has been dramatic and where much of the growth has been generated by domestic rather than foreign firms. Over the 1990s the sector expanded at an average annual rate of over 40 per cent. And although by 2000 the software sector only accounted for around 1 per cent of national income and less than 0.5 per cent of total urban employment, exports accounted for over 75 per cent of sales and around 7 per cent of the total value of Indian merchandise exports.[2] Further, export growth has remained strong at around 30 per cent for 2002. This expansion has occurred in a period of economic liberalisation, but – it is important to note – one where trade restraints and limitations on competition have remained pervasive. Indeed, some commentators consider it to be an anomaly.[3]

Yet India has not been alone. Brazil and China have seen sharp increases in growth for their software sectors and a steep rise in the skill content of output, if not necessarily of exports. In both instances, there has also been strong growth in IT manufacturing. In the Chinese case, in particular, their strength has principally been in hardware and manufacturing. Again, while liberalisation has been proceeding over the period in which such growth has been strongest, these local environments remain marked by substantial regulation and constraints on trade. Moreover, the fact that all these settings suffer from major deficiencies in the protection of intellectual property rights makes these changes all the more remarkable, given the danger that investors may have their ability to appropriate returns undermined by such deficiencies. Then there is the case of Israel. While hardly a developing country, Israel nevertheless provides some interesting lessons for developing countries that seek to raise the profile of their software – and more generally their high-technology – sectors, not least through the mix of openness to external markets and ideas, as well as supportive public policy.

This chapter provides an overview of these disparate developments and locations – Brazil, China, India and Israel. As will become clear, despite a common engagement with software, they remain very heterogeneous in their attributes, as well as in the local dynamics of the industry. The chapter concentrates on trying to answer three important questions. Why is it that some developing countries have successfully spawned and sustained dynamic software industries? Is the industry likely to act as an engine for growth in these developing countries or is it likely to be a set of enclaves? Finally, what – if any – lessons concerning replicability do these examples hold for other developing countries?

The chapter is organised as follows: Section 1.1 provides some basic information on the four countries. Section 1.2 contains an overview of what the software industry looks like in these different countries and any changes that have occurred over time. Section 1.3 then turns explicitly to the role of public policy in sponsoring or impeding the growth of the industry over the recent past. Section 1.4 looks at the locational features of the industry – in particular, the strong agglomeration that has occurred – and the degree to which it has induced spillovers to the rest of the economy. Section 1.5 looks at how some emerging market firms have managed to build reputation and exposure in export markets. Section 1.6 turns to the important issue of the mobility of skilled software labour across borders and, in particular, looks at whether this constitutes a brain drain for developing countries. Section 1.7 concludes.

## 1.1 COUNTRY CHARACTERISTICS

Table 1.1 brings together some summary numbers for the four countries as well as for some advanced economy comparators. What is evident is that the four countries under review have some very different properties. In terms of income per capita and other indicators, the distance between Israel and the advanced economies of Europe and North America is relatively slight. By contrast, India's income per head (in purchasing power parity terms) remains under 7 per cent of the USA level while China's income is only just over 11 per cent. Brazil is an intermediate case. Two commonly used measures of human capital – gross tertiary enrolment rates and average years of schooling – similarly show wide divergences. In India and China enrolment rates are no greater than 6 per cent, as opposed to 50 per cent in Israel and France, while average years of schooling are also notably lower than in the advanced

Table 1.1  *Country characteristics*

| | Brazil | China | India | Israel | USA | France |
|---|---|---|---|---|---|---|
| **GDP and Education** | | | | | | |
| GDP per capita in 2000 (PPP$) | 7300 | 3920 | 2400 | 19 930 | 34 100 | 24 420 |
| Education, Gross Tertiary Enrolment rate (1998) | 14 | 6 | 6 | 49 | 77 | 51 |
| Average Years of Schooling (1999/2000) | 4.9 | 6.4 | 5.1 | 9.6 | 12.0 | 7.9 |
| **PC and Internet Access (2000)** | | | | | | |
| PCs (per 1000 population) | 44.1 | 15.9 | 4.5 | 253.6 | 585.2 | 304.3 |
| Internet Users (% population) | 3 | 2 | 0.5 | 20 | 34 | 15 |
| Service Provider Charge ($) | 22 | 7 | 10 | 11 | 5 | 20 |
| Telephone User Charge ($) | 0.9 | 0.14 | 0.18 | 0.18 | 3.5 | 0 |
| ICT Expenditure to GDP (%) | 8.4 | 5.4 | 3.8 | 7.4 | 8.1 | 8.7 |
| **Telecommunications (2000)** | | | | | | |
| Telephones (per 1000 population) | 182 | 112 | 32 | 482 | 700 | 579 |
| Mobile Phones (per 1000 population) | 136 | 66 | 4 | 658 | 493 | 398 |
| Cost of Local Calls ($ per 3 minutes) | 0.03 | 0.0 | 0.01 | 0.05 | 0.0 | 0.10 |
| Cost of Call to USA ($ per 3 minutes) | 108 | 6.7 | 4.2 | 3.3 | n.a | 1.0 |

*Notes:*
Per 1000 population.
Service Provider Charge: costs for 30 off-peak hours of dial-up Internet access per month.
Telephone User Charge: costs of 30 off-peak hours of telephonic use while logged on to Internet.

*Source:*  World Bank (2002).

Table 1.2 Macroeconomic data, 1999-2002

| | Brazil | China | India | Israel |
|---|---|---|---|---|
| **GDP growth** | | | | |
| 1990-2000 (av) | 2.9 | 10.3 | 6.0 | 5.1 |
| 2001/2002 | 1.0 | 7.5 | 5.0 | -1.1 |
| **Inflation** | | | | |
| 1990-2000 (av) | 199.5 | 8.6 | 9.1 | 9.7 |
| 2001/2002 | 7.4 | 0.2 | 4.0 | 3.8 |
| **Overall budget balance (% of GDP)** | | | | |
| 1990-2000 (av) | -6.1 | -2.1 | -5.5 | -3.0 |
| 2001/2002 | -7.6 | -3.0 | -5.6 | -4.3 |
| **Foreign direct investment (% of gross capital formation)** | | | | |
| 1990 | 1.1 | 2.8 | 0.2 | 1.1 |
| 2000 | 26.9 | 9.5 | 2.1 | 20.6 |

Source: International Financial Statistics (various years).

countries or in Israel. Turning to communications infrastructure – a key requirement for high-technology industries and software in particular – it is also evident that access to telephones and personal computers remains very restricted in Brazil, India and China. Indeed, in India telephones and personal computers per thousand population remain as low as 32 and 4.5 respectively. And only between 0.5-3 per cent of India, China and Brazil's populations are Internet users. However, in all these countries the share of ICT expenditure in GDP has risen and, for example, in the case of Brazil is now comparable to the advanced countries.

In terms of macroeconomic aggregates, Table 1.2 shows that since the 1990s there have been some similarities – notably a trend toward lower inflation rates – but also significant differences in performance across this group of countries. Growth in China has been particularly robust, while – at least when compared with the previous decade – Indian growth also accelerated notably. Both countries have maintained high growth even after 2000. By contrast, Brazilian growth remained modest through the 1990s with further recent deceleration as the economy was held back by major fiscal imbalances and substantial debt accumulation. In Israel, the impact of the slowdown, particularly in the USA, has been significant and combined with the conflict with the Palestinians has led the economy to decline in size. All countries have run fiscal deficits with off-budget obligations – as in China and Brazil in the 1990s – swelling the size of the imbalance. Interestingly, the table also shows that over the last decade the share of foreign direct investment in gross capital formation jumped massively in both Israel and Brazil, and grew significantly in China and, to a lesser extent, in India. This has been part of the wider opening of these economies over the decade. Certainly, in both Brazil and Israel, these large jumps in investment were the fruit of successful stabilisation programmes and these in turn were, as will become clear, key in driving the IT sector forward in both places, but particularly in Israel.

Table 1.3 provides some basic information on the software economies in these countries. It can readily be seen that all have experienced very strong growth through the 1990s with, however, a significant deceleration after 2000. From a low base, Chinese software grew at over 65 per cent per annum through the 1990s. Further, both Chinese and Indian software sales have continued to grow at over 20 per cent per annum after 2000. What also stands out is the particularly strong export profile of the Indian and Israeli software sectors. By 2001 nearly 80 per cent of India's software sales were exports. By contrast, both Brazil and China have had very small export exposures and, at least in the case of Brazil, a relatively small change over the past decade.

In short, the software industry has expanded very rapidly from a low base in these four countries over the last decade. However, this growth has

*Table 1.3 Software industry descriptive statistics*

| | Brazil | China | India[*] | Israel |
|---|---|---|---|---|
| Total software sales 1991 | $0.3bn | $0.06bn | $0.56bn | $0.65bn |
| Total software sales 2001 | $7.7bn | $9.1bn | $9.0bn | $7.1bn |
| Annualised growth rate 1991-2001 | 38.1% | 65.0% | 43.1% | 29.9% |
| Growth rate 2000-2001 | 6.9% | 26.4% | 23.0% | 12.7% |
| Export share 1991 | n.a.- | n.a.. | 58.9% | 42.3% |
| Export share 2001 | 2.0% | 8.9% | 79.0% | 42.3% |

*Note:* * 1993 for India.

*Source:* chapter authors.

occurred in contexts (with the exception of Israel) where access to tertiary education has remained limited and where the aggregate level of human capital has not been high but where pockets of skills have formed. As the industry has grown, however, these localised skill-intensive places have in turn attracted other skilled individuals, as well as expanding the local demand for skills acquisition and training. Later, the chapter asks whether these pockets have in effect been successful enclaves with only limited linkages to the rest of the economy.

## 1.2  INDUSTRY ATTRIBUTES AND EVOLUTION

The global software industry took off in the mid-1980s, initially in the developed countries with the provision of packaged software and, later, with a mix of systems applications as well as increased demand for integrating software and solutions for larger firms. In common with the broader ICT sector, software growth accelerated dramatically in the 1990s only to hit the buffers at the end of the decade as the 'tech bubble' burst. While globally, software represents less than 10 per cent of the aggregate ICT market, its growth – even post-2000 – has been particularly robust, both for packaged software and software related services. Innovation in the sector has remained strong, leading to the development of new products but also major change in terms of market structure, through entry, mergers and alliances. The main challenges for the industry now concern systems integration and product compatibility, while growing use of the Internet and network computing have required new approaches to supplying software by applications providers. Indeed, some argue that over time the Internet will facilitate a shift towards computing being provided more as a utility and software as a service, with much of the latter being outsourced. This implies that applications will move away from being software running on individual computers towards a combination of web-based services with programmes written not for operating systems but application servers instead. These changes are likely to have major implications for the software industry and the way it operates, not only at the leading edge – most of which is unequivocally USA based – but also for emerging market firms looking at finding their niche. Indeed, changes have already occurred that have led to a dramatic increase in the size of the IT services industry servicing businesses and individuals over the Internet. Moreover, growing use of outsourcing has itself generated new software requirements.[4] These combined factors suggest that demand for software is likely to remain strong, even if the way in which software is supplied, priced and paid for undergoes change.

The software industry currently embraces a wide variety of activities. For a start, a distinction can be drawn between customised software and more generic products. The latter may, however, include a fair share of customisation before they can be applied by an individual client. As such, the industry encompasses a variety of activities with very different relative profitabilities and levels of technical difficulty. A simple hierarchy of complexity would rank product development at the top, followed by development of packages, then customisation and finally, maintenance, coding and other more repetitive tasks. For obvious reasons, product development generally requires strong intellectual property rights protection. Most of the major product space is occupied by firms operating in developed economies with just such protection and technological infrastructure. These various activities involve different levels of skills. At the top end of the skill distribution lie the conceptualisers. Programming, coding, testing and support activities are the realm of less-skilled workers and this is naturally reflected in their wage differences.[5]

In the case of the four countries, it is clear that very different niches have come to be occupied, although there is some evidence that over time firms have tried – but not always succeeded – in moving up the value chain. At risk of simplification, Israel has largely concentrated on products, nearly 40 per cent of China's software output has been in products, while Brazil and India have concentrated more on services. In the Indian case, most of the firms have been involved in relatively less complex, relatively low-skill activities such as coding, maintenance and other services. However, there is also additional evidence that some of the larger Indian software firms have been trying to diversify and develop the product side, as well as offering software solutions. The following sub-sections now try to provide an overview of developments in each of the four countries.

**Brazil**

The origins of the Brazilian software industry lie with the protection instituted by a nationalist, military government in the 1970s. While much of their focus was on hardware, an associated effect was the training of a labour force that was able later to provide the bedrock of the nascent software industry. This occurred when protection for the hardware sector was finally phased out in the early 1990s.

Although the software sector remains small in terms of its contribution to output and employment (0.1 per cent of formal employment), what has been striking in Brazil is that, firstly, the sector has largely developed for the domestic market and, secondly, that it remains quite heterogeneous in terms of skill content and firm organisation. Thus, most firms are small and involved in customised software development or packages, although there appears to be comparatively little specialisation. However, there are a number of major software ventures – mainly linked to the banking industry – which have developed highly complex software products. For example, Brazil remains something of a leader in offering Internet-based banking and other forms of networked transactions. The two major private banks – Itau and Bradesco – have operated successful, captive software development units. E-commerce has flourished despite some regulatory obstruction. There has also been innovation in a variety of domains, including the management of Linux networks, security firewalls and the broader use of e-networks, particularly by government. Interestingly, there has been little attempt to market these products beyond Brazil's borders and the industry as a whole remains almost exclusively devoted to the domestic market. Part of this can be attributed to language and other barriers, but also to apparent deficiencies in business strategies, including a weak client focus. In the domestic market, competition from foreign software companies in recent years has also increased, putting downward pressure on revenues. This has been exacerbated by the problem of lack of intellectual property rights.

In short, Brazil has developed a widely networked economy, a hardware sector – albeit one increasingly dominated by foreign owned firms – but a relatively restricted software industry.    Although liberalisation of the economy has been occurring throughout the past decade, there remain strong traces of the more autarkic features that earlier governments had imposed. At the same time, a number of important labour market features – including employment protection and high payroll taxation – have combined with the underlying income distribution to limit the supply of skills and talent necessary for the IT sector as a whole to grow.

## China

Chinese software grew very robustly in the 1990s but from a small base. The industry has the potentially important advantage of being located in an economy that has overall experienced substantial growth, including in the hardware and IT economy more generally. Indeed, there has been very strong growth in IT manufacturing in the recent past, including a shift from Taiwan to South China and the growth of a semi-conductor manufacturing centre around Shanghai. There are signs that in the future, linkages from the software to the IT manufacturing sector will be important.

The software industry remains oriented almost entirely to the domestic economy with exports accounting for no more than 6 per cent of sales. While foreign firms have entered and dominate the product market, over 60 per cent of output is accounted for by services and this is where Chinese firms are dominant. However, there are a number of large and growing Chinese firms that concentrate mainly on products. As in Brazil – but here mainly due to the particularities of the local accounting system – Chinese firms have built an important niche in financial software. Supply chain management is another area where Chinese firms have developed strong competence. Even so, the domestic industry remains highly fragmented with most firms small and involved in developing niche applications, such as systems integration, as well as adapting products to the Chinese language. The predominance of small firms can be related not only to the characteristics of the financial sector but also to the relative lack of integration between markets.

Preferential treatment – more than trade protection – has been an important factor behind the growth of the software industry. Government institutions have systematically favoured domestic software firms over foreign competition. Public resources have also been allocated, by various layers of government, to domestic firms in a conscious attempt to build local players. The inexact boundaries between public and private interests have also played a part. Given the size and role of government in China – including its role in granting licences, permits and other requirements for business activity – the evidence suggests that private firms need commonly to cultivate and maintain close connections with public agencies and decision makers. Not surprisingly, this has tended to be associated with non-transparent decision making and allied inefficiencies. The same underlying weakness in the way decisions are made and the limited scope for judicial oversight has also been manifest in the pervasive presence of software piracy. As such, lack of adequate protection for intellectual property rights continues to be a major problem in China, particularly for firms offering products. This helps explain some of the changes in the structure of output – for example, the strong relative growth of systems integration firms where piracy is less of a problem. Further, despite large investment in human capital and R&D by the public sector, it appears that managerial skills remain scarce and a constraint on the operations of firms in the sector. There is some anecdotal evidence that multinationals have played a positive role in expanding the managerial labour pool but the size of the effect is unclear. In sum, Chinese software has experienced impressive growth and there are signs of emerging linkages with the more established domestic IT manufacturing sector. Yet, in many key respects, the industry continues to be held back by the vestiges of the planned economy and its subsequent mutations.

## India

The Indian software industry was originally oriented largely to the domestic market. A greater export orientation was initially helped by a shift in public policy, whereby import entitlements for hardware were made conditional on exports. Later, in the 1990s, both hardware and software imports were liberalised – as part of a wider abolition of import licensing for capital goods – and joint ventures were encouraged. At this time, the dominant players were spin-offs from established Indian businesses, but some of the new entrants were multinationals. In this phase, offshore development operations generating software for their own use were often established and this was helped by English being the common language. Innovations in communications, such as the use of satellites – VSATs – and better telecommunications, were critical in allowing greater decentralisation, reducing the need for proximity between suppliers and users. Over time, there has also been a dramatic increase in outsourcing of IT functions and tasks by firms in developed countries. The example of leading airlines outsourcing back-office functions to India is a case in point.[6] The use of outsourcing has been driven not simply by technical facility but by important cost differences. In the late 1990s, Indian firms were pricing programming labour at roughly 20-30 per cent of rates in either the USA or UK, although the cost differential was smaller for more skilled labour, particularly for on-site work. This cost advantage has been sustained post-2000.

While much of the initial growth in Indian software was relatively low value added – involving mostly on-site services, including sending workers abroad to work on site on a temporary basis, a phenomenon widely known as 'body shopping' – there has subsequently been greater substitution of labour in India for labour on site. Clearly, knowledge of English was an important factor in enabling this cross-border flow of labour. There has also been a clear attempt by firms since the mid-1990s onwards to try to operate further up the value chain. A number of the larger firms – NASSCOM estimates suggest that by the end of the 1990s the top 25 firms accounted for nearly 60 per cent of exports – are now first tier contractors for software projects from customers in developed countries. Even so, the majority of Indian software exports comprise maintenance tasks, development of small applications and e-commerce solutions with projects being mostly small and technologically unsophisticated.[7] A number of the leading domestic players nevertheless have clear aspirations for entry into the more lucrative ERP and software development markets. Although Indian firms have proven strong at process innovation – such as the management of large software projects – the evidence regarding product innovation seems to have been mainly limited to tools, and on a fairly narrow basis.

In conclusion, the Indian software industry remains a largely export-oriented services sector. The industry has throughout retained very strong links to the North American market and hence to a powerful source of demand for services.[8] This link has been principally organised around India's advantage as a supplier of relatively low-cost labour, rather than as a product competitor. This source of advantage appears to be eroding and as such the industry has made a concerted attempt to focus on reputation and quality. Visa restrictions – particularly in the USA – have also had an adverse impact. At the same time, there has been growth in outsourcing – particularly of IT-related services – to India to exploit labour cost advantages. However, in software, labour productivity in India – as measured by software revenue per employee – though greatly superior to that in manufacturing, remains at under 10 per cent of levels in either Israel or the USA. Most of the services provided by Indian firms are still relatively unsophisticated and the share of solutions or products in total output is still small. Linkages between the export and domestic sectors remain limited. Deepening of the domestic economy will be desirable, by producing more domain expertise and allowing greater market diversification.

**Israel**

Israeli software took off in the 1990s, fuelled by a massive inflow of foreign direct investment and equity investment. The timing was not fortuitous: it required a prior stabilisation of the economy and a movement away from high and volatile inflation. At the same time, strong domestic demand for security software was key in giving the industry an initial impetus, often with a substantial public financing component. Over time, however, growth of the software sector was mainly driven by exports with bilateral and regional trade agreements enabling most of that trade to be with North America and Europe. While the performance of the sector was very strong, it is important to emphasise that this was part of a broader structural change in the economy. By 2000, information sectors accounted for nearly 15 per cent of GDP. A striking feature of the Israeli software industry is that it operates in a large number of technology niches with almost all firms being relatively high-end players. Product innovation and a competitive technology edge have been central to the Israeli story. As such, software applications have been developed for a wide and diverse range of activities, including Internet security and e-commerce, and most domestic markets remain strongly competitive. The strong export orientation of the sector has also been important in maintaining market-based discipline and incentives. The content of software exports has been quite varied – the largest shares have been for application development tools, middle- and server-ware – but it has mostly been at the higher end of the product spectrum. In stark contrast to the Brazilian example, successful Israeli firms have placed a strong emphasis on marketing and attention to clients.

An important – and idiosyncratic – stimulus to the sector was the large immigration of talent from the former Soviet Union to Israel over this period. Aside from bringing appropriate skills to the sector, the enhanced supply of skills had beneficial effects on the domestic labour market, reducing upward wage and cost pressures.

In common with the larger economy, the software industry has been hit hard by the downturn after 2000. Exports and investment in the sector have declined substantially. And in the Israeli case this has been compounded by the political and military uncertainty arising from the Palestinian conflict. Many software firms have failed or dramatically scaled back operations, while there are now signs of greater migration of skilled labour out of Israel.


## 1.3 ROLE OF PUBLIC POLICY

In common with earlier East Asian experience, it appears that the combination of an absence of high and volatile inflation, alongside a stable exchange rate regime, have been critical ingredients in stimulating growth in the software economies of these four countries. Certainly, in both Brazil and Israel, it was only after successful macroeconomic stabilisation that investment began to pick up. But all have been characterised by persistent fiscal and quasi-fiscal problems and, particularly in the case of Brazil and China, by high levels of debt. In India and China, the continued presence of controls and restrictions remains quite pervasive, even if the software sector has been relatively unaffected. Certainly, an argument that these places have succeeded in developing a software economy simply by conforming to the so-called Washington Consensus would be highly misleading. In addition, other aspects of government policy have also been important.

Following Gerschenkron (1962), it has been common to emphasise the institutional dimensions behind episodes of accelerated development and, in particular, the case – or lack of it – for government intervention. Thus, it has been widely argued that the East Asian growth spurt from the 1970s onwards was attributable not only to a rapid growth in investment but also the use of specific financing and coordinating mechanisms. These tended to favour concentration, economies of scale and long-run relationships between financial institutions, firms and government. Some – such as Shleifer and Vishny (1998) – have argued that even if such interventionist policies succeed in raising investment, they are likely to do so at significant cost and to have major dynamic disadvantages, not least the associated growth of vested interests and the crony relationships that, for example, became so powerful a feature in East Asia. Such interests may ultimately act to conserve inefficiencies and dull the ability of an economy to adapt.[9] Some of this long-standing debate has evident relevance for the software economy, not least because of the prolonged attempts of various governments to stimulate investment-based growth through a mix of subsidies and competition-reducing measures. However, the software example also highlights the apparent ability to shift into innovative, (near) cutting-edge activity rather than simply strategies of imitation, and this in itself raises a number of interesting questions.

The country studies highlight a number of areas in which public policy has been significant in either stimulating or retarding the software sector. They can broadly be grouped under three titles: (1) protection, subsidies, preferential finance and trades; (2) infrastructure – particularly communications and investment; and (3) investment in education and training.

## Protectionism

All the four countries have pursued, in one form or another, protectionist policies that have had a significant bearing on the evolution of the industry. Such policies have comprised not only the erection of trade barriers but also the use of preferential fiscal and financial incentives to local firms. However, there have been major differences across countries.

In India, wider IT adoption was initially held back by the presence of embargoes and protection of domestic hardware producers or assemblers. Such protection was reduced or eliminated in the 1980s giving an important stimulus to the sector. Subsequent liberalisation further helped the sector shift from a supplier of labour to a complex constellation of domestic and foreign firms providing, for the most part, services to foreign clients. Of course, conventional trade restrictions would be difficult to implement for software exports once communications infrastructure was established. As such, the Indian and Israeli cases together appear to provide a strong argument for why trade liberalisation and an absence of non-transparent financing have been important in raising the longer-run growth rate of the industry. However, in the Indian case, it is clear that the industry still faces major impediments to business – principally in terms of restrictive hiring and firing rules – and that the sector has been far from immune to the more general deficiencies in the overall business environment. As always, there are some important nuances to these arguments – notably the role of government as a provider of education and as a source of demand for products and services, of which more below.

By contrast, the origins of Brazilian software and the IT sector in general, unequivocally can be traced back to the period of high protection and the so-called market reserve policies of the 1970/80s. While there is little doubt that this policy did not ultimately provide secure foundations for the domestic software industry, it did have a number of important consequences. In the first place, the IT sector as a whole remained very much domestically oriented, shielded as it was – in part – from competition. Once that protection was finally lifted in the 1990s, the market share of domestic producers declined substantially. More positively, the market reserve policy appears to have created a demand for IT-related training and contributed to an important increase in the supply of skilled personnel for the sector. Further, it led to a more general uptake in IT use and networked activity. In some sectors – such as banking – this was further stimulated by the challenge of managing assets under regimes of high and unstable inflation.   Successive Brazilian governments since the 1970s have also pursued a policy of export promotion, using a mix of instruments, such as tax rebates and credit subsidies. More generally, this did lead to a tremendous increase in exports throughout the 1970s, but a later export initiative particular to the software sector and focused on products – Softex (started in 1992) – has been generally unsuccessful. Further, as in India, employment in the sector has continued to be adversely affected by the presence of substantial payroll and other taxes that have effectively discriminated against sectors that are labour intensive.

The most pervasive and long lasting involvement of government has undoubtedly been in China. It was only in the 1980s that a partial liberalisation of the economy started and there is plenty of evidence that it remains incomplete. What is indeed striking is that while barriers to the entry of foreign firms have been progressively lifted, discretionary policies to raise the market share of local players have become a key feature of the Chinese software economy. Indeed, public policy has explicitly set the target of building a large domestic software industry. This policy has manifested itself in a variety of forms, running from subsidised credits to both public and private firms (ownership boundaries remain blurred in many cases) to tax breaks, tariff exemptions for imports and incentives for exporters. And while the framework in which such incentives are allocated may not be consistent with WTO rules, they mark a clear shift away from earlier protectionist policies. What is far less clear – given the lack of transparency in both ownership and business practices – is the extent, let alone the consequences, of government preferences when granting licences and contracts. Certainly, there are explicit cases where domestic-industry-first policies have been pursued: for example, the Beijing government's purchase of local (Kingsoft), as against Microsoft, software. The pervasive role of government and the public sector has contributed to restricting the range of firms and their competitiveness. The allied failure to safeguard intellectual property rights has undermined the willingness to try to innovate as well as more general investment in the sector.

In short, in the early years of the industry protectionism has been important, particularly in Brazil and China. This has predictably skewed the sector toward a stronger focus on domestic markets. There appears to be little evidence that public enterprises have played an important role in raising returns to private investment by ensuring that key inputs were available locally for private producers downstream. As such, the gains from coordination that have been argued to be a feature of East Asia do not appear to have been significant in the Chinese case. Further, whatever the exact mechanism for support, a key question concerns the ability of public agencies to reduce or eliminate support when appropriate, not least because of political economy considerations and rent-seeking.

Public sector financing of the software industry has met with very mixed success. In Brazil, support has either proven to be too episodic or limited, while in China the principal problem remains a lack of transparency. The pervasive interference of government in financing and other important commercial realms has contributed to the slow growth of alternative financing sources, such as venture capital, equity and bank finance. Bank finance has also been restrained by the common insistence on collateralisation. As such, much public funding has been ineffectual and ultimately wasteful of resources. In India – perhaps surprisingly – the software sector has not been the recipient of any direct large order public financing or allocation of discretionary resources. Some of the regional governments made land easily available for software parks, while in Bangalore, the relative ease by which property can be transacted has also been a further stimulus to the industry. Profits from exports across industry (not just for software) remained tax-free until 2000 – these tax incentives are being phased out by 2005 – and this provided a further, powerful incentive for a strong external orientation.

One striking exception can be found in Israel, where primarily through the use of matching funds programmes, public resources have been made available for high-technology firms. Such resources have had enforceable repayment conditions attached. Other support to the industry has come through time-bound support for the creation of a venture capital industry. In this instance, an initial allocation of $100 million in 1992 under the Yozma programme was critical in jump-starting the domestic venture capital industry and enabled public resources to be withdrawn five years later. This appears to be a rare case of public funding being used for a specific objective over a limited time horizon. However, the Israeli venture capital industry has grown in tandem with a local capital market and on the back of offshore – principally North American – listings, a feature that is generally attenuated or missing in most developing countries, yet critical in providing effective exit from venture investments.

## Infrastructure

Good communications are essential for the software industry. Yet, as the figures cited earlier in Table 1.1 show, countries such as China and India have relatively low levels of telecommunications and other infrastructure when compared with developed countries and overall their economies remain weakly networked. However, such numbers disguise a number of salient features relevant to the industry. Firstly, they disguise the substantial improvements in communications that were a prerequisite for the industry to develop and subsequently expand. In this regard there is clear evidence that while secure, well priced and efficient communications have best been provided by the private sector – often following privatisation – the public sector has been able to provide significant infrastructural support to the industry. Secondly, they camouflage the fact that telecommunications infrastructure looks significantly different and better in the main software locations than in the economy as a whole.

In the Indian case, the shortcomings of the state-owned telecommunications system were effectively bypassed by the Government of India in 1991 through the creation of the Software Technology Parks of India. Aside from providing specific locations for their business, these parks were a way of circumventing the public sector's monopoly on telecommunication. VSATs could be located within these parks and with them efficient and cost-effective external communications links. Shortly thereafter firms located outside these parks were also allowed access to the satellite connections, as well as the import of capital goods and inputs on a duty-free basis. Without these changes, the software industry would have been stillborn.

Of course, a more effective longer-term solution would have been to privatise and allow new entrants to telecommunications provision – as later happened – but at that time, this would likely have been a difficult political proposition. The software parks arrangement was an interim measure that was politically feasible, had the additional feature of encouraging greater spatial agglomeration in the industry and also facilitated the supply of complementary inputs, not least a reliable energy supply. The advent of the Internet, coupled with privatisation, subsequently improved access further.

In Brazil, China and Israel, major upgrading of communications infrastructure occurred in the 1990s, although this was not necessarily a precondition for software sector growth. In China, most of the improvement was financed and managed by the state-owned telecommunications company – China Telecom – and this appears to have been important in allowing the software sector to expand. However, in Israel the greater part of the investment in communications infrastructure came after 1996 and has proceeded alongside deregulation of the industry. This disguises differences in the level and coverage of communications services across these two countries. In China, prior upgrading was required – as in India – for a basic threshold for activity in software to be crossed. However, good communications – while important – have not been a sufficient recipe for rapid growth of the industry. It is interesting to note that in both China and Israel initiatives involving software parks or zones have been tried, albeit with different degrees of success. In Brazil, a government agency – Softex – originally set up to raise software exports, moved into sponsoring incubators and regional software nuclei. However, this does not appear to have been particularly successful. Certainly, most of the industry continues to be located in south-east Brazil near the major sources of demand, while the incubator programmes run by Softex have continued to suffer from weak market orientation and inability to launch viable projects. In Israel, numerous software parks have been set up by regional development authorities throughout the country, but these have never just housed software firms. It appears that while being of some importance in peripheral areas, such parks have not been a central feature of the Israeli software industry. Interestingly, in 2001 the Chinese moved to consolidating a group of software centres with a view to giving them priority in the allocation of support services, finance and other inputs. It is too early to know whether these will be effective mechanisms for coordinating support and realising gains from agglomeration.

**Education**

Common to Brazil, India and China is the large absolute number of educated workers. For while the share of the total labour force with tertiary education remains small – particularly in China and India – a rough estimate for India in the mid-1990s placed the number of scientists, technicians and engineers in India at over 170 000, while annual growth in the number of software professionals at the end of the 1990s was estimated at around 67 000. The obvious questions are what factors account for the rate of enrolments and the extent to which this was dependent on public investments in education?

The answers are, predictably, far from formulaic. It is certainly the case that public resources have been critical in all these countries in financing the tertiary sector. In Brazil, the years of protectionism were also ones in which significant resources were ploughed into higher education and training. The number of universities and course offerings increased and this has been maintained into the more recent period. At the same time, IT technical education has been increasingly provided at secondary or non-university levels and this has raised the effective supply of labour to the software sector, albeit at the lower end of the skill spectrum. The picture at postgraduate level is less positive. Relatively low exposure to education abroad, and a weaker science orientation than for India or China, has limited the availability of high-end skills for the sector. In addition, while Brazilian universities – rather than firms – have tended to produce the major stream of R&D, much of this work has had limited market application, while serious legal difficulties in assigning patent rules for work done in universities has also had adverse consequences for incentives.

The Indian example also speaks strongly to the initial importance of a high quality publicly funded educational system. Indeed, the role of Indian Institute of Technology graduates – primarily engineers – has been widely discussed. While a significant share of such graduates has been among skilled migrants to advanced economies – primarily the USA – this has often resulted in important and positive gains in terms of networks, investment and establishment of commercial relationships with firms and individuals remaining in India. At the same time, education abroad, mainly in the USA, has also raised skill levels. Section 5 explores in more detail the various ways in which such a beneficial brain drain could have resulted, not least through the rapid growth in enrolments as individuals sought to acquire marketable skills.

Enrolments in software-related training – principally engineering – rose dramatically as the sector expanded. Between 1992 and 2002 the number of Indian graduates trebled for engineering, IT degrees and diplomas. And it is here, in both India and Israel, that some important innovations on the supply side were made in the 1990s. With the public system unable to provide a sufficient flow of skilled labour, private institutions were allowed to enter and offer training on a fee basis to applicants. Particularly in the south of India, there was a rapid growth in the share of engineering graduates coming out of self-financed colleges.[10] These institutions have received notably lower subsidies than the state-financed institutions. In addition, private firms have emerged to provide non-degree training. In India, the largest such provider, NIIT, established a strong market niche – often through franchising – in providing workers with basic coding and other skills. As such, innovative private sector training initiatives raised the supply of lower-level skill groups while the public tertiary system and self-financed colleges continued to provide a flow of graduates. At the height of the 1990s boom, the diversion of graduates, mainly engineers, into the software industry did indeed force up wages in other parts of the economy but these effects – not least after the 2000 slowdown – were not long lasting.

In Israel, the relatively high quality of public universities and the large resources channelled to R&D by the public sector – civil and military – were fused with the dismantling of the state monopoly on education and led not only to a proliferation of educational institutions but also to higher enrolment rates. Thus, between 1980 and 2000 degrees conferred by private colleges jumped from under 5 per cent to nearly a third of all first degrees granted. While the state kept tight control over accreditation, this liberalisation of the educational market, both domestically and to foreign institutions, was important in raising the supply of skilled labour. This, coupled with the large inflow of skilled workers from the former Soviet Union, was central in ensuring that skill shortages and wage pressure were not strong constraining factors. Training abroad by Israelis – particularly in the USA – has also been important in helping to build strong networks and links to best practice.

Although the role of public institutions in education remains overwhelmingly dominant in China, the number of graduates who have studied abroad – and increasingly have returned – has grown substantially over the past decade. Furthermore, the blurred distinctions between public and private control have increasingly extended to the education sector and to the allocation of public resources. By the late 1990s the government was allocating resources for science and technology not just to universities but also to private firms, at the same time as controls over the selection or import of technology were being eroded. Even so, it appears that Chinese public universities have a rather weak record, not only in R&D but also in taking innovations to the market. Further, their ability to provide an adequate supply of IT-trained graduates and diploma holders has been restricted. Shortages exist at both the high and low ends of the software skill distribution, leading – among other consequences – to private firms, such as India's NIIT and APTECH, beginning to offer training, as well as the selective use of migrant labour. At the same time, the evidence points to strong growth in enrolments in science and engineering degrees in the traditional universities.

In short, the software industries in these countries could not have got off the ground without a strong, prior set of investments in human capital. That investment was almost entirely made by the public sector. However, over time – and essential in ensuring that pervasive skill shortages did not emerge – governments have tended to reduce the barriers to entry for private suppliers of education, domestic and foreign. Such providers have increasingly operated over the full skills spectrum with some effectively internationalising their training programmes. At the same time, the acquisition of education abroad has become an important channel for skills and networks acquisition and knowledge transfer.

## 1.4 AGGLOMERATION AND SPILLOVERS

The software industry has been characterised by significant spatial concentration. In India the great bulk of activity is concentrated in no more than five urban centres,[11] in China agglomeration along the eastern coastline has occurred, while in Brazil over half the employment of the sector is concentrated in the southeast of the country, most particularly in and around São Paulo. More generally, the economic geography literature has argued that it is the combination of economies of scale and transaction costs that determine the level of concentration. The former are necessary for concentration to happen at all, the latter will limit concentration by raising the benefits to locating production close to demand. Software provides an interesting case in that the principal transaction costs – associated with the use of telephone lines, satellites or the Internet – have not necessarily been low but have still been associated with concentration. In India, for example, agglomeration has also been driven by the ways in which high transaction costs on account of infrastructural constraints have been dealt with. The establishment of software parks with dedicated access to VSATs was itself a powerful factor favouring agglomeration. Further, there is clear evidence that there are non-trivial spillovers between skilled workers – through knowledge sharing, teamwork and the like – and that these features of the industry also raise the return to agglomeration.

It has been argued that software generates few linkages with other sectors in these emerging markets, although the demonstration effects may be far from trivial.[12] In India, for example, the sector is commonly held up as an example of good corporate governance and entrepreneurship. At the same time, the sector has been noted for changes to the internal organisation of firms that have placed less reliance on hierarchy, and applied incentive wages to induce effort. These can in part be attributed to the strong market discipline exercised on the sector on account of its predominant export focus. Foreign listing – principally on North American exchanges – has also been accompanied by use of GAAP accounting and other reporting rules. Further, the strong income effects of the industry in its main locations has provided a powerful stimulus to the growth of services and the housing sectors and this, in turn, has created employment opportunities for unskilled as well as skilled labour from neighbouring areas.

However, Patibandla and Petersen (2002) have also argued that multinationals operating in India – by bringing in differentiated inputs, technologies and working norms – have induced significant and positive spillovers, particularly at the higher end of the technology spectrum.[13] While this may be plausible, technology spillovers are always difficult to identify and their evidence is drawn from a very small sample of firms. Other work suggests that multinationals – including through work experience abroad – can play a positive role through training and improving the skills of managers.[14] There is some evidence that this has been the case in China.

A further possible channel for productivity gain is likely to be the reduction in technology mismatch. To the extent that the relative success of the sector has induced a clear outward shift in the demand for education, the increase in human capital would tend to raise skill levels allowing firms in emerging markets to match workers to new generation technologies more easily. Over time, this should lead to falling income differentials across countries, although it might be expected to raise inequality within the country, as returns to the skilled increase.

What is clear, however, is that there have been major differences across countries in terms of the linkages – as principally determined by the rate of overall ICT diffusion – to other parts of the economy. In India, such inter-industry linkages remain attenuated on account of the generally low quality of infrastructure, including low access to telephony – mobile and fixed line – as well as problems with bandwidth, pricing and energy shortages. As such, domestic demand for software products remains very limited on account of the combination of income levels and other constraints, such as labour legislation, and the relatively slow and regionally patchy adoption of ICT by government and the public sector. Not surprisingly, links between work on export projects and on domestic work remain quite restricted. Indeed, what is striking is the effective segmentation of firms serving domestic and export sectors. Even so, as liberalisation of markets proceeds, there is evidence of wider restructuring in the economy, not least as the manufacturing sector adapts to an environment of greater competition. This should in due course raise the demand for software in the domestic economy. It is also likely to be aided by the investments in the sector made by incumbent industrial entities.[15]

In Brazil, China and Israel, government policy has been explicitly aimed at raising the networked level of the economy and encouraging wider ICT diffusion. In Brazil, ICT adoption is widely diffused, as exemplified by both the levels of e-commerce and the integration in industrial production, as well as the level of e-government, that have been attained. Certainly, this has been associated with increased local demand for software. In China important linkages have been established to the finance and telecom sectors, which have been the main sources of demand for software. This has been helped by active public promotion and financing of infrastructure. However, in both Brazil and China, income barriers obviously remain significant at the level of households while organisational impediments, combined with deficiencies in the business environment, principally piracy, have come together to limit, in particular, the market for software products. This has meant that demand has largely been driven by government, but this itself – as will be discussed in more detail in Section 1.5 below – has brought its own problems, not least through a lack of transparency in the allocation of contracts. On the positive side, increasing linkages to local educational institutions and research laboratories have been evident in all the four countries, most particularly in Israel.

Finally, the 1990s boom in software clearly placed strong upward pressure on wages in the sector, particularly for the higher skill categories subject to a more inelastic supply and to poaching from abroad. This increased demand for skilled engineers does appear to have induced ripple effects to other industries through wage pressure, particularly in China and India and to a lesser extent elsewhere. However, this has subsequently been offset by the slowdown after 2000 so that wage emulation effects appear not to have been long lasting. In addition, given the high level of firm or process-specific knowledge associated with the industry, high levels of turnover – including through migration – should have imposed a cost on firms. This is certainly a common perception in China, at least with regard to higher skilled software developers. There has also been much anecdotal discussion of turnover costs in the Indian context. Section 1.5 below takes this issue up in more detail, where empirical evidence actually suggests a relatively limited adverse impact on firms on account of increased turnover.

## 1.5 BUILDING REPUTATION IN EXPORT MARKETS

In both the Indian and Israeli cases software exports have been an essential component. Both Brazilian and Chinese policymakers appear to place a strong emphasis on increasing exports, albeit with limited success, at least to date. This brings to the forefront the issue of how firms from emerging markets can effectively shift into export markets given lack of experience and reputation. Experience elsewhere also suggests that any shift from price to quality as the source of competitiveness involves significant changes in industrial organisation. It could be argued that for such a shift to occur larger firms may be better placed insofar as they could find it easier to deal with the important reputational issues associated with moving into high quality export markets. Indeed, there is some evidence from Korea and Taiwan to suggest that scale may have helped in reducing negative reputational externalities, although small size did not impede Taiwanese firms entering high-technology/high quality markets.[16]

From the four countries covered in this project, the Indian and Israeli cases stand out as the ones that have had high export exposure. In the Indian case, a significant share of the activity has been in the type of work – customised software – where hold-up could easily be prevalent and where the cumbrous and non-transparent Indian legal process would provide limited or non-existent remedy. So the obvious question to ask is: how have Indian software firms and their clients managed to circumvent or limit these tricky contracting problems?

For a start, there is clear evidence that many Indian firms have moved to getting quality certification, either ISO9001 or the Carnegie Mellon Capability Maturity Model (CMM) to signal quality to clients.[17] Indeed, certification is likely to become more important as Indian firms attempt to shift into higher-end activity. It also seems to have been accompanied by a strong emphasis on the quality of processes of software development and methodology. There also appears to be some patterns with respect to pricing and contract design. Banerji and Duflo (1999) found that younger firms tended to use fixed price contracts. However, repeated association with a client was associated with greater use of cost-plus or time-and-materials contracts. Indian firms in dealing with foreign clients also appear to have fairly scrupulously adhered to cost sharing on overruns. As overruns are common and significant, this latter aspect has been central to the accumulation of reputation. A complementary conjecture is that contracts have been conditional on the type of work and its predictability in terms of labour input. The greater the predictability, the more contracts have largely involved specified payments for labour time. However, it is clear that by the end of the 1990s the larger Indian software firms – such as Infosys, Wipro and TCS – have managed to accumulate sufficient reputation for reliability and price advantage for firms in the advanced economies to trust them with complex and often repeat projects. As such, reputation has been accumulated by implementing repeated contracts for the same clients, with reputation and contract size positively correlated over time. These projects appear to have been mainly organised around cost-plus contracts. Margins have been materially affected by the slowdown in the industry.

## 1.6 A CONDUIT FOR BRAIN DRAIN FROM DEVELOPING COUNTRIES ?

The software industry has been notable for the high degree of cross-border migration by skilled labour. In particular, the migration of talent to the USA – and especially Silicon Valley – has been widely cited. In addition, in the 1990s the rapid growth in customised software applications, involving greater on-site interaction between supplier and customer, as also for turnkey projects, led to greater mobility of labour across borders, including from developing countries.[18] These features have led many to question whether this is not an aggravated case of a brain drain from these emerging markets. By contrast, others have argued that due both to the nature of the industry and the often temporary nature of migration – as illustrated by the earlier widespread use of 'body shopping' from India – that this is more a case of 'brain circulation' than an example of brain drain.[19]

In addition, a body of literature – largely analytical – has emerged in recent years that places emphasis on the possible demonstration effects that migration abroad may induce and, in particular, the impact on the demand for education.[20] The key argument is that if the possibility of emigration encourages more acquisition of skills than loss of skills, sending (or home) countries might increase their stocks of skills as opportunities to move or work abroad open up. If, in addition, this accumulation of skills has beneficial effects beyond the strictly private gains anticipated by those who acquire the skills, the whole economy can benefit: a beneficial brain drain, in short. For example, increased investment in human capital should raise skill levels, in turn allowing firms to match workers to new generation technologies more easily. Certainly, anecdotal evidence from the software sector shows workers in developing countries working with very similar technologies as their counterparts in the advanced economies. Over time, this should reduce the productivity – and wage – gap between developing and developed countries. This, in turn, will lower income differences across countries, although within-country inequality in incomes may well rise.

In all these models, it is of course assumed that wages for given levels of skills are higher abroad than at home: a fact that is clearly true in the case of the software industry. For the beneficial brain-drain argument to hold, however, requires that the increased incentive to acquire education still results in some skilled workers remaining at home; only some fraction of those who acquire education can migrate abroad.[21] However, if the developed country or organisation can effectively screen migrants for ability, this will have an impact on the willingness to acquire education.[22] Indeed, a necessary criterion for a beneficial brain drain is that the marginal person in education has a positive probability of emigrating.

Although it is clear that developed countries cannot practise perfect screening of talent, the organisation of visa programmes – such as the USA's H1-B visa and other similar initiatives in Canada, the UK and other countries in Western Europe – indicates that such countries actively attempt to screen.[23] However, if the sending/developing country has some unexploited capacity for education, in the sense that the returns to education are primarily determined by the demand for skilled workers rather than the ability of the population, in this case even a perfectly screened emigration would generate net benefits. What empirical evidence exists that can throw some light on these issues and help sort out the net impact of skilled migration on the developing country?

Commander et al. (2004) use evidence from a detailed firm-level survey of 225 software firms in India to shine some light on a number of these issues. They find that there is evidence of both short and longer run migration of skilled Indians from software firms, particularly pre-2000. Clearly, the principal motivation for migration was generally perceived as being the wage advantage from moving abroad and, to a lesser extent, career opportunities. In response, the majority of firms in the sample had raised salary levels to try to retain workers. However, it is striking that only 15 per cent of the firms that were interviewed considered that migration had imposed a major cost on their firms over the previous three years. Further, less than 10 per cent of respondents thought that skilled migration had significantly affected their main activity. Indeed, over 60 per cent of respondents thought that skilled migration had been of benefit to the Indian software industry and their firm, principally by allowing contact with cutting-edge technology, changing working habits and providing access to new markets and customers.

The evidence from posted visa requirements and national policies certainly points to screening by the developed countries, with possible implications for the demand for education in the sending country. The presence of screening is further confirmed by evidence from sending firms. For those firms that had lost a high-skill employee – conceptualiser – or manager abroad, between 7 and 22 per cent ranked those employees that left as being in the top 1 per cent of their employees respectively for conceptualisers and managers, while 51 and 58 per cent put them in the top 10 per cent respectively. One conjecture is that the loss of top talent to firms in developed countries might induce software firms in developing countries to choose to work lower down the value chain: this could in part explain, for example, why Indian firms concentrated on maintenance and legacy work. Further, high turnover of skilled workers could lead to firms making production and technology decisions that matched to skill levels with lower poaching probabilities. High poaching probabilities from foreign firms should make firms unwilling to internalise training costs. Yet the survey suggests that neither has been the case. Indeed, to help reduce turnover, over half the sampled firms had actually increased training for their workers.

Furthermore, even if the developed countries appear to be able to cherry pick, it is important to emphasise the positive impact on the demand for education. Educational enrolments have continued to grow significantly. As already mentioned, in India between 1992 and 2002 the number of graduates trebled for engineering, IT degrees and diplomas. Of course, it is problematic to infer that this was driven primarily by migration possibilities, but it seems very probable that this was one contributing element. And interestingly, over 80 per cent of the Indian software firms surveyed in 2003 noted that the skill level of the workforce had unequivocally increased over the previous five years. This can be attributed in part to the demonstration effect that resulted in shifting outwards the demand for education.

With respect to possible network effects linked to migration, about a quarter of firms had retained links with workers that had gone abroad, although there was little evidence from this sample of emigrants investing in firms at home. However, over 10 per cent of respondents reported that emigrants or their firms were now customers of their firm, suggesting that commercial links could result.

In short, the migration of skilled labour from the software industry does not generally appear to have imposed a major cost on software firms in India. Indeed, the case that had many of the attributes of a classic brain drain was the migration of Jews from the former Soviet Union to Israel in the 1980s and 1990s. While in the Indian case, it is true that the top part of the talent distribution appears to have moved permanently to advanced countries – principally the USA – this has not necessarily been the case for other skilled labour in the sector. Further, it is not obvious that the developing countries would have been able to match the top talent to appropriate jobs or activities at home. In addition, the severe slowdown in the industry post-2000 has actually resulted in a number of skilled migrants returning home. For example, there is some evidence that returnees have been increasingly important in China in filling the ranks of middle management, while in Israel a significant number of returnees from Silicon Valley branched into entrepreneurial activity. The relative absence of such return flows in the case of Brazil has been one element in explaining the relatively weak performance of the industry. Finally, there is evidence that movement abroad has often been associated not only with remittances, but also with the establishment of business relationships and networks. These have generated positive results for the sending countries.


## 1.7  CONCLUSION

The software industry is still overwhelmingly dominated by firms from North America and Europe. Yet a number of firms from emerging markets have made significant headway in this market and in the current post-boom period have even consolidated their positions on account of major cost advantages. This chapter has attempted to explain the factors behind these developments.

What emerges is that software and emerging markets have come together for a variety of factors, not least the availability of relatively low-cost skilled labour, low start-up costs and enabling infrastructural investments. Prior investment in educational services and infrastructure, often by the public sector, has been critical. Measures to improve the quality of communications infrastructure by the public sector have been a powerful contributory factor, although greater private provision has been – and will be – critical in the longer run.

To date, the international division of labour that has been associated with the growth of IT and the software sector in particular has largely involved the developed countries concentrating on the higher value products and services, with firms from developing countries providing outsourcing and on-site labour services to firms from developed countries. India, for example, has strongly benefited from being closely linked to the North American market and firms. In addition, emerging market firms have provided software services, and to a far lesser extent, products and applications, in their domestic markets. With the exception of Israel, productivity levels in the industry have remained low compared with developed country firms. There are some signs that this is changing as developing country firms try to shift into higher-end products[24] – including by establishing subsidiaries in developed country markets – but such changes have as yet not been that dramatic. However, software firms with significant exposure in export markets have had to place a major emphasis on quality control and reliability, as well as increasingly seeking certification, in order to build reputation and clients. There have been other allied changes. For example, Indian firms have begun to outsource to China, signalling the advent of a more complex set of trading relationships.

The software industry has been generally characterised by its striking openness: openness to ideas, trade and labour flows. These have generally been powerful and positive features. Yet the greatly increased cross-border mobility of skilled labour from the sector has provoked fears that talent has been siphoned off from the developing to developed countries. But there are good grounds for scepticism. One feature that stands out – notably in the cases of China, India and Israel – is the importance of networks and, in particular, the commercial and other links associated with flows of humans across borders, as well as within countries. Links between diasporas and the originating country have been important – and are likely to remain important – through a variety of channels, including remittances, investment and enhanced knowledge flows. As such, the migration of skilled workers from the industry appears not to have constituted a classic brain drain, but one where the positive impact on the demand for education at home, as well as these network effects, has helped offset any loss of talent to the developed countries.

Can software act as an important engine of growth for the larger economy? Here, despite significant gains, there are reasons for being cautious. Firstly, the industry rarely accounts for more than a small share of GDP – even in the USA, software accounts for no more than 1 per cent. Secondly, high growth over the 1990s in these four countries has come from a shallow base. Thirdly, the industry is generally very concentrated spatially and with limited inter-industry linkages. This can change over time but – in China and India, particularly – this will require further liberalisation and changes to the business environment in the rest of the economy. Nevertheless, it is striking how rapid has been the growth of the sector – particularly in China – even when handicapped by such deficiencies. This may suggest that small improvements to the business environment will tend to be associated with substantial further growth in activity. Already, through its ability to project good corporate governance, its lack of hierarchy and widespread use of motivating working practices and compensation schemes, the software industry has exerted a powerful demonstration effect on other sectors in these emerging market economies.

## NOTES

1. Note that trade in software tends to be significantly underestimated as, for example, it is commonly measured in terms of the value of supports, such as CD-ROMs, rather than content.
2. Note that for the European Union software comprised around 0.07 per cent of GDP; in the USA that share was just about 1 per cent. see OECD (2002).
3. Hausmann and Rodrik (2002), who note low levels of IT penetration, obstructive government policies and a strong endowment in unskilled labour.
4. For a general discussion, see OECD (2002).
5. A common ordering of activity has the following ranked categories: requirements analysis, high-level design, low-level design, coding, testing and post-production support.
6. Arora and Athreye (2002) find that 185 out of the Fortune 500 outsourced software production to India.
7. Arora et al. (2001).
8. A point emphasised in Bresnahan et al. (2001).
9. See also, Acemoglu et al. (2002).
10. Arora and Athreye (2002).
11. They are Bangalore, Mumbai, Chennai, Hyderabad and Delhi.
12. As argued, for example, by Arora and Athreye (2002). Of course, the absence of backward linkages can be an advantage to the extent that the sector may avoid being held back by reliance on domestic inputs.
13. The channels include demonstration effects, direct investments in local R&D and strong research, and other links to universities and institutes in the region.
14. Bresnahan et al. (2001).
15. A point made by Arora and Athreye (2002).
16. Rodrik (1994).
17. Arora and Asundi (1999).
18. For instance, at the top end of the skill chain network administrators in India cost roughly one-third of their USA counterparts and the gap was substantially higher for less skilled staff.

19. Saxenian (2001).
20. For example, Mountford (1997); Beine et al. (2001).
21. A critical assumption is that the probability of migration is fixed and exogenously given for any individual aspiring to migrate. This implicitly arises because foreign firms cannot screen migrants to distinguish the able from the less able and it is this market failure that makes it possible for the brain drain to be beneficial for the developing country.
22. See Commander et al. (2004) for a more detailed discussion.
23. OECD (2001).
24. Arora et al. (2000) who cite figures for India showing that revenues per employee jumped by around two and a half times in dollar terms between 1993 and 1999.

# 2. India

## Ashok V. Desai

---

### INTRODUCTION

The perception of an industry is generally shaped by official statistics. In the case of the Indian information technology (IT) industry,[1] the statistics are not official. All statistics on it are generated by the National Association of Software and Service Companies (NASSCOM). This energetic industry association had 850 members at the end of 2002 (NASSCOM 2003a: 17); it claimed that they accounted for over 95 per cent of the industry's revenue. There are clearly many firms in the industry that are not members of NASSCOM; a single directory, for instance, lists over 4000 firms (EFY Enterprises 2002). Although there is no reason to expect a bias in NASSCOM's estimates, they are projections from its members' figures. A comparison with IT export figures recently by the Reserve Bank of India shows that NASSCOM's figures are within 10 per cent of gross exports. Imports, not estimated by NASSCOM, are less than 10 per cent of exports. The official and NASSCOM figures are comparable; the differences between them could be the result of leads and lags.

In the rest of the chapter we will use the NASSCOM figures. But we should point out the shortcomings of defining the Indian IT industry in terms of what happens within India's borders. Thus defined, the industry includes the subsidiaries of multinational companies, which are an integral part of their global operations. NASSCOM estimates their share in the sales of the Indian industry in 2001-2002 at 26.6 per cent. On the other hand, Indian companies have affiliates and subsidiaries abroad. The accounts of selected IT companies show financial investments to have been 24 per cent of their gross assets in 2001-2002; virtually all of those would be abroad. If we think in terms of Indian entrepreneurs, 21 of the 25 Indian entrepreneurs chosen by Naroola (2001) achieved their success in the USA IT industry. Saxenian (1999) found 774 high-technology firms in Silicon Valley, with 1998 sales of $3.6 billion, that were headed by persons with Indian names. Indian firms' IT sales in 1998-1999, in comparison, were $3.9 billion, and exports were

$2.7 billion. And in 1999-2000, when NASSCOM estimated the number of software professionals working in India at 284 000 (including those employed by IT user organisations), there were about 200 000 working in the USA on H-1B visas. The two overlap to the extent that Indian companies were using H-1B visas to send professionals to the USA. But a large proportion of the Indian IT workforce was engaged abroad, and competition from abroad for labour was one of the crucial factors that shaped the Indian industry in the boom years. Nationality no longer defines boundaries. In this industry, enterprise, labour and capital are dispersed across the world, and each of them interacts with the industry located in India.

With that qualification, Figure 2.1 shows the growth of the industry's sales based on NASSCOM's figures. The industry's sales grew at a compounded average annual growth rate of 41.2 per cent in the nine years to 2002-2003.[2] In the same period, real GDP grew at 6.2 per cent per year, merchandise exports (in USA dollars) at 8.9 per cent, and current account receipts (including software exports) at 12.8 per cent. Exports propelled the growth of the IT industry; their share in revenue grew from 58.9 per cent to 79.3 per cent in those eight years. They rose from 1 per cent to 10.3 per cent of current account receipts, from 1.5 per cent to 18.8 per cent of merchandise exports, and from 0.2 to 2.7 per cent of GDP. No other industry has experienced such rapid export-led growth.

However, the growth rate of the industry declined sharply after 2000-2001. Industry sales grew only 47 per cent per year in the seven years from 1993-1994 to 2000-2001; in the next two years, their growth rate fell to 22.5 per cent per year. Export growth halved from 52.1 per cent to 26 per cent; growth of domestic sales declined from 37 per cent to 11.3 per cent per year. These declines are partly due to a fall in charges for services; the real growth has been higher than these figures suggest. But there has been a slowdown even in real terms; the almost complete cessation of campus recruitment in 2002 is one indicator. The deceleration is part of the slowdown in the global IT industry, in particular of the USA industry that has been the major market for Indian software. But it has raised questions about whether India's competitive advantage is declining.

India's advantage has rested on the low wage costs of Indian software professionals. Other low-wage countries are training their own IT labour forces, often with Indian training companies, NIIT and APTECH, participating. China and the Philippines have been seen as strong potential competitors. Countries with higher wages, such as Israel and Singapore, have acted as offshore warehouses for Indian software workers, whom they have used to do contract work in Europe and South-East Asia. Both could undermine the growth prospects of the India-based industry.

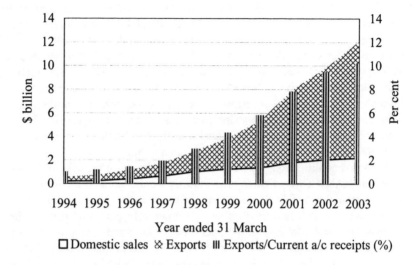

1994 1995 1996 1997 1998 1999 2000 2001 2002 2003
Year ended 31 March
☐ Domestic sales ⊠ Exports Ⅲ Exports/Current a/c receipts (%)

*Figure 2.1  Information technology exports and domestic sales*

This chapter, based inter alia on over 60 interviews with Indian IT firms, reviews the growth of the industry and evaluates its prospects. It aims to go beyond the received wisdom about the Indian industry, which includes the following misconceptions amongst others.

- *India has succeeded in software because of low wages:* Actually, wage costs are a small component of the industry's revenue – 20-25 per cent, less than its profit margin – and there are many countries where programmers' wages are not much higher than India's.
- *Use of English in India has made it easy for its firms to penetrate anglophone markets:* While it is true that India's software exports are heavily concentrated in anglophone markets, so is global software consumption. Programming requires only the most elementary English, with a very limited vocabulary and simple syntax. India's specialisation in finance explains which markets it has served.
- *India's human capital – especially its stock of engineers – enabled it to make a substantial entry into the software market*: Actually, emigration of programmers as well as the software export boom caused a serious labour shortage by the early 1990s, which was alleviated only by a rapid expansion of the education system.
- *India's geographical position, exactly halfway round the world from the USA West Coast, made it the ideal location for firms wanting to work*

*round the clock*: A location in the USA remained superior to one in India, as is evidenced by the persistence of onshore working in Indian IT firms' business.

- *The presence of a large number of Indians, especially engineers, in the USA gave India an easy entry into the US software market*: Whilst it is true that Indian engineers in the USA were often instrumental in outsourcing work to India and were involved in body-shopping, Indian software firms were almost entirely the creation of indigenous entrepreneurs. Indians in the USA have found it easier to operate in the USA than to set up enterprises in India where red tape remains daunting and infrastructure poor.

The chapter develops a less prejudiced explanation of the emergence of India's IT industry than that embodied in the preconceptions listed above. It gives due weight to historical accidents, namely that the exit of IBM in 1978 left India with a few thousand programmers familiar with mainframes, and that the presence of a few thousand Indian engineers in the USA led USA firms to turn to India at a time of programmer shortage. It points to the role of a new technology, namely wireless satellite links, which made it unnecessary for programmers to be located on-site and enabled Indian firms to work at home for clients abroad; it thereby enabled them to move up the value chain from being suppliers of labour to contract producers of software. It highlights the industry's main success, namely conversion of fresh engineering graduates into reliable programmers within weeks of induction. Finally, it describes the irreversible change brought about in the global industry by the US downturn beginning in 2000, and its impact on the markets and the structure of the industry.

The rest of this chapter is organised as follows: Section 2.1 maps the software product space and the position of Indian firms within it. Section 2.2 traces the exodus of programmers from India in response to shortages in the USA beginning in the late 1980s. Section 2.3 describes the resulting labour shortage faced by the Indian IT industry and the practices it developed to circumvent the shortage. Section 2.4 describes the emergence of an IT export industry from the early 1990s following the advent of VSAT radio links with the major markets. Section 2.5 describes the impact on the industry of the end of the IT boom in the USA in 2000. Section 2.6 shows the strong profitability of the industry and the impact on its development. Section 2.7 covers the industry's infrastructural requirements. Section 2.8 describes how the educational system responded to provide the rapidly rising manpower requirements of the industry. Section 2.9 discusses government policies impacting the industry, and Section 2.10 analyses the industry's share in global markets for various types of software, and from it draws some conclusions on what it needs to do to meet potential competition and secure its markets.

## 2.1  INDIA'S SOFTWARE SPECIALISATION

The most striking feature of the IT industry in the past 50 years worldwide, has been the fall in the cost of information processing, as semiconductors or 'chips' have become cheaper, smaller and more powerful. This has led to three major trends. First, computers have been designed to take up ever-larger data storage and processing tasks. Second, they have been miniaturised and commoditised. Finally, chips have been divorced from computers, and embodied in diverse equipment to make it more automatic, versatile and less demanding of human attention. There has been a parallel and related trend in telecommunications. Partly as a result of the use of processors telecommunications have become cheaper, can carry more information faster, and to more remote locations. Telecommunications have thereby made integration of management possible in companies with multiple locations.

With these developments, the room-sized computers of 50 years ago have given way to three types of equipment. Powerful mainframe computers – servers – that can handle the information-processing requirements of large and dispersed organisations and that will be connected by routers – coordinating devices – to area networks consisting of a number of workstations; varieties of small, stand-alone personal computers (PCs) designed to serve individuals or small offices; and microprocessors or chips embodied in various intelligent machines, ranging from machine tools to washing machines.

Specialised software is written for these three types of devices. Mainframe computers typically use elaborate software. The servers and routers have software written into them by their manufacturers but the software is flexible enough for the customer to expand, modify and connect it with other software. Since the number of large computers is small, the number of copies of their programmes sold is also small, so the programmes are expensive. Mainframe manufacturers improve the programmes in successive generations of computers but it is rare for owners of old computers to replace their software; they generally modify it incrementally as their needs change and networks grow. Thus large computers create a demand for complex software built into new ones, as well as for repair, maintenance and modification of installed software.

Personal computers also come with 'operating system' software initially written into them. In their case, however, it is unusual for the software to be modified after installation as suppliers embody the capabilities commonly required by users in the original copy. The operating systems have a capacity to accept add-ons, limited by their compatibility with the operating system, and there is a distinct market for such specialised software for use on PCs. Thus PCs support a very large market for built-in software, plus a market for various add-ons. Machines and consumer durables embody processors that can interpret a limited number of commands and are controlled by a relatively simple console. The software for these is called system-on-a-chip (SOC) or embedded software.

Thus, each of the three types of equipment has a corresponding type of software. In addition, two other types are important. Large organisations have specialised needs, and software is created specifically to cater to those needs. The special activities of such organisations are called domains and domain-specific software is created for hotels, airlines, banks and so on. And finally, software has begun to be written for programmers to increase their productivity, reduce errors and take the tedium out of programme writing. Known as software tools this type of software often comes written on a shrink-wrapped CD.

These five classes of software are not mutually exclusive. Tools are also designed for PC owners. In the initial years of the Internet there was a flood of tools in the market to help PC owners set up their own websites. Similarly, much domain software is marketed retail, off-the-shelf, instead of being written for customers.

One distinction is between product software, either written into computers or sold shrink-wrapped or on the Internet, and services, which are contracted by and delivered to particular users. Few products require no service at all, and services often yield reusable or resaleable components akin to products. By and large, Indian firms provide services rather than products. Another distinction is between embedded software and computer software. Indian firms are largely involved in the latter, having only a small presence in embedded software. A third distinction is between information technology (IT), which encompasses all the types of software described above, and IT-enabled services (ITES), which are commercial activities using IT. India entered IT first, but has made an entry into ITES since 1998.

## 2.2 BODY-SHOPPING

The demand for programmers in the USA began to spill over to India in the late 1980s and programmers began to leave their jobs and move to the USA. Table 2.1 shows the wage differentials in 1995. Figures for 1997 show even wider differentials (Arora et al. 2000). The differential was the greatest for programmers, Indian relative wages being higher for more senior staff.

Programmers were easier to train or replace and firms took fresh engineering or IT graduates and trained them in-house, but experienced managers or specialists were scarcer, and were paid more in an effort to retain them.

*Table 2.1   IT industry wages elsewhere as a multiple of Indian wages, 1995*

|                              | USA | UK  | Ireland | Greece |
|------------------------------|-----|-----|---------|--------|
| Project leader               | 2.3 | 1.7 | 1.9     | 1.0    |
| Business analyst             | 1.8 | 1.8 | 1.7     | 1.3    |
| Systems analyst              | 3.4 | 2.4 | 2.6     | 1.1    |
| Quality assurance specialist | 3.6 | 2.4 | 2.1     | 1.1    |
| Programmer                   | 5.1 | 3.6 | 2.6     | 1.6    |

*Source*:   Calculated from Heeks (1996).

The early stages of the body-shopping market are now lost in obscurity. It was dominated by individuals and small firms, most of which did not admit to being body-shoppers. Laws passed in the 1970s, when Indians began to work in the Middle East, placed stringent obligations on firms sending workers abroad. The firms have to be registered with the Custodian of Emigrants, submit periodic information, and meet the cost of repatriation in certain circumstances. The firms that had sprung up to recruit manual workers died out in the 1980s, and none were set up, when the demand arose in the late 1980s. Those that did emerge posed as consultants and software producers. A large proportion of the recruiting was not done by firms in India. People close to the potential employers in the United States – mostly but not necessarily Indian engineers – used contacts in India to recruit for them. Large American auditing and consulting firms often recruited for their clients. In the heyday of the boom in the late 1990s, it was not uncommon for persons or firms from the USA to advertise in Indian newspapers, hold interviews in hotels and recruit directly without any infrastructure in India.

The presence of Indian engineers in the USA was the primary reason that recruiters looked to India, which was otherwise remote from the USA in location as well as in economic relations. The fact that English was widely used in India was also important. Computer languages use a limited vocabulary and the fact that it is in English does not give an anglophone programmer an edge. However communication with the customer and with other members of IT teams is crucial. This is where Indian programmers' knowledge of English helped.

We have no estimates of the number of programmers who were body-shopped or of their earnings. However, the money they sent back shows up in the Indian balance of payments as remittances. Private transfers from abroad rose sharply from $2.08 billion in 1990-1991 to $12.4 billion in 1996-1997, and fluctuated between $10 billion and $16 billion till 2002-2003. Inflows of bank deposits from non-resident Indians provided another $1-3 billion a year through the 1990s. These two figures give upper estimates of programmers' remittances. Most of the deposits are term deposits and were withdrawn at the end of the period. Thus programmers' remittances in the early years, and even very recently, were comparable to and could have been higher than software export receipts.

We have one other indicator of the outflow of programmers – from the USA Immigration and Naturalisation Service (Table 2.2). H-1B visas are issued to workers from abroad coming temporarily to the USA. They are issued for a term of six years to either the workers or their employers and a worker who stays on longer can proceed to get a Green Card and, eventually, citizenship, while working on an H-1B visa. The USA issued 51 000 H-1B visas to Indian programmers in fiscal year 2000, 136 000 in 2001 and 47 000 in 2002; the number of visas to Chinese programmers, the next largest group, was 5000 in 2000, 12 000 in 2001 and 5000 in 2002. We do not have comparable figures for previous years; but in 1996, 1998 and 1999, a total of 179 000 H-1B visas were issued to Indians. If the proportion of programmers had been the same in those years as later, some 120 000 of the visa holders would have been programmers. That gives 1 355 000 in the six years for which there are some data – as against 192 000 programmers in IT firms in India at the end of March 2002 (NASSCOM 2002b). Many of the H-lB visa holders would have been working for Indian IT firms and some may have commuted between India and the USA. But even allowing for these, the numbers who were involved in body-shopping were comparable to programmers working in India on software exports.

## 2.3 RESPONSE OF INDIAN FIRMS

From the 1950s, IBM had a virtual monopoly of computers in India. Its 360 Series, released in the 1960s, became the workhorse of large organisations, which maintained batteries of programmers to write software for the machines. In 1978, however, George Fernandes, then Minister of Industries asked IBM to take local shareholders into its subsidiary. It refused, and wound up operations in India, the government set up a company to employ IBM's ex-employees on maintainance of the installed computers.

From then until the opening up of the early 1990s, the only mainframes being imported into India were Russian. Western computers could not be

*Table 2.2 Visas issued to temporary and exchange workers and intra-company transferees (USA, fiscal years 1996, 1998-2001)*

|  | 1996 | 1998 | 1999 | 2000 | 2001 | 2002 |
|---|---|---|---|---|---|---|
| Computer workers – total | n.a. | n.a. | n.a. | 74 551 | 191 397 | 75 114 |
| - from India | n.a. | n.a. | n.a. | 50 587 | 136 646 | 47 477 |
| - from China | n.a. | n.a. | n.a. | 5276 | 12 009 | 5377 |
|  |  |  |  |  |  |  |
| All workers - total | 227 440 | 240 947 | 302 326 | 136 786 | 331 206 | 197 537 |
| - from India | 31 417 | 62 544 | 85 012 | 60 757 | 161 561 | 64 980 |
| - from China | 6181 | 7746 | 11 367 | 27 331 | 12 333 | 18 841 |

*Notes:*
n.a. = not available.
The fiscal year in the USA runs from October to September; for instance, fiscal year 2001 is October 2000 to September 2001.

*Source:* USINS (1997-2002).

imported because of an American embargo on export of high-technology equipment to India, which was considered an ally of the Soviet Union. When Rajiv Gandhi became prime minister and visited the USA in 1985, he asked to be allowed to import Cray computers, then the most powerful computers available. Eventually, a licence was issued for one for the Indian meteorological office. It did not arrive. Instead the government's Centre for Development of Advanced Computing (CDAC) connected together a string of less powerful computers to create the first powerful parallel computer. CDAC continues to sell a 1-teraflop version (CDAC 2003).

Meanwhile, computers were finding commercial applications in India as in western countries – in materials planning, airline scheduling, CAD/CAM and so on. Programmers got training in working out these applications on ageing and heterogeneous computers. In this way, a stock of technological capability was built up (Evans 1992). In the 1980s, programmers were employed by three types of organisations. First, there was Computer Maintenance Corporation, which employed software engineers who worked for IBM before it closed shop in India in 1978. Then there were producers or suppliers of computers. The 1970s and 1980s saw the evolution of computers into mini-computers and PCs, and the number of their producers grew in the USA, Europe and Japan. India's import substitution policies reserved the domestic market to whoever could 'produce' a product in the country. The definition of production was vague: it could consist of assembly of imported components, with a few being produced within the country or bought from another domestic supplier – who could get his own import licences. Thus a large number of licensees emerged who, for instance, imported the motherboard of the PC and put it into a box welded by themselves. Finally, since mini-computers did not come loaded with user-friendly programmes, users also employed programmers. Amongst the users were consultants, large firms and government institutions. Thus, of India's software producers today, TCS started as a consultancy in 1968, whilst Tata Infotech (1977), Patni Computer Systems (1978) and Wipro (1980) began as computer manufacturers. Programmers were also employed by large companies and government laboratories. They began to lose programmers as the USA demand for programmers spilt over to India in the late 1980s. Loss of workers was their prime worry well into the 1990s; the survey done by Arora et al. (2000) showed labour shortage and attrition to be the foremost problem. They responded to the exodus in a number of ways.

First, they turned themselves into labour suppliers. USA importers of programmers, whether they were software producers or users, did not know or have a presence in India; they had to rely on someone to select Indian programmers and deal with the procedures related to their import. A new type of intermediary arose who did this for them. Some of them were Indians settled in the USA; some were programmers who had been to the USA and established contacts. But Indian employers of programmers also turned to this business and to facilitate it; the larger ones set up branches in the USA. They would hire out their employees on an hourly or daily basis and would take them back when the work was over. Many employees found jobs in the USA and left their Indian employers, but some stayed with their employers. In 1988, 90 per cent of Indian software exports consisted of on-site work. With the coming of satellite links in 1992, it became possible to work for clients abroad without physically sending the programmers abroad – or at least to do part of the work in India. Then the share of on-site work in exports declined (Figure 2.2), it fell to 66 per cent in 1995 and 56 per cent in 2000 (Kumar 2001: 4280) and in 2002-2003 it came down to 39 per cent (NASSCOM 2003a).

The second response to the exodus was to structure wages so as to discourage the most essential people from leaving. As Table 2.1 shows, Indian wages as a proportion of wages abroad were the lowest for the bottom-of-the-rung programmer. They were higher for programming specialists, and still higher for domain specialists and project managers. The organisation of the typical Indian software firm was outwardly egalitarian; workers and managers had similar cubicles, ate together and played together. But there was a hierarchy – more pronounced at any rate than in a typical firm in the USA. Workers kept a log of time spent and work done that went into a common server and they were assessed on the basis of productivity, quality, record maintenance and the project audit report.

Third, they developed active and anticipatory recruiting techniques, the standard method of which was campus recruitment. The favourite campuses were those of engineering colleges. The fact that most people at the top of IT firms were engineers may have played a part in this, but preference for engineers rested on the fact that selection at engineering colleges was more rigorous, and that engineers were likely to have had some courses in computing and to have worked with computers.[3] Fourth, with the recruitment of fresh graduates they also developed short, focused training programmes designed to bring them up to speed quickly with training mirroring problems that the firm had worked on previously. Fifth, they made the working conditions attractive. They built comfortable dedicated offices, which often embodied sports and entertainment facilities, and they organised community activities like tournaments and picnics. Finally, they recorded the progress of work, defining the process and documenting it so that if a worker left before a job was complete, someone else could immediately continue the work. A client would normally look for these precautions; they are embodied in various certification procedures such as the Capability Maturity Model (CMM) of Carnegie Mellon University's Software Engineering Institute. In

2003, NASSCOM (2003a) listed 225 firms with ISO9000 certification or one of its variants, 48 with CMM5 certification, and 45 with CMM3 or 4 certification.

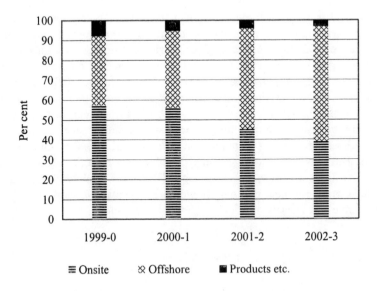

≡ Onsite      ⊗ Offshore      ■ Products etc.

*Figure 2.2*: *Proportion of on-site and offshore work, 1998-1999 to 2001-2002*

These process innovations were not, of course, entirely indigenous. Indian firms worked closely with their clients abroad. The clients often paid on a time-and-materials basis. To ensure that the time spent led to maximum output, clients provided the working environment and practices for programmers who were body-shopped, and set standards for them in offshore development. In particular, the flat hierarchical structures, round-the-clock working and the stress on incentive payments were borrowed from American practices.

Whereas body-shopping for large IT users imparted managerial and work-related practices to Indian firms, working for foreign IT firms familiarised them with OEM software and its architecture. Several kinds of relationships between Indian and foreign IT firms developed (Patibandla and Petersen 2002). For instance, Nortell and Cisco set up joint ventures with large Indian firms; essentially, parts of the Indian firm's facilities and manpower were dedicated to work done for their partners. Motorola and Hewlett Packard outsourced work to a number of small satellite firms. Firms with proprietary software, such as Motorola, Oracle and Texas Instruments, did not work with or give out work to local firms. Patibandla and Petersen regressed the revenue of 20 large Indian IT firms in 1990-1999 on foreign firms' share in Indian IT sales and on royalty payments by the Indian firms, amongst other variables, and concluded that there was considerable spillover of technology, work practices and so on from foreign to Indian firms. Our observation, based on interviews with Indian firms, suggests that the contact between local firms and Indian subsidiaries of foreign firms varied considerably. Whilst some outsourced work or partnered large local firms, others had no contact at the firm level at all; in particular, those that did high-level R&D kept to themselves. Most Indian firms were exporters; spillovers to them from abroad – from clients, foreign IT firms, and through employees recruited abroad – were more important than from foreign firms within India.

The process innovations were made in order to cope with the rapid loss of workers. But they were more generally valuable. It is these innovations that give Indian firms a competitive advantage. They were exhibited to potential customers to assure them that quality would be maintained, work would be done on time and security of information would be assured.


## 2.4 OFFSHORE DEVELOPMENT

The alternative to body-shopping, namely writing the software in India and exporting it, was uneconomic. The software had to be exported on tapes or disks that were subject to heavy import duties that raised costs, and duty rebates did not work well. The only profitable way to export software was through people, who were all too likely to stay on in the USA.

Satellite links made the disembodied export of software possible and the first link was set up in 1985. At that time, the government did not allow private links so Texas Instruments gifted it with the equipment, which it then proceeded to use from its Bangalore establishment. IBM, which wanted to set up a link in 1988, ran into the same problem: the government insisted on retaining its monopoly in telecommunications, the rates offered by its Department of Telecommunications were exorbitant, and it was completely inexperienced in running VSAT links.

The newly set-up Department of Electronics broke this impasse when in 1991 it created a corporation called Software Technology Parks of India (STPI), which, being owned by the government, could provide VSAT communications without breaching its monopoly (see section 2.7 below). STPI set up software technology parks (STPs) in different cities, each of which provided satellite links to be used by firms with wireless connections to them. In 1993 the government began to allow private dedicated links as well. These links allowed work done in India to be transmitted abroad, and lessened the need for programmers to travel. However, Indian firms still had to convince their American customers that a satellite link was as reliable as a team of programmers working in a client's office. To do so, one body-shopper moved its team to a building across the road first, then, once he had proved to the customer that distance was no handicap, he was allowed to move the team to India.

Another important change was in the import regime. In the 1980s, an importer of hardware had to obtain an import licence from the Chief Controller of Imports and Exports, who in turn required a no-objection certificate from the Department of Electronics. That meant going to Delhi, waiting for an appointment and trying to persuade the bureaucracy. In the 1992 import policy, computers were freed from import licensing and import duties on them were reduced in the same year. As a result, it became possible for Indian software firms to work on the same computers as their clients. A bonding facility even made it possible for clients or parent firms to lend computers to Indian firms.

These two changes – satellite communications and import liberalisation – made offshore development possible and firms began shifting out of body-shopping. This development had a number of implications. When programmers were sent abroad, they worked on fragments of programmes assigned to them; they could seldom get an idea of the entire programme and what it was meant to do. Offshore development now made it possible for firms to take orders for complete programmes. Indian firms could work for final clients; now the bulk of the work came from them, and it became possible for firms to market their products. The availability of complete jobs from clients led to a change to sale of services by results instead of labour time only. Work for final clients also led firms to specialise in work for particular industries or verticals: it led in particular to India's specialisation in software for banking, insurance, airlines and so on, giving India a brand value and a reputation.

The next big technological change was the web. Even when satellite links became available, they could be used only by exporters who had their own dishes or shared those of STPs. The Internet offered the same links on telephone lines and as the number of firms using the Internet expanded, the potential market for software expanded correspondingly. Since it was far easier and cheaper to obtain telephone lines than satellite links, the Internet greatly increased the number of potential exporters. It also opened up a new field of work. Earlier, IT users could connect geographically separated locations only with satellite links but once they could use the web, setting up of integrated systems became possible for dispersed locations and new work to connect such locations became available. The web provided a considerable advantage for resource-poor Indian firms. It had even greater influence on businesses that required frequent interaction with clients such as banks, airlines and sellers of consumer durables. By offering a new channel of communication, the web made their services cheaper and more convenient.

## 2.5  END OF THE IT BOOM IN THE USA

The stock market boom in the USA ended in April 2000 and with it, the high valuations of IT firms and the easy availability of capital for the industry. Growth in the USA slowed, and profits of firms came under pressure. The slowdown was bound to affect the growth of the Indian IT industry, since North America accounted for 62.7 per cent of India's software exports in 2000-2001. But a number of other things happened at the same time. The labour shortage eased and since the Indian IT industry paid lower wages and lost programmers to the USA, the fall in demand for them brought down the rate of attrition. IT costs came under pressure everywhere, which increased the demand for Indian software services as against more expensive sources, but also led clients to look for even cheaper sources. Finally, the downturn affected different IT services differently – in-house IT activities in the USA, which absorbed most body-shopped programmers, declined, and more in-house work was outsourced in the form of ITES and business processes. But in India, as programmers became cheaper and more easily available, in-house activities increased at the expense of purchased services. The impact of these changes varied with the size of firms.

Export growth halved between 2000-2001 and 2001-2002 (Table 2.3), but growth of domestic sales slumped even more. With a less tight market for programmers, large Indian clients could afford larger IT departments in-house. Consequently the industry oriented itself even further towards exports after the downturn in the USA.

Amongst markets for exports, the USA share went up from 61.2 per cent in 2000-2001 to 65.6 per cent in the following year, and the UK's share from 11.8 per cent to 14.1 per cent (NASSCOM 2002a: 33-5; NASSCOM 2003a: 28-9). The share of the rest of the world went down from 27 per cent to 20.3 per cent; this fall was widely distributed. The USA and the UK were the two countries with the most liberal labour import regimes. Table 2.2 shows a huge increase in the number of H-1B visas issued to Indian programmers in 2001-2002. Some of these visas were no doubt taken by Indian IT export companies. In markets other than the USA and the UK, visa regulations discriminated more strongly against foreign programmers so when demand growth slowed down, demand for Indian IT services fell disproportionately.

Exports of ITES saw hardly any slowdown. Their share in exports rose from 12.1 per cent in 2000-2001 to 16 per cent in 2001-2002. ITES used relatively less educated labour; India's labour pool in such labour was much larger, and the wage differential greater. Hence as cost pressures increased, ITES began to move to India.

Some of these IT-enabled services were located in India by foreign ITES providers and some by large users of ITES. GE Capital was the biggest as it employed 12 000 workers (NASSCOM 2003a: 71). Banks and financial companies which had earlier bought Indian IT services or set up IT operations, also set up large ITES centres: Standard Chartered employed 2500, JP Morgan Chase 3000, and AMEX and HSBC 2000 each. NASSCOM (2003b) put the share of foreign companies in ITES revenues at 45.1 per cent. ITES were not the only services foreign companies relocated in India; their share in services exports also went up from 14-15 per cent in 2000-2001 to 22 per cent in 2001-2002 (NASSCOM 2002a: 31; NASSCOM 2003a: 40). Earlier, the major activity of foreign companies was reported to be R&D (Patibandla and Petersen 2002). Their Indian affiliates were not services exporters as they did only in-house work for the parents. After 2000, however, foreign companies have set up profit centres in India that do work for outside clients. Thus there was migration of foreign IT activities to India's low-wage base. Amongst the large companies abroad that were clients of India's software industry, there was pressure on IT budgets. They reduced the number of suppliers, made them compete for business, forced down their rates and made them give more comprehensive services. These cost-cutting moves affected the smaller suppliers more severely; they were less capable of taking on broader responsibilities and were edged out. They were also more vulnerable as they had fewer clients – many worked for a single client – and loss of clients sent more of them into bankruptcy and closure. NASSCOM's estimates, fragile as they are, indicate the extent of the pressure (Table 2.4). They show a rise in the export share of foreign firms from 14-15 per cent in 2000-2001 to 22 per cent in 2001-2002, and a corresponding fall in the share of Indian firms exporting less than Rs1 billion from 14-15 per cent to 10-11 per cent. But specialist product firms, which had an export share of 3-4 per cent in 2000-2001 disappeared the next year, although it is unlikely that they ceased to export altogether. Insofar as they retained a share of the market, the share of small firms must have fallen even more sharply. Thus 2001-2002 saw a substantial rise in foreign firms' export share, at the expense of small Indian firms. The former did not take away the market of the latter. Changes in the market were unfavourable to small firms; and the rise in the share of large firms was due to relocation of their activities to India. Small firms were also adversely affected by the flight to safety amongst employees. Employment in the industry was suddenly proving to be precarious, and programmers had developed a preference for working in big companies who chose the more experienced of them.

Table 2.3 Indian software sales, 1990-2000 to 2001-2002

| | Revenue ($ million) | | | | Growth (%) | | |
|---|---|---|---|---|---|---|---|
| | 1990-2000 | 2000-2001 | 2001-2002 | 2002-2003 | 2000-2001 | 2001-2002 | 2002-2003 |
| Export | 3962 | 6217 | 7647 | 9875 | 56.9 | 23.0 | 29.1 |
| Software | 3397 | 4737 | 5597 | 6575 | 39.4 | 18.2 | 17.5 |
| ITES | 565 | 930 | 1475 | 2400 | 64.6 | 58.6 | 62.7 |
| R&D | n.a. | 550 | 575 | 900 | | 4.5 | 56.5 |
| Domestic sales | 1577 | 2081 | 2311 | 2580 | 32.0 | 11.1 | 11.6 |
| Software | 1330 | 1737 | 1923 | 2203 | 30.6 | 10.7 | 14.6 |
| ITES | 247 | 344 | 388 | 377 | 39.3 | 12.8 | -2.9 |
| Turnover | 5539 | 8298 | 9958 | 12 455 | 49.8 | 20.0 | 25.1 |
| Share in turnover (%) of | | | | | | | |
| Exports | 71.5 | 74.9 | 76.8 | 79.3 | | | |
| ITES | 14.7 | 15.4 | 18.7 | 22.3 | | | |

Source: NASSCOM (2002, 2003a, b).

48

NASSCOM's 2000-2001 figures cover only its members, whereas the following year's figures cover all exporters. Hence it is likely that the earlier figures overestimate the shares of large and medium firms as well as perhaps foreign firms. If they do, the share of small firms fell even more sharply than Table 2.4 suggests.

## 2.6  FINANCES

Beyond the export and revenue figures that NASSCOM collects, little information on the finances of the software industry is available. Many of the firms are offshoots of conglomerates or hardware firms and information concerning their software activities cannot be separated out. A significant proportion are branches of multinational firms whose finances are not always transparent. The biggest firm, Tata Consultancy Services (TCS), was fully owned by the Tatas until late 2004 and gave out little beyond its revenue information. The only firms for which some figures are available are those incorporated as Indian companies, which constitute a tiny fraction of the firms and account for less than half of exports. Amongst them, the financial accounts of the biggest, which have floated equity on the New York Stock Exchange or NASDAQ, are models of detail and clarity; the rest are variable. However, the scanty figures available yield some illuminating conclusions. Table 2.5 gives the consolidated profit and loss account of such firms.

The accounts confirm the intensity of competition for labour in the late 1990s: the share of wages in income rose 5 percentage points between 1997-1998 and 2000-2001. Still, wages were only 20.7 per cent of income in 2000-2001. Low Indian wages gave the firms an advantage. This, however, was not because the software industry was a labour-intensive one, but rather because the difference between Indian and USA wages, converted at the current exchange rate, was enormous (Table 2.1). The difference in the cost of living explained much of the difference in wage. However, the wage costs of Indian firms could have doubled without them being forced out of business as profit margins exceeded wage costs.

Despite the rise in wages, the mean profit margins increased due to the fall of other costs. As exports came to be made increasingly through electronic communications, and the share of body-shopping, with its attendant costs of travel and accommodation, dropped, non-wage costs fell, and profit margins rose. The bulk of the profits were retained as dividends took less than 3 per cent of revenue. Higher profits enabled the companies to pay off debts quicker and as a result, their interest costs fell (Table 2.6). This too added to net margins.

*Table 2.4 Size and ownership structure of the software export industry, 2000-2001 and 2001-2002*

| | Annual exports | Number of firms | | Share of exports (%) | |
| | Rs bn | 2000-2001 | 2001-2002 | 2000-2001 | 2001-2002 |
|---|---|---|---|---|---|
| Large Indian firms | >10 | 5 | 5 | 33-35 | 32 |
| Medium Indian firms | 1-10 | 49 | 47 | 33-35 | 35 |
| Small Indian firms | <1 | 762* | 2858 | 14-15 | 10-11 |
| Subsidiaries of overseas firms | | | | 14-15 | 22 |
| Product makers | | | | 3-4 | |
| Specialist service providers | | | | 3-4 | 3-4 |

*Note:* *NASSCOM members only.

*Source:* NASSCOM (2002a, 2003a).

*Table 2.5  Income and expenditure of selected software companies, 1997-1998 and 2000-2001*

| | 1997-1998 | 2000-2001 | 1997-1998 | 2000-2001 |
|---|---|---|---|---|
| Number of companies | 148 | 255 | 148 | 255 |
| | Rs billion | | Percentage | |
| Income | 73.4 | 227.3 | 100.0 | 100.0 |
| Expenditure | 55.2 | 155.5 | 75.2 | 68.4 |
| Materials and stores | 19.1 | 20.4 | 25.9 | 9.0 |
| Wages and salaries | 11.5 | 46.9 | 15.7 | 20.7 |
| Gross profit | 18.2 | 71.8 | 24.8 | 31.6 |
| Interest and lease rent | 3.2 | 4.2 | 4.4 | 1.8 |
| Depreciation | 3.4 | 11.1 | 4.6 | 4.9 |
| Provision for income tax | 1.4 | 4.4 | 1.9 | 1.9 |
| Net profit | 10.2 | 52.1 | 13.9 | 22.9 |
| Dividends | 2.1 | 5.6 | 2.9 | 2.5 |
| Retained earnings | 8.1 | 46.5 | 11.0 | 20.5 |

*Source:* CMIE Prowess Database (2003).

*Table 2.6  Consolidated balance sheet of selected IT companies, 1997-1998 and 2000-2001*

|  | 1997-1998 | 2000-2001 | 1997-1998 | 2000-2001 |
|---|---|---|---|---|
|  | Rs billion | | Percentage | |
| Total assets | 82.2 | 323.0 | 100.0 | 100.0 |
| Land        and buildings | 4.6 | 16.7 | 5.6 | 5.2 |
| Equipment | 20.3 | 55.1 | 24.7 | 17.1 |
| Investments in group companies | 13.7 | 77.6 | 16.6 | 24.0 |
| Other investments | 1.9 | 17.7 | 2.4 | 5.5 |
| Inventories | 5.7 | 7.4 | 6.9 | 2.3 |
| Receivables | 13.7 | 58.8 | 16.8 | 18.2 |
| Cash and bank balances | 5.1 | 43.6 | 6.3 | 13.5 |
| Total liabilities | 82.2 | 323.0 | 100.0 | 100.0 |
| Paid-up capital | 4.5 | 12.7 | 5.5 | 3.9 |
| Reserves | 15.6 | 95.4 | 5.6 | 6.1 |
| Net worth | 20.1 | 108.1 | 24.5 | 32.5 |
| Borrowings | 28.2 | 14.1 | 34.2 | 4.4 |

*Source*:  CMIE Prowess Database (2003).

Table 2.4 covers only exports so we have no data on the market structure in the domestic market, but IT directories list thousands of firms, many of whom have not exported at all. They do IT work for local industry, hospitals, governments and so on. Some combine software consultancy with the sale of hardware and packaged software. Thus, below the software export industry is a large base of smaller firms serving the domestic market, which have moved from one speciality to another as market changes have required.

## 2.7  INFRASTRUCTURE

The most important component of infrastructure for body-shopping was air connections. India was well connected with Europe and East Asia but the demand for programmers came from the USA. Besides this, the connections were constrained by factors other than distance. India had only four international airports in 1990 through which all international traffic was funnelled. Of the four, international airlines preferred Bombay and Delhi, which generated the most traffic. Despite the government's manipulation of landing rights, few international airlines were prepared to fly to Calcutta or Madras. There was also the question of reciprocity. Landing rights are negotiated through bilateral bargaining between governments and the government gave its own airlines, Air India and Indian Airlines, monopoly of international flights. However, they could neither afford the investment required nor attract the traffic necessary to use all these landing rights abroad, which limited the flights foreign airlines were allowed to fly.

As seat shortages emerged from 1996 onwards, the government allowed foreign airlines to increase the number of flights. The conversion of airports into international ones took longer as new terminals with aerobridges had to be built, and customs had to set up screening facilities. Over the 1990s, international flights were allowed into Goa, Cochin, Hyderabad, Bangalore and Amritsar, but the number of flights into those airports remained small, and so did the range of their connections. Thus programmers continued to fly chiefly through Bombay and Delhi. The two cities housed a pool of programmers, who were instrumental in turning them into major centres of the IT industry. Singapore Airlines connected Madras to San Francisco via Singapore. This flight to Silicon Valley became popular with programmers. Madras also developed into a major industry centre.

Next to airline connections, telecommunications were the most important resource. Here, the Telegraph Act of 1885 gave the government a monopoly of telecommunications. The Department of Telecommunications strongly resisted pressures to relax the monopoly and in the 1980s, its high charges and unfamiliarity with VSAT technology deterred IT companies from setting up offshore development centres. Finally in 1991, the Department of Electronics, found a way of getting around the difficulty – it conceived Software Technology Parks. The model for STPs was Export Promotion Zones which were areas of land cordoned off by the Customs Department, specialised in exporting and allowed to import inputs and capital goods duty-free for export production. STPs were initially set up in defunct industrial estates, each of which was equipped with a dish antenna and leased out rooms to software exporters. Soon, however, duty-free status was granted to firms located outside the STPs as well and they were allowed to set up radio links and use the STPs' dish antennas for transmitting and receiving data. The costs of registration with the STPs were low resulting in many firms being registered that did not export, and many more that had negligible exports. Once private firms were allowed to uplink directly in 1995, all the larger firms did so; in 1998-99, the average exports of firms in software technology parks were only Rs 21 million (Table 2.7). STPs provided a cheap link for smaller firms, and their share of exports increased from 8 per cent in 1992-1993 to 68 per cent in 1999-2000 – the last year for which figures are available.

*Table 2.7  STPI clients and their exports, 1998-1999*

|  | No. of clients | Exports (Rs bn) | Exports (%) | Exports per client (Rs m.) |
|---|---|---|---|---|
| Bangalore | 746 | 43.2 | 37.2 | 57.9 |
| Noida (Delhi) | 1103 | 24.5 | 21.1 | 22.2 |
| Madras | 535 | 18.9 | 16.3 | 35.3 |
| Hyderabad | 977 | 10.6 | 9.1 | 10.8 |
| New Bombay | 755 | 9.6 | 8.3 | 12.7 |
| Poona | 474 | 5.7 | 4.9 | 12.1 |
| Calcutta | 131 | 1.5 | 1.3 | 11.5 |
| Bhubaneswar | 152 | 0.9 | 0.8 | 5.9 |
| Trivandrum | 188 | 0.6 | 0.5 | 3.0 |
| Gandhinagar (Ahmedabad) | 295 | 0.3 | 0.2 | 0.9 |
| Jaipur | 95 | 0.2 | 0.1 | 1.6 |
| Mohali (Chandigarh) | 131 | 0.2 | 0.1 | 1.1 |
| Total | 5582 | 116.1 | 100.0 | 20.8 |

*Source*:  STPI (2000).

In 1995, the government gave licences to private telephone companies – one fixed-line and two mobile competitors were licensed in each of the 24 circles into which the telecommunications department divided the country (a licensee could hold multiple licences). Soon after the new licences were issued, the government telephone providers gave telephone connections to whoever wanted one, depriving the private licensees of a market. Some licensees were liquidated or sold off and the agitation of the remaining private licensees induced the government to migrate from licence fees to a share of revenue. There were also recurrent quarrels between the public and private providers over interconnection fees. The policy changes did not however help the fixed-line providers, who still have very limited networks. Despite the acrimony, competition did increase the number of telephone lines and bring down the charges. The cost of leased lines for software export also came down.

Every IT company needed a continuous, steady, high-quality electricity supply. No state except West Bengal provided an uninterrupted power supply – even West Bengal did not guarantee quality. Hence, IT companies required power backup. The kind of backup depended on the frequency and length of blackouts. In the southern states, where blackouts lasted only a few hours and were well spread out, IT companies generally set up a bank of inverters to provide for 8-12 hours of power. Elsewhere – and everywhere in businesses that could not tolerate an interruption, such as call centres – the companies set up diesel generators.

State governments owned the power supply companies. Subsidies to farmers and domestic users led to losses and made it impossible for the companies to attract funds for expansion. Many states were incapable of giving firms uninterrupted power. But spurred by competition, they devised an answer to the power problem, which also solved the IT companies' accommodation problem. As discussed in the finances section, getting the right kind of accommodation, which could house good communications, provide a comfortable working environment and adequate parking space, was a major concern for IT companies.

Some state governments converted old industrial estates into IT estates, others set up new specially designed industrial estates with communications, central air conditioning, restaurants, shops and entertainment. In those states that were attractive to the IT industry – especially Karnataka and Tamil Nadu – the new IT estates attracted big companies. Elsewhere they acted chiefly as nurseries for small companies.

The large tracts of land on which the new estates were set up were generally not available in the cities, but were located on the outskirts or even further away. Those companies that moved to such remote sites found it more difficult to attract workers and many of them transported workers in their own buses. Land costs outside cities were low so companies built large establishments there with restaurants, sports facilities, gardens and swimming pools. The 120-acre Satyam campus for instance, 38 kilometres out of Hyderabad, has a small zoo, an aviary, and a botanical garden besides the usual gym and restaurant.

## 2.8 EDUCATION

As shown in section 2.2, the USA issued about 307 000 H-1B visas to Indian programmers in 1996 and 1998-2002; adding figures for 1997, the figure would rise to 350 000 for 1996-2002. Then there were IT workers who migrated on visas other than H-1B visas, estimated by NASSCOM at 20 per cent of the total or 25 per cent of those who obtained H-1B visas – approximately 90 000. In addition, there were those who got visas before 1996, whose number we may conservatively put at 50 000. Thus programmers who obtained USA visas alone were at least half a million. NASSCOM estimated 298 250 IT workers in India in 2001-2002 – 170 000 in exports, 22 000 in domestic software production, and 224 250 in IT user organisations (NASSCOM 2003a: 63). Thus we get a total of migrant and India-based programmers of 800 000. Insofar as some of the H-1B visas were issued to employees of Indian IT companies and to programmers who commuted from India, and given that some of the H-1B visas would have expired without being replaced by a Green Card or citizenship, the total number of programmers would be fewer; even so, it would be in the range of 600 000–700 000. NASSCOM placed the number of IT workers in 1985-1986 at 6 800 (NASSCOM 2002a: 63). Hence, although the available stock of programmers may have induced recruiters from abroad to come to India in the first place, the growth of the Indian industry – and in the USA – was sustained for over a decade by the supply of freshly trained programmers. A 2002 survey showed that the median age of software engineers was 26.5 years, and that 58 per cent of them had less than three years' experience (NASSCOM 2003a: 138-9). Whilst more experienced people were to be found at more senior levels, the typical programmer was likely to be in his or her twenties and just a few years out of college. Interviews suggest that emigration was also strongest amongst young software engineers – visa requirements would have ensured that they were graduates at least. How was the required supply of programmers created?

Entrepreneurs in the IT industry are predominantly engineers, and although many firms are owned by businessmen or business houses, the chief executives are almost always engineers. They have recruited other engineers by preference, and when engineers were not available they recruited science graduates with a master's degree in computer applications (a degree that was developed to meet the shortage of programmers). According to a NASSCOM-Hewitt survey of recruitment practices, 88 per cent of the firms visited engineering campuses, and 47 per cent recruited only there. The other important method of recruitment was through employee referrals and 68 per cent of the firms recruited this way; 94 per cent of those would pay employees for every recruit they brought.

By the early 1990s the demand for programmers exceeded the supply of engineers. The IT industry had to compete with other industries for engineers who once recruited, had to be trained. It was necessary to expand supply

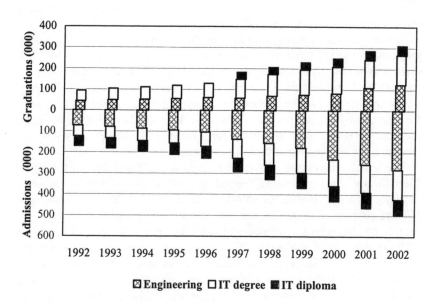

**☒ Engineering ☐ IT degree ■ IT diploma**

*Figure 2.3  Engineering, IT degrees and diplomas, 1992-2002*

beyond engineers and to impart training in computer applications in the universities. In response to the demand, a number of universities started masters and diploma courses in computer applications (MCA and DCA). According to NASSCOM (2002a, 69-70), engineering colleges offered 73 000 places in 1992, only some of which were in computer science. But there were 98 000 places in MCA and diploma courses. By 1996, the number of places in engineering courses had risen to 104 000, and in MCA and diploma courses to 122 000. But there were no graduates from the newly started MCA and diploma courses; the number of engineering graduates increased from 44 000 to 61 000. In 1997, however, the first students of MCA and diploma courses graduated, and added 76 000 to the 59 000 graduating engineers; the total number of potential programmers more than doubled within a year, to 135 000. It nearly doubled again, to 250 000 by 2002 while the number of places had increased to 498 000. The system was thus capable of supplying some 400 000 graduate programmers a year, allowing for wastage and for engineers not entering IT (Figure 2.3). NASSCOM's figures are not entirely accurate as the duration of diploma courses was shorter than degree courses. But the general point, illustrated by Figure 2.3, is correct: that the supply of potential programmers showed a marked increase in the second half of the 1990s.

This expansion of supply initially benefited Indian firms that were losing programmers to USA firms as programmers were likely to be hired by USA firms only if they had some proven skills, which they could acquire only by working for firms in India. Once they had worked for 2-3 years in India, they would have developed the contacts necessary to get a job in the USA, and the experience to improve their marketability. This is why there was a huge increase in H-lB visas in 2000-2001 (Table 2.2), when the supply of programmers employable in the USA increased.

The supply situation in 2001-2002 is shown in Table 2.8. In that year, 133 000 new workers entered the industry, while 64 400 left the country, resulting in a net increase of 65 600 or 18.2 per cent. By then, university training courses in IT and related subjects were well established, and they provided 55.9 per cent of the new entrants – 32.1 per cent were graduates and 23.8 per cent held diplomas. Almost a quarter were engineers without university training in IT, although they may have gone to private training institutes, and a fifth were neither engineers nor trained in IT. The last set of recruits would have gone into management, marketing and accounting. Many of them would be from management institutes, where 47 per cent of the firms recruited. It would not be advisable to read more into the figures, which are based on somewhat sweeping assumptions regarding the proportions of disciplines and of those entering the industry.

However, there were considerable regional variations. To cope with the shortage, both Karnataka and Andhra Pradesh freely allowed private colleges to be set up. Karnataka also set uniform standards and thus ensured that quality remained above a set minimum. This was one of the major factors behind the rise of Bangalore as the IT capital of India. The other was the presence of the Indian Institute of Science and many companies and laboratories that employed engineers. Bangalore was also very open to outsiders – as were Bombay, Poona and Delhi. By comparison, relatively parochial cities such as Calcutta suffered.

The expansion of graduate numbers was accompanied by a fall in quality. Engineering teachers found more lucrative employment in the IT industry, leaving colleges with fewer good teachers, who tended to skip over the curricula. In addition the number of computers per student was modest and although the students were supposed to learn CAD/CAM and other computer-based engineering applications, most of the teaching was done at the blackboard.

*Table 2.8  Balance sheet of Indian IT labour force, 2001-2002 (thousands)*

|  | Total | Entering the industry | Total | Per cent |
| --- | --- | --- | --- | --- |
| Number of IT workers at the beginning of the year |  |  | 360.0 |  |
| Graduates in IT (1) | 53.4 | 42.7 |  | 32.1 |
| Computer science and IT | 32.0 |  |  |  |
| Electronics and telecommunications | 21.3 |  |  |  |
| Diplomas in IT (2) | 41.1 | 31.7 |  | 23.8 |
| Computer science and IT | 22.2 |  |  |  |
| Electronics and telecommunications | 18.9 |  |  |  |
| Non-IT graduate engineers (3) | 106.7 | 32.0 |  | 24.1 |
| Non-IT, non-engineering entrants |  | 26.6 |  | 20.0 |
|  |  |  | 133.0 |  |
| Sub-total |  |  | 493.0 |  |
| *Less* workers leaving India |  |  | (64.4) |  |
| Total |  |  | 428.6 |  |

*Notes*:  It is assumed that (a) 60% of the graduates were in computer science and IT, and 40% in electronics and telecommunications, and 80% of the graduates entered the IT industry; (b). 54% of those with diplomas studied computer science and IT, and 46% studied electronics and telecommunications, and 77% of those with diplomas entered the industry; (c) 30% of the non-IT engineering graduates entered the industry.

*Source*:  NASSCOM (2002a: 67-8).

This is where private training institutes, which grew in the 1990s in their hundreds, filled the gap. The dominant model was to set up corner shops, on franchise, which provided a number of computers and one or more instructors. Students used these 'cybershops', which were open all hours, for practice. The two biggest training providers, NIIT and APTECH, which offered courses in software training on franchise across India, were the best known. They gave their own degrees, which were not officially recognised but were nonetheless extremely popular. Their role was somewhat ambiguous as although their trainees ran into hundreds of thousands, most IT firms deny having recruited programmers trained by them.

The private training institutes have fulfilled four functions. First, they gave potential programmers the facilities to learn and practise close to their homes. Even when engineering and science colleges gave courses in programming, the number of computers they had was generally too small to allow the students much practice and students made up for the shortages by going to their local training shop. Second, the training institutions served as bases for training and certification of foreign software companies with their own specialist software, such as Microsoft, IBM, Cisco and Oracle. Third, they trained young people for jobs involving the use of PCs and computers, such as word processing, calculation, and accounting. Finally, they took on software-related contracts such as consulting and setting up of IT systems for clients, using both teachers and students for the purpose.

The training institutes filled a gap in the late 1980s and early 1990s when the supply of graduates and those holding diplomas fell short of requirements. That was when they upgraded their training from operation of PCs to programming. The qualifications they imparted would not on their own be sufficient for obtaining work visas and hence could not be used in body-shopping, but VSAT links brought work offshore to India, which could be done by people trained in informal institutes.

This demand declined in the second half of the 1990s when the supply of university-trained graduates and those with diplomas increased. However by that time, the training firms were picking up a considerable volume of IT-related work on which they could use their students as cheap labour. There was also considerable demand for certification in proprietary programming systems such as those of IBM and Microsoft.

The slowdown of 2000 hit the training companies hard. Most of the small ones closed down, and the corner training shops they had franchised became cybershops offering web surfing and e-mail facilities. Both NIIT and APTECH went through painful restructuring, and expanded their software business to compensate for the contraction of training.

## 2.9  GOVERNMENT POLICIES

As discussed in the previous section, both the central and the state governments noted the growth of the IT industry in the 1990s as a foreign exchange earner and a creator of incomes and employment, and responded with policies to help it. The new BJP government that came to power in 1998, however, went further. It decided to give priority to the industry, to set up a ministry of information technology, and to appoint a task force both to find out what the industry needed and to translate it into policy. Although the industry used the process to ask for many special favours, the reports of the IT Task Force (Ministry of Information Technology 1999a-c) provide a good picture of the obstructions faced by the industry (Table 2.9).

Customs and import control were the subject of many complaints. Import duties on computer hardware were substantial and although an exporter could avoid them, he thereby subjected himself to vexatious policing. He had to set up a bonded warehouse and the movement of goods into and out of the warehouse was subject to detailed rules and could lead to harassment. The industry sought an end to the policing and arbitrariness, and proposed that the customs and import licensing authorities should rely on ex-post audits.

Exporting companies were allowed to hold dollar accounts, but there were many restrictions on how money in the accounts could be spent. Here too, investigations by the Reserve Bank of India or the Enforcement Directorate could lead to much worry and loss of management time. The companies wanted greater freedom in investing and divesting abroad, in incurring expenses and using credit cards abroad.

The industry had a problem in raising finance: banks required a material asset as collateral, and a large proportion of the IT companies' assets were immaterial, such as programming work in progress and credit to customers. The government's financial institutions were prepared to fund on the basis of fixed assets, but computers and equipment were often leased, and when they were not, they were subject to rapid obsolescence. Hence the industry wanted the lending rules to be changed, and to be given credit on the basis of their turnover.

Soon after the IT Task Force reported, the Prime Minister's Council on Trade and Industry appointed a Subject Group on Knowledge-based Industries (SGKI 2000). Its report revealed widespread harassment based on labour laws. For instance, the Shops and Commercial Establishments Act 1961, and the rules framed under it, limited working time to no more than 9 hours per day and 48 hours per week, requiring a break to be given at least once every 5 hours, limiting the total length of a working day to no more than 12 hours, and requiring that hours worked beyond 9 per day or 48 per week had to be paid at twice the normal wage. The hours of work and wage rates had to be displayed, as also the applicable minimum wage and dearness allowance (cost-of-living adjustment).

Every worker who had worked more than 240 days had to be given one day's leave for every 20 days he worked. Before he went on leave, he had to be paid wages in advance for the leave period. Advances could not exceed two months' wages without the labour inspector's permission. Every establishment had to whitewash all inside walls, passages and staircases with lime and paint all internal structural iron and steelwork at least once a year. Wages could be paid only in coins or banknotes. Registers had to be maintained to record attendance, the hours worked, overtime, leave taken with wages, dates of whitewashing and painting, fines or deductions for damage or loss imposed on workers, and advances.

*Table 2.9  IT Task Force's recommendations*

|  | Total | Per cent |
|---|---|---|
| **Laws** | **14** | **4.3** |
| **Simplification of rules** | **56** | **17.3** |
| Central government | 26 | 8.0 |
| Customs | 24 | 7.4 |
| Other | 6 | 1.9 |
| **Relaxation of rules** | **45** | **13.9** |
| Exchange control | 21 | 6.5 |
| Banks and financial institutions | 10 | 3.1 |
| Other | 7 | 4.3 |
| **Favours** | **50** | **15.5** |
| Central government subsidies | 5 | 1.5 |
| Increase in financing | 12 | 3.7 |
| Reduction in taxes | 20 | 6.2 |
| Other | 13 | 4.0 |
| **Government purchases** | **29** | **9.0** |
| **Training** | **28** | **8.7** |
| **Remove government monopolies** | **7** | **2.2** |
| **Other government support** | **61** | **18.9** |
| **Other** | **36** | **11.1** |
| **Total** | **323** | **100.0** |

*Source*:  Ministry of Information Technology (1999a-c).

The task force asked that the permitted length of the shift without the need to pay overtime should be increased to 12 hours, and that women should be allowed to work night shifts. The Subject Group on Knowledge-based Industries asked for exemption for those industries from the above restrictions. The Cabinet approved night work by women in February 2003 but the rest of the demands were ignored.

Employers sought to evade the rigours of the labour laws by employing temporary labour. Temporary labour is legally defined as employment lasting not more than 240 days out of a year. Thus employers either employed a worker and dismissed him within 240 days, or they engaged a contractor to provide labour on contract. To prevent this, the government passed a Contract Labour Abolition Act in 1976, which made contract labour illegal in a wide range of circumstances. It also amended the Employees' State Insurance Act 1948 and the Employees' Provident Fund Act 1952 to ensure that an employer of contract labour, and not the contractor, became liable for paying workers' health insurance and provident fund contributions. The government is still debating whether to relax the law on casual labour for firms employing fewer than 200 workers.

The task force recommended that the Contract Labour Abolition Act should not apply to the IT industry, and that temporary status should be defined as 720 days in three years instead of 240 days in a year. It also asked that IT firms should be allowed to dismiss 10 per cent of the employees in a year without permission. The SGKI asked that knowledge-based establishments should be exempt from the liability for the health insurance and provident fund contributions of contract employees. None of these demands were met; however, retrenchment, overtime and night work were common throughout the industry; despite legal constraints.

Thus India's administrative style, consisting of complicated laws and rules and numerous bureaucrats, affects the IT industry as much as any. That it has grown within this environment suggests that it has found the same ways of dealing with red tape as every industry that preceded it.

## 2.10 MARKETS AND MARKET SHARE

The industry consists of three sections: body-shopping, offshore development, and specialised products and services. Body-shopping straddles frontiers, and its dimensions are indeterminate. All that is known about specialised firms is that hundreds exist – exactly what they do is uncertain. We have relatively reliable information only about the business of Indian IT firms, which have a foot each in body-shopping and offshore development. An estimate of their share in the world software market is given in Table 2.10.

Starting from virtually zero, ten years earlier, India took a 2.2 per cent share in the world software market – three times India's share in world merchandise trade. In custom applications, towards which much offshore work is directed, India had a 14.6 per cent share. In application outsourcing it

*Table 2.10 Global IT services market and India's share, 2001*

|  | Global market | | India's exports | | India's share |
|---|---|---|---|---|---|
|  | $ bn | (%) | $ bn | (%) | (%) |
| Professional services (total) | 128.6 | 36.8 | 2.9 | 37.5 | 2.2 |
| IS consulting | 20.2 | 5.8 | 0.1 | 0.7 | 0.2 |
| System integration | 71.0 | 20.3 | 0.2 | 2.0 | 0.2 |
| Custom applications | 18.2 | 5.2 | 2.7 | 34.8 | 14.6 |
| Network consulting & integration | 19.2 | 5.5 |  |  |  |
| Product services (total) | 111.1 | 31.8 | 1.5 | 19.9 | 1.4 |
| IT training and education | 22.7 | 6.5 |  |  |  |
| Hardware support & installation | 44.8 | 12.8 | 1.2 | 15.9 | 2.7 |
| Packaged software support & installation | 43.6 | 12.5 | 0.3 | 3.9 | 0.7 |
| Outsourcing services (total) | 109.3 | 31.3 | 3.2 | 42.7 | 3.0 |
| Application services | 1.8 |  |  |  |  |
| System infrastructure services | 11.1 | 3.2 |  |  |  |
| IS outsourcing | 63.6 | 18.2 |  |  |  |
| Application management | 11.2 | 3.2 | 1.8 | 23.0 | 15.6 |
| Network & desktop outsourcing | 21.6 | 6.2 | 1.5 | 19.7 | 6.9 |
| Total | 349 | 100.0 | 7.6 | 100.0 | 2.2 |

*Source:* Calculated from NASSCOM (2003a: 35-6).

had an even higher share – 15.6 per cent. This may be surprising since India entered the outsourcing market only after 1999, but it is in fact an outgrowth of Indian firms' work on custom applications – the same clients, having developed confidence in their Indian developers, have begun to outsource more comprehensive services. These are amongst the biggest corporations and financial institutions of the USA and the industry prides itself on the number of the largest clients it works for. It has also taken a 6.9 per cent share in relatively simpler outsourcing of services like call centres, transcription services and document processing and has a modest share of 2.7 per cent in product design, embedded software and the like.

These figures are uncertain and approximate but still they show where India has a foothold and where it has not. When big clients install new computers and want new software systems, they call IBM, Cisco, Oracle or other such large, established firms; so also when they want to connect up offices across the globe. But when those systems need to be repaired, maintained or expanded, they are more likely to call an Indian firm. It requires painstaking examination of existing software and 'stick-and-paste' reconstruction, but does not call for review of the overall architecture. Indian firms are just beginning to enter embedded software and product design, but that market is largely unpenetrated. Amongst outsourced processes, Indian firms have made no inroads into system management, but have picked up some jobs to manage applications, and some outsourcing of calls and office processes.

Amongst applications, Indian firms have specialised in work for banks, insurance and financial institutions, which accounted for 35 per cent of their revenues in 2001-2002 (NASSCOM 2003a: 30). In product software, they were particularly strong in telecommunications software accounting for 12 per cent of their sales. Manufacturing accounted for another 12 per cent of revenue; but here their world market share was not much more than 1 per cent. Half of their work was distributed across a wide range of other verticals.

Less information is available about work in the domestic market, but it is clear that the areas of specialisation were the same at home and abroad (Table 2.11). Thus, finance and insurance were the most computer-intensive industries and services followed. The automobile industry was a relatively heavy user, the manufacturing industry in general lagged behind. The scope for software applications increases with the size of operations, the number of transactions and the complexity of products and inputs. All these combine to put banking and insurance at the top in terms of software-intensity. The number of components and the complexity of assembly also puts automobiles in this class. One of the firms that have put IT to good use is Micro Ink, which produces 5000 different products and sells them to 60 000 customers.

Thus, Indian firms had specialised in custom applications, but within that field they were fully versatile, doing whatever jobs came to them. The reason was that the software boom kept them extremely busy. Once India was established as a low-cost source, clients of all sorts rushed to Indian firms and used them for a great variety of jobs, resulting in Indian firms becoming jacks-of-all-trades. They were too busy to accumulate and exploit knowledge in particular areas, with the exception of finance.

*Table 2.11  Expenditure on information technology in Indian industry, 2000-2001*

|  | Workers/PC | IT expenditure /worker (Rs 000) | IT expenditure /revenue (%) |
|---|---|---|---|
| Information technology | 1 | 95 | 1.60 |
| Insurance | 3 | 29 | 2.49 |
| Services | 6 | 16 | 0.24 |
| Finance | 6 | 17 | 0.09 |
| Automobiles | 9 | 10 | 0.50 |
| Other manufacturing | 15 | 7 | 0.15 |

*Source*:  Varma (2001).

## 2.11  BROADER ECONOMIC EFFECTS

The software industry's 2001-2002 sales came to 2.2 per cent of GDP. Although thousands of small IT firms are spread through all India's cities, the export industry, accounting for 79 per cent of sales, is largely concentrated in half a dozen cities, all of which, apart from Delhi, are in the peninsula (see Table 2.7). In these cities, the large exporting firms acquired a highly visible presence. They pioneered a new trend in office architecture – compact, air-conditioned buildings clad in heat-reflecting glass, soothing colours inside, facilities for eating, sports and recreation as well as underground car parks. The incomes they generated locally led to the emergence of new shopping malls, restaurants and bars. Signs of poverty – beggars, shanties and manual labour – receded. The southern cities came to look newer and neater than northern ones.

Taxes in India are widely evaded, and the income-elasticity of tax revenue is low. Further, the most income-elastic taxes – income tax and excise – are the remit of the central government. So the prosperity of the industry was not immediately reflected in that of the cities or states of its location. To get around this problem, the Karnataka government set up a Bangalore Agenda Task Force in 1999. It was a meeting point between the state authorities active in Bangalore – the civil administration, Bangalore Municipal Corporation, Bangalore Development Authority, Bangalore Telecom, the local police, and the Karnataka Power Transmission Corporation – and the major companies and their executives. The latter promised resources as well as technical and administrative help, and in return the public authorities promised to improve their facilities and services. In the course of this partnership, the local IT industry helped in modernising the administration of the public authorities. Their century-old single-entry accounting system was replaced by a double-entry system that recognised and kept track of assets. It turned the chronic deficits of Bangalore Development Authority into surpluses. A Geographic Information System was set up for solid waste management. In 2003, the Karnataka government set up a Mysore Agenda Task Force for its second city on the model of Bangalore. On a more limited scale, IT firms set up a Poona Software Exporters' Association and whenever a member was asked for a bribe or met bureaucratic obstruction, the Exporters' Association went on the member's behalf to the superior of the erring government servant. This tactic was generally successful. At the national level, NASSCOM, the industry association, played a similar role in lobbying the government for helpful changes in affecting the industry.

Recruiting from engineering colleges, the industry was faced with a labour shortage throughout the 1990s. Its pressure led to considerable changes in tertiary education, including the rapid expansion of engineering education, dedicated degrees and diplomas in information technology, and changes in the curricula of engineering and science courses. It was also involved in setting up the Indian Institutes of Information Technology in Bangalore and Hyderabad. Hewlett-Packard funded research and helped train researchers in universities and colleges in and around Bangalore. Motorola took in teachers from engineering colleges during sabbaticals (Patibandla and Petersen 2002). Globsyn Technologies ran its training courses in the engineering colleges of West Bengal; one of the courses it offered was in entrepreneurship for engineers. The alumni of Indian institutes of technology raised $12 million to improve facilities.

## 2.12  CONCLUSION

As we showed in section 2.10, Indian firms had succeeded by first providing manpower to large clients in the USA, and later by doing custom applications for them – in other words, by taking on any kind of work that the USA was prepared to give. They developed a loyal roster of clients amongst the largest firms, but were unspecialised in terms of the types of work they were doing. Can this continue? According to a NASSCOM projection made in 2001, 90 per cent of America's 1352 largest corporations used outside service providers; of those, 44 per cent used overseas providers in 2001 (Table 2.12). Now suppose that the proportion were to rise to 67 per cent and the IT budget rose from 8 to 20 per cent, and suppose some of the smaller corporations started sourcing services overseas. On these assumptions, demand for Indian IT services could easily quadruple. In other words, there is considerable scope for expansion in India's major market. However, as mentioned in section 2.5, there was a major redirection of India's IT exports between 2000-2001 and 2001-2002. The share of exports going to the USA, the UK and Singapore increased from 74.9 per cent to 81.8 per cent; it fell from 3.6 per cent to 2.5 per cent for Japan, from 3.2 per cent to 2.6 per cent for Germany and from 1.2 per cent to 0.8 per cent for Switzerland (NASSCOM 2002a: 33-5; NASSCOM 2003a: 28-9). What this shows is that Indian exports are heavily dependent on the movement abroad of programmers, and hence on visa regimes. The share of exports to the three countries that have liberal visa regimes for Indian programmers rose but the share of exports to countries with stricter regimes fell. Programming is eminently teachable, there are bound to be pressures to replace labour imports, and as labour shortages ease, countries will replace imported with domestic labour. In addition, access to labour markets is a political variable – countries discriminate between programmers from different source countries. The USA, the UK and Singapore remain open to Indians. Germany has issued far more 'green cards' to East Europeans than to Indians and Japan has imported Chinese in preference to Indian programmers. Elsewhere, official prejudices against Indian programmers have been expressed in other ways. In March 2003, the police in Kuala Lumpur raided a housing estate and arrested many Indian programmers who had visas, while ostensibly searching for illegal immigrants. In the same month, the Netherlands government expelled 13 programmers working for i-Flex Solutions, an Indian subsidiary of Citigroup that was marketing Flexcube, a product it had developed for international banks, and had for that purpose set up an office in Amsterdam in 2000.

*Table 2.12  NASSCOM projections, 2001-2002 to 2004-2005*

|  | 2001-2002 | 2002-2003 | 2003-2004 | 2004-2005 Optimistic | 2004-2005 Minimum |
|---|---|---|---|---|---|
| No. of large USA companies | 1352 | 1352 | 1352 | 1352 | 1352 |
| - who will use offshore providers | 535 | 681 | 815 | 676 | 669 |
| Average software purchases ($m) | 65 | 68 | 71 | 75 | 75 |
| - of which from offshore providers | 7.8 | 12.2 | 20 | 23.2 | 18.7 |
| Total offshore purchase | 4160 | 8339 | 16 295 | 20 357 | 12 541 |
| Small companies' purchases | 42 | 250 | 815 | 1425 | 627 |
| Total large & small companies | 4202 | 8589 | 17 110 | 21 782 | 13 168 |

*Source:*  Extracted from NASSCOM (2002a: 66).

*Table 2.13   Comparative IT industry size and programmers' wages*

|              | Industry revenue $m | Average wage/year $000 | Relative wage (India = 100) |
|--------------|:-------------------:|:----------------------:|:---------------------------:|
| Romania      | n                   | 2.4                    | 40.8                        |
| India        | 6.2                 | 5.9                    | 100.0                       |
| Czech Rep    | 0.7                 | 6.4                    | 108.8                       |
| Philippines  | 1.0                 | 6.5                    | 110.5                       |
| Malaysia     | n                   | 7.2                    | 122.4                       |
| Vietnam      | n                   | 7.2                    | 122.4                       |
| Ukraine      | n                   | 8.0                    | 136.1                       |
| China        | >1.0                | 8.9                    | 151.4                       |
| Israel       | 2.6                 | 25.0                   | 425.2                       |
| Ireland      | 6.7                 | 28.0                   | 476.2                       |
| Russia       | <1.0                | 6.0                    | 102.0                       |

*Note*:  n = negligible.

*Source*:  NASSCOM (2003a: 85-7).

Movement of labour is subject to discretionary non-tariff barriers.  It is customary for industrial countries to reject visa applications without giving reasons. Hence entry of Indian programmers can be arbitrarily restricted at any time, and the market for body-shopping will remain vulnerable to such actions.

Apart from this, India's wage advantage itself is vulnerable. There are countries like Romania where the average programmer's wage is lower than in India, at current exchange rates (Table 2.13). In other potential competitors such as the Czech Republic, the Philippines, Malaysia and Vietnam it is within 25 per cent of the Indian average wage.  If there were another crisis like the 1998 East Asian financial crisis, India's wage advantage could disappear.

This implies, first, that India's competitive advantage would depend on its macroeconomic policies – on how well it maintains the difference in the cost of living between itself and other countries at the current exchange rate. India did not follow the extensive devaluations in East Asia in 1998 and as a result, it lost competitive advantage in industries such as textiles and steel. It could similarly lose competitive advantage in IT if relative prices in India were to rise.

The second implication is that the Indian IT industry must find sources of competitive advantage other than low wages. Some Indian firms have developed such sources in their process technology. Meticulous planning shortens development lags and makes them predictable; extensive documentation reduces vulnerability to staff departures and other accidents; 'Chinese walls' ensure security of work done for clients; designed buildings and campuses increase labour productivity. In these process innovations, the Indian industry has an advantage it should preserve and develop. In addition, it should adopt process innovations from elsewhere, and generate its own. The development of tools that increase productivity and control quality is of utmost importance for Indian firms. The quality and reliability of their software distinguishes the world's leading firms from Indian ones – Indian firms must bridge the gap. The days of cheap, labour-intensive programming are nearing their end and Indian firms must take a lead in process innovation and increased productivity.

Third, the industry must learn from and document the domain knowledge arising from the work it does. It has worked for a very broad range of industries, but, except for some financial software, it has not codified or utilised the domain knowledge that it has been exposed to. It should exploit all sources to acquire domain knowledge – the work it does, buying into firms abroad that have such knowledge, and investing in firms that can yield domain knowledge. It is in such knowledge that it must seek to differentiate itself from its competitors, who are not far behind.

Finally and crucially, the world IT industry has passed through a phase of extreme fragmentation of work, which is now nearing an end. In the initial stages, the upper end of the industry was a craft business. The software used by big businesses had grown incrementally, and its varied provenance and resulting complexity were such that marginal additions and patches were the best that could be done. Since it belonged to an era when software was not standardised, large users employed software managers who preferred to buy incremental packages of software services. It was this porous structure of legacy software use that enabled Indian firms to penetrate the market.

This phase is now ending, and so is the opportunity that Indian firms exploited. To survive and grow, they will need to tap the more durable sources of demand for information technology. IT is essentially used to mimic real-world processes, and to use computer models to automate, control and improve those processes. This work is a variant of old-style consultancy, but instead of advising firms, it requires close involvement with them while they reconfigure their processes. The two basic components of this type of work are intimate knowledge of real-world processes – domain knowledge – and capacity to make robust conceptual models of it. The firms that do this kind of work globally are large and there are few. The smaller Indian firms, in comparison, are handicapped by their different experience. They could reduce this handicap by getting practice at home. Hitherto they have neglected the domestic market because its capacity to pay was low and because Indian client firms were less capable of making systemic changes. Though no more attractive than before, Indian industry and services are more or less a captive market for the Indian IT industry. The domain knowledge they can provide could be applied to work for clients abroad – the domestic market can provide the intellectual capital for entering the global market. For this reason, the IT industry should increase the work it does at home, and if necessary, should cross-subsidise it.

## NOTES

1. This chapter refers to information technology, and excludes communications, which have their own complex story in India. It covers software-related services, ranging from simple code-writing to setting up, managing, maintaining and modifying information systems. Although Indian firms have worked on telecommunications software, they have virtually no links with the Indian telecommunications companies, which are mostly joint ventures between Indian business houses and overseas telecommunications operators.
2. Fiscal year runs from April to March in India.
3. Arora et al. (2000) show that although few CEOs of IT firms admitted to recruiting non-engineers, the growth of the IT labour force far exceeded the output from engineering colleges. The difference is explained by the fact that the industry recruited a large number of older engineering graduates, and many non-engineers for jobs that did not require knowledge of programming – management, marketing and domain-oriented jobs. Science graduates were taken after they had done Master of Computer Applications (MCA). Only exporting firms needed to employ engineers; firms that worked for them or for the domestic market were under no pressure to employ engineers and the non-engineers they employed could be absorbed into exporting firms once they had acquired specialist programming skills.

# 3. China

## AnnaLee Saxenian and Xiaohong Quan

## INTRODUCTION

*Five years ago the Chinese software industry pretty much didn't exist. Today, in Beijing and Shanghai and some of the major cities, it is about 5 to 6 years behind; in the countryside it's about 500 years behind.*

Ya-Qin Zhang, Director, Microsoft Research Asia

*Government policy is like the moon. It is different in the middle of the month than it is on the first day of the month. Government policy is also like the sun. When it shines on you, you flourish.*

Chinese proverb

China's tenth Five-Year Plan (2001-2005) identifies software as a critical or 'pillar' industry that is essential to economic progress and national security, hence deserving of government promotion, along with more established industries such as computer manufacturing, telecommunications, lasers and aerospace. This targeting reflects the recognition that software remains a small and underdeveloped sector. It is an extremely fragmented industry that consists of thousands of small, undercapitalised firms with few competitive advantages relative to the foreign corporations that dominate the market. Its exports are negligible. At the same time, Chinese software output has grown at an average annual rate of 30 per cent since 1995 and is predicted to continue this rapid growth for several more years. The industry appears to be a threat to more established producers like Japan and India because it is located in the world's fastest growing market alongside a dynamic Information Technology (IT) manufacturing sector.

These contradictory trends in the Chinese software industry are best understood as products of the country's incomplete transition from a centrally planned to a more market-oriented economy. Chinese policymakers have accelerated the introduction of market mechanisms for over two decades, however the recent vintage of the reforms means that institutional change is uneven and fragmentary, and that the entrepreneurial, managerial and technical skills required for developing globally competitive firms remain scarce. At the same time as government control over the economy is being reduced, there are few signs that China is creating a Western style laissez-faire market economy.

The Chinese leadership has repeatedly affirmed its deep commitment to national economic autonomy. Deng Xiaoping's often-repeated words 'Science and Technology are the Chief Productive Forces' reflect the significance of indigenous mastery of technology to their vision of a modern, powerful economy. This perspective is reinforced by military and strategic concerns. An editorial in the *People's Liberation Army Daily* during 2000, on 'information colonialism', argued for example, that China must develop its own software because 'without information security there is no national security in economics, politics, or military affairs'.[1] Taking it one step further, one official argues: 'maintaining independence and keeping the initiative over our own operating system will be the "Two Bombs and One Satellite" [i.e. the intercontinental missile] of the new era'.[2]

These commitments provide ideological justification for the 'techno-nationalism' that characterises contemporary Chinese policy toward software and other high-technology industries.[3] The shift to market-coordination thus coexists with the aggressive promotion and preferential treatment – either explicit or implicit – of domestic producers or 'national champions'. One Chinese engineer concludes: 'Most high-tech promotion in China is just old wine in new bottles; an attempt to grow entrepreneurship using the tools of the planned economy.' Moreover the identification and promotion of select producers, by providing government contracts, preferential access to capital, and regulatory priority, leaves open a multiplicity of opportunities for bureaucratic discretion and corruption.

These contending pressures contribute to the unpredictability of the business environment in China. A Western lawyer warns of 'the apparent schizophrenia in the evolution of law and practice in the PRC (People's Republic of China) technology-sector over the past few years (late 1990s/early 2000s) ...'. The impression of schizophrenia derives, in part, from the lack of transparency in regulation and policymaking: state agencies and actors can (and do) change the rules of the game with little warning. Moreover the actions of different agencies and different levels of government in China are often contradictory. The government is organised around a complicated inner network of personal relationships that do not correspond to a standard organizational chart or Western bureaucracy. In theory the Communist Party controls the government, yet no individual or committee rules in a predictable top-down fashion. Decisions are the product of continuous and complex two-way negotiations between individuals in different ministries (horizontally) and levels of government (vertically). These internal debates remain inaccessible to all but select insiders.

In spite of the rapid pace of change in the Chinese economy since 1978, the creation of stable regulatory and legal institutions will likely take decades. In the interim the legacies of prior economic and political structures continue to affect most aspects of economic life. Personal relationships, or *guanxi,* have historically served as an important organising principle for Chinese economic and political life; trusted friends and family often provide the only reliable partners in an uncertain and unpredictable environment. Scholars have noted a renewed role for such personal connections in China's transitional economy – particularly for entrepreneurs seeking to advance in its evolving market system (Gold et al. 2002). Reliance on social networks and trust appears to be a characteristic of shortage economies with weak legal infrastructures, like Russia and China, where powerful officials control access to resources. In such an environment the accumulation of *guanxi* is necessary to achieve most goals, from acquiring housing to starting a business. Entrepreneurs in China, for example, typically need official assistance to gain access to licences, financial resources, facilities, protection, favourable interpretation of regulations and other favours.[4]

If personal relationships are a mechanism for coping with institutional instability and the absence of a formal and reliable system of laws and regulations, the emergence of a market economy and rational law might be expected to diminish the importance of *guanxi.*[5] However the experience of the Chinese software industry suggests that the need to cultivate relationships with powerful state actors remains critical for businesses even in regions that have aggressively adopted market mechanisms (Wank 1999). Local officials in China control resources that are essential for entrepreneurs and businesses, including, most notably, land (which is owned by the state and controlled by local governments). Their administrative authority includes allocation of financing, infrastructure, access to licences and permits, and the enforcement of contracts.

At the same time government officials in China depend upon local businesses to demonstrate their own capabilities. Political advancement in China's new reform economy is tied closely to growth, and the decentralisation of state authority has fuelled intensifying competition between localities – particularly in the critical IT sectors. This creates powerful incentives for officials to favour local technology firms in the interest of stimulating growth; and local enterprises recognise the advantages associated with devoting time and energy to building these relationships. This is particularly the case for private entrepreneurs who typically have no official connections: they are rarely officials or members of the Communist

Party and their firms are not part of the state. A manager of one of the leading US software companies in China notes: 'The most important factor for business success in China is not technology, it is relationships'.

These relationships are not necessarily limited to the highly personalised *guanxi* of an earlier era – particularly given the aggressive efforts by the central government to combat corruption. Most observers concur that government officials are particularly vigilant in the new technology industries, insuring that software is among the sectors least affected by corruption. On the other hand, if overt corruption is minimised, it is clear that once a firm reaches a certain scale it is scrutinised, and often controlled by government agencies and bureaucrats in more subtle ways. In the new technology sectors, these relationships are likely to take the form of 'reputational practices' such as hiring Party members or formerly prominent top officials for managerial positions and seats on the board of directors.

This chapter begins with a brief history of the evolution of China's science and technology system, and its information technology sector in particular, to highlight the widespread institutional changes under way in the transition from a planned to a more market-oriented economy. It then focuses on the development of the Chinese software industry – the market, labour force, sources of capital, ownership and management, and its regional distribution. The analysis highlights the persistent role of non-market factors, the government and *guanxi*, alongside the ongoing reforms oriented toward introducing market mechanisms into the economy. The conclusion focuses on the effects on the software industry of China's entry into the World Trade Organisation (WTO) and on the emerging trends in an economy where the pace of change is unparalleled.

## 3.1  THE DEVELOPMENT OF INFORMATION TECHNOLOGY IN CHINA

### The Evolution of China's Science and Technology System

#### Science and technology in the planned economy
China's leaders began to develop a science and technology base immediately after the formation of the People's Republic. From 1949 until 1977 all research, development and engineering activities were controlled and coordinated by the State Development Planning Commission and the State Science and Technology Commission. The State Development Planning Commission controlled the detailed annual and five-year plans that allocated resources throughout the economy. Each administrative and productive unit made investment, production, pricing, distribution and other operational

decisions according to these guidelines. The State Science and Technology Commission oversaw the funding and administration of science and technology activities in Chinese research institutes, firms and universities.

Research and development was conducted by state-owned research institutes such as the giant Chinese Academy of Sciences, dedicated to basic research, and the hundreds of industrial and local institutes that conducted more applied R&D. The latter focused on the needs of particular industries such as defence and other heavy industries like machinery, iron and steel, or mining. In most cases, the relevant ministries of the central government administratively governed the R&D institutes, controlling both funding and personnel, as well as the state-owned enterprises, or manufacturing firms, that were to implement and exploit the new technology.

Approximately fifty major state-owned research institutes were the driving engine for technological innovation and the development of heavy industry in China. Since civil use technologies accounted for only a very small portion of both research and production activities of the country before the 1980s, it is not surprising that the most significant technological achievements of this era were high priority strategic weapons such as guided missiles and artificial satellites. China's system of higher education was organised in the same period to both create and disseminate scientific and technological knowledge. By 1965, fifty-five universities had been established across the country but their focus was almost exclusively on teaching rather than research.

The entire system of science and technology research came to a halt during the Cultural Revolution (1967-1976), with the exception of the development of military technologies such as nuclear weapons, guided missiles and satellites. This created an enduring gap in the age structure of China's technical community that has yet to be overcome. On one hand, three-quarters of 'senior scientists' such as full professors and senior engineers were due to retire early in the twenty-first century; on the other, half of Chinese scientists were under 35 years of age in the late 1990s, and only a small percentage held ranks higher than 'junior' (for example, assistant professor). In the 1990s China fell behind the advanced countries in development of its IT industries.

## Abandoning central planning, 1978-1992

China's policymakers initiated market-oriented economic reforms in the 1980s in order to address the shortcomings of the nation's science and technology system, which combined weak R&D, poor technical skills, a lack of efficiency and a dated focus on defence and other heavy technologies. The new policy initiatives that were developed to enhance China's technological capabilities in this period fall into three categories:

- Exploiting the international environment by acquiring foreign technology, attracting foreign investment, and sending students abroad for training.
- Promoting university-based research, which barely existed in the pre-reform era, and encouraging closer ties between research and production through horizontal, market-mediated ties linking research institutes, universities and enterprises. This included providing greater managerial autonomy to new 'high-tech' enterprises without changing ownership.
- Funding schemes and institutional innovations to improve the focus and coherence of R&D and technology diffusion efforts, including most famously the '863 Plan' (named for its approval date of March 1986), which allocated approximately RMB5 billion between 1986 and 2000 to projects designed to monitor the world's high technology frontier, train a new generation of researchers, and advance Chinese capabilities in fields such as biotechnology, information technology, energy, robotics, new materials, space and lasers.

The proliferation of programmes in this period reflected in part the competitive bureaucratic entrepreneurship among Chinese officials seeking to insure a continued role in a rapidly changing system, as well as an underlying frustration with the quality and efficiency of existing research and innovation practices.

These reforms significantly improved the infrastructure for domestic research in China and reduced the direct control by the central government over decisions made by firms and research units. Many decisions regarding administration and resource allocation were shifted to the provincial level, and reliance on market-based resource allocation decisions increasingly replaced administrative fiat at both central and local government levels. The '863 Plan', for example, introduced the concept of peer review for the first time in technology research, and focused primarily (but not entirely) on civilian objectives. In most state-supported organisations there were comparable attempts to shift evaluation criteria from political to economic goals.

Chinese policymakers also led the development of the domestic information technology infrastructure (Guo 2001). From 1988 to 1992 the State Economics Committee, the newly formed Ministry of Machine and Electronics, and the State Science Committee focused their joint efforts on developing Electronic Data Interchange (EDI), CAD/CAM and Management Information Systems (MIS) to propel the broader application of electronics and information technology. And in the early 1990s the State Informatisation Expert Group invested heavily in accelerating the adoption of IT in key sectors of the Chinese economy and infrastructure through large-scale projects such as the 'Golden Card' (adoption of IT in banking), 'Golden

Bridge' (construction of the national telecommunications backbone and other networks) and 'Golden Customs' (computer networking for foreign trade and other related issues).

The 'Torch Plan' was also proposed in the 1980s, by the State Council, to create a supportive environment for development of new technology enterprises. The plan, undertaken by the Ministry of Science and Technology, has focused most prominently on the establishment of national high-tech industrial development zones that provide firms with first-rate infrastructure (including roads, buildings, electric facilities and so on) and a variety of preferential taxes and collective services. The first of these zones was established in 1988 as a trial in Beijing's Zhongguancun area (sometimes referred to as China's Silicon Valley).

The reforms of the 1980s, while far-reaching, failed to develop consistent technology policy or a coherent system of innovation in China. Progress was disjointed and uneven. Funding for R&D and education remained low by international standards, policy continued to reinforce the concentration of applied research in public research institutes rather than industry, and the weight of policy – hence the flow of resources – remained biased toward state-owned enterprises rather than the potentially more creative and innovative non-governmental technology enterprises (Suttmeier and Cao 1999).

The '863 Plan', for example, trained thousands of new researchers and contributed to development of a network of research centres.[6] However it had little success in bringing new products to market, largely because the research institutes had few connections with commercial enterprises; and the enterprises had little incentive to look to these institutions for innovation. Furthermore resources were often spread too widely: for example, the average funding for every '863' researcher between 1988 and 1994 was only about US$5000 due to more than 1000 programmes receiving funding annually (Naughton and Segal, 2001). Moreover the majority of students and scholars who had gone abroad to study (approximately 200 000) since the beginning of the reform period remained abroad, making it difficult to staff research facilities and university science and engineering departments with a new generation of well-trained personnel capable of providing scientific leadership.

## Market reforms to accelerate science and technology development: 1992-2002

Chinese technology policy through the early 1990s favoured the large state-owned enterprises (SOEs) and government research institutes, following the model of Japan and Korea. However most Chinese ministers lacked understanding of both the technologies that they sought to develop and the needs of Chinese industry, and Chinese SOEs and research institutes were unable to abandon the practices and structures of the planned economy. China also faced a different international environment from Korea and Japan a decade or so earlier, one characterised by an accelerating pace of innovation and intensifying global competition. As a result, the strategies of the 1980s and early 1990s produced very little success.

Policymakers began in the 1990s to experiment with more extensive loosening of government control as well as opening of the economy to new actors and new forms of ownership. The accelerated growth of Shenzhen (in Guangdong province), which had been given policy autonomy during the 1980s as a Special Economic Zone, demonstrated to the central government the economic benefits of market opening. Following Deng Xiaoping's famous 'Southern Tour' in 1992, China liberalised market access and initiated more favourable policies toward foreign investment, recognising that it could play an important role in developing technological leadership. These reforms triggered a dramatic inflow of foreign investment in all sectors of the economy, particularly from Taiwan and Hong Kong. By the late 1990s China was one of the world's leading recipients of Foreign Direct Investment (FDI) and multinational corporations had become a dominant mechanism of technology transfer as well as an important source of new management models and training in the technology sector.

Policymakers also took steps toward promotion of non-state technology enterprises and signalled a new willingness to embrace alternative forms of ownership. The 1993 'Decision on Several Problems Facing the Enthusiastic Promotion of Non-Governmental Technology Enterprises' recognised that non-state enterprises could play a role building a new, more market-oriented economy (US Embassy, Beijing 1996). Influenced by the successful growth of the small start-ups in the US technology-based industry, Chinese policymakers began to encourage the formation of a 'new' generation of technology firms – typically entrepreneurial spin-offs from universities or government research institutes. While the start-up capital for these ventures typically came from friends or personal savings, the initial technology and offices came from the university or research institutes. They were thus viewed as neither 'private' nor 'public' but rather 'collectively-owned' enterprises. The Legend Group (a spin-off from the Chinese Academy of Sciences) and the Founder Group (a spin-off from Peking University; see box 3.1) are two of the leading successes of this generation of 'non-governmental' technology firms.

BOX 3.1: CASE STUDY THE FOUNDER GROUP: A 'NON-GOVERNMENTAL' ENTERPRISE

Peking University Founder Group Corp. was one of China's early 'collective enterprises'. Professor Wang Xuan, a mathematician at Peking University, started the firm with university support to develop Chinese-language electronic publishing software. Founder now controls over 80 per cent of China's desktop-publishing system market and it is a dominant supplier to overseas Chinese newspapers. While top government officials are not involved in allocating funding or corporate investment decisions as in a traditional SOE, it is typical for the university to maintain ownership and control in university spin-offs. Founder's seven-person board of directors, for example, includes three Peking University professors and five graduates of the university. Professor Wang Xuan, who remained Chairman of the Board until 2002, is Communist Party Secretary for the university and a member of the Standing Committee of the 9th National People's Congress. The close connection to the university and to the Party gives the company an advantage in competing for contracts from state-owned businesses. Founder's leading customers include state-owned newspapers, banks, the tax bureau and television stations. And the strong university and Party ties also create pressure to make decisions based on political rather than purely economic/efficiency considerations. In short, despite its apparently innovative ownership, Founder appears to be a new variant of state enterprise. The original business, Founder Holdings Ltd, was listed on the Hong Kong stock exchange in 1992 but Peking University remains the largest, and majority, investor, through a diversified holding company called Beijing Founder. The Founder Group is now a highly diversified business, like most leading Chinese IT companies. It includes three other listed companies (including not only software development but also IT equipment and new materials) along with 17 wholly owned businesses and joint ventures in businesses ranging from manufacturing its own brand of PC hardware and developing broadcast and TV systems to network security and mobile Internet communications. Founder is also one of China's leading systems integration firms. In 2000 it had 5000 employees and RMB10.1 billion ($1.2 billion) in revenues.

By the late 1990s, the Chinese government was supporting private firms as well as university or research institute spin-offs, instead of directing resources for science and technology solely to state-owned enterprises.[7] All domestic enterprises designated by the government as technologically advanced began to receive the same preferential treatment (including preference in procurement decisions, access to low interest credit and so on) regardless of ownership status. The expansion of the types of technology enterprises receiving preferential treatment was accompanied, during the 1990s, by the establishment of 52 more national high-tech industrial development zones, which were designed to provide an environment conducive to technological innovation and entrepreneurship.

The opening of the technology sector to private and other forms of ownership was paralleled by substantial reductions in the manpower and mandates of government ministries. A major restructuring of the Chinese Academy of Sciences (CAS) and its research institutes, for example, included dramatic reductions in the workforce and the introduction of competition in hiring decisions. The Institute of Software, which performs research on fundamental software theory and applications, reduced its workforce from over 500 to 125 between 1999 and 2001. Many individuals whose jobs were eliminated found jobs in private enterprises with the training they had received at the institute. Salaries were increased from an average of RMB2800 to RMB5000 per month, with top salaries around RMB15 000 per month. This insured that programmers and technicians at the Software Institute were paid more than their counterparts at private firms such as Legend. These salary increases reduced staff turnover from 30 per cent in the late 1990s to around 10 per cent in 2001.

By the end of the 1990s the Chinese government had abandoned most of its control over the process of selecting or importing technology. Private firms and venture capital were increasingly identified as keys to domestic technology development in this period. A 1999 decision summarised a wide range of policies developed to foster new technology enterprises, including a fund to support Science and Technology innovation in Small and Medium-sized Enterprises (SMEs), preference for domestic products and equipment in government and enterprise procurement, partial tax deduction for R&D expenditures, tax exemption for all income from the transfer or development of new technologies, a preferential 6 per cent value added tax rate for software products developed and produced in China, the deductibility of payroll expenditures for software development and manufacturing firms, VAT exemption and subsidised credit for high-tech exports, preferential tax treatment for imports of cutting-edge technologies and equipment, the listing of new technology companies on the Shanghai and Shenzhen stock exchanges, and interest subsidies for technological restructuring projects of strategic scientific importance by large and medium-sized SOEs deemed as profitable.

Policy in this period also focused on accelerating development of the venture capital industry as a means to finance new technology enterprises as well as increasing investments in R&D. Total R&D expenditure in China increased steadily during the 1990s, reaching a total of RMB89.6 billion ($10 billion) in 2000, or 1.01 per cent of GDP compared with only 0.60 per cent in 1995. The 10th Five-Year Plan sets the goal of raising R&D spending to 1.5 per cent of GDP by 2005. If achieved this would be very high for a developing economy: India in 1999 was 0.86 per cent, Mexico was 0.40 per cent, and the ratio in most advanced economies is in the 2-3 per cent range (US Embassy; Beijing 2002). The available data does not allow us to disaggregate by sector; funding for software research is primarily through initiatives such as the '863 Plan', which allocated RMB15 billion ($1.8 billion) for 2001-2005, and the Informatisation Programmes. While R&D expenditure has increased significantly, China's companies, universities and research institutes still remain relatively isolated from the market. As the president of a Dallas-based software company, puts it, 'In China, research is too far from being applied to real life. For example, we can barely find one out of five hundred PhD dissertations (e.g. in computer science) with research findings useful for commercialisation. While in the United States, one dissertation out of one hundred can be turned into a real product.'

*Table 3.1   Adoption of IT in China and comparator countries, 2000/2001*

|  | China | India | Brazil | Israel | USA |
| --- | --- | --- | --- | --- | --- |
| Personal computers (per 1000 people), 2000 | 15.9 | 4.5 | 44.1 | 253.6 | 585.2 |
| Internet users ('000), 2000 | 22 500 | 5000 | 5000 | 1270 | 95 354 |
| Internet secure servers, 2001 | 184 | 122 | 1028 | 301 | 78 126 |
| ICT expenditures % of GDP, 2000 | 5.4 | 3.8 | 8.4 | 7.4 | 8.1 |
| Telephone mainlines (per 1000 people), 2000 | 112 | 32 | 182 | 482 | 700 |
| Mobile phones (per 1000 people), 2000 | 66 | 4 | 136 | 702 | 398 |

*Source*:  The World Bank, *2002 World Development Indicators*, 5.9 and 5.10.

Two decades of change in China's science and technology infrastructure have been both disruptive and remarkable at the same time. The Chinese economy is stronger today than most would have predicted in the 1980s, with impressive achievements in building a national telecommunications infrastructure and widespread adoption of IT, particularly wireless phones and related telecommunications products (Table 3.1). The new technology regime has been extremely successful in the development of IT manufacturing capabilities, where relationships between domestic firms and foreign investors – particularly from Taiwan and Hong Kong – have contributed to rapid development of the domestic capacity for low-cost manufacture of computers, consumer electronics and communications equipment. While initially these ventures were restricted to lower technology, intensive-intensive (so called) processes, over time their technical capabilities have increased. China is now manufacturing laptop computers and sophisticated electronic components for export. In 2002 the country received $59 billion in FDI and was ranked the third largest IT manufacturing centre in the world, following only the USA and Japan (Figure 3.1).

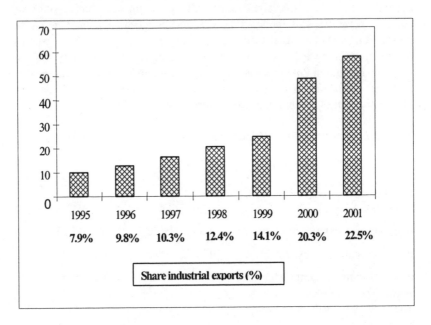

*Sources*:   China Science & Technology Statistics Data Book 2000 Ministry of Science and Technology of The People's Republic of China; Liu, Xielin. 'The Achievement and Challenge of Industrial Innovation in China', Proceedings of Third International Symposium on Management of Innovation and Technology. Conference Hangzhou, China, October 2002.

*Figure 3.1 China's high technology exports ($ billion); 1995-2001*

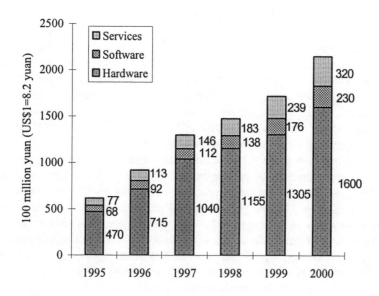

*Source*: Tsao (2001).

*Figure 3.2 Market structure of Chinese IT industry*

Software remains the weakest link in China's IT sector. In 1995, software products accounted for only 10 per cent of total Chinese IT output, or RMB68 million (only $8.2 million), and the share had barely increased by 2000. Software services outpaced the growth of products somewhat, increasing from 10 per cent in 1995 to about 15 per cent of the total by 2000 (see Figure 3.2). The development of a dynamic software industry, unlike computer or even semiconductor manufacturing, requires more than the ability to mobilise resources quickly; it requires soft and intangible skills such as creativity, technical experience and managerial know-how as well as the capacity for commercialisation skills which are scarce in China. Moreover the technology transfers achieved in IT manufacturing through large-scale Taiwanese investments are not likely to be repeated in software, as Taiwan lacks software capabilities as well.

## The Origins of the Chinese Software Industry

The Chinese software industry barely existed before the 1990s. The Institute of Computing Technology (ICT), at the Chinese Academy of Sciences, built China's first computer in 1958. However the government devoted most of its financial resources and limited pool of skilled labour to reverse-engineering key hardware such as integrated circuits and technologies with mixed military and civilian importance. There were, to be sure, scattered software development projects in state-owned research institutes, but commercial R&D was largely non-existent because of the organisational and institutional barriers separating these research institutes from the market.

In the late 1980s a few Chinese computer firms, including Founder and Legend, were authorised to commercialise software products. This allowed Founder to establish its early dominance of the market for Chinese-language publishing systems. Chinese programmers at the Institute of Software at the Chinese Academy of Sciences and other research institutes also began to develop simple information systems, typically by directly manipulating a database for a limited set of functions such as searching and reporting, or providing the ability to update information interactively. These systems were developed separately for particular end-users and little attention was given to integration or overall design.

The Internet bubble, as elsewhere in the world, brought both hype and money to China's emerging software industry. It appears that the effects of the bubble were more severe than on the software industries in developed economies because of its immaturity. The inflated salaries and funding, as well as the impractical expectations for growth, distracted Chinese software developers from the necessary focus on mastering the processes and techniques needed for mature software design and integration – including systems thinking, component-based design, and object-oriented design and development capabilities. The attitudes of customers, financiers and policymakers were also distorted by the experience. In short, the bursting of the bubble left all of the actors in China's fledgling software sector with limited capabilities and superficial understanding of software processes and technologies (Brizendine 2002).

These weaknesses were masked, however, by the industry's growth: an average annual growth rate of over 30 per cent from 1992 to 2000, albeit from a very small base (Figure 3.3). The International Data Corporation (IDC) forecasts the Chinese software market will continue to grow at a compound average annual growth rate of over 30 per cent between 2000 and 2005 (IDC 2001). Nevertheless, industry output of $7.2 billion in 2000 remains small relative to the booming IT hardware manufacturing industry, and China lags behind countries like India, Ireland and Korea in software output (Table 3.2).

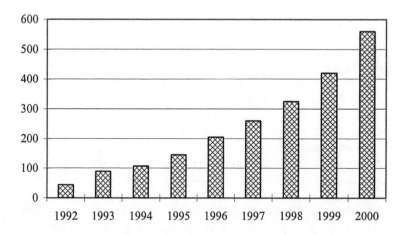

*Source*: CSIA (2001, p.4).

*Figure 3.3  China's software market (RMB100 million)*

*Table 3.2  Software output: China and other countries, $ billion*

|  | China | USA | Japan | Ireland | India | S. Korea | Global |
|---|---|---|---|---|---|---|---|
| Sales 1999 | 5.3 | 220 | 54 | 8.4 | 6.8 | 5.9 | 527.4 |
| World market (%) | 1.0 | 42 | 10.2 | 1.6 | 1.3 | 1.1 | 100 |
| Sales 2000 | 7.2 | 240 | 57.2 | 8.9 | 8.9 | 8.3 | 596 |
| World market (%) | 1.2 | 40.2 | 9.6 | 1.5 | 1.5 | 1.4 | 100 |

*Source*: CSIA (2001, p.3).

The Chinese government, recognising these weaknesses, has targeted software, along with integrated circuits, in the 10th Five-Year Plan. The plan sets a target of 30 per cent annual growth rates for the software and IT industries combined, which would bring total sales to nearly $20 billion by 2005. It specifies two main goals for software: (1) increasing domestic companies' share of the Chinese software market to 63 per cent, current share and; (2) growing annual software exports to $1.5 billion by 2005. These goals will be achieved, according to the plan, by building 20 domestic firms with revenues exceeding RMB1 billion ($120 million) and more than 100 'famous software brands' (SIIA-USIT 2002). The government has allocated a total of RMB4 billion ($480 million) to achieving these tasks.

The most important central government policy for the software industry is the June 2000 announcement of State Council Document 18, formally known as 'Notice of Certain Policies to Promote the Software and Integrated Circuit Industry Development'.[8] The document's policies for software companies include most notably:

- Value added tax (VAT) refund for R&D and expansions of production, reducing the effective VAT for software firms from 17 per cent to 3 per cent;
- No enterprise income tax (EIT) for two years for new enterprises, once approved, and 50 per cent EIT for the next three years, beginning with the first year of profitability;
- Tax rate of 10 per cent EIT for companies designated as 'key software enterprises' in the plan, that do not qualify for the 10 per cent EIT;
- Fast-track approval of software companies seeking to raise capital on overseas stock markets;
- Exemption from tariffs and VAT for all imports of technology and equipment;
- Direct export rights for all software firms with over $1 million in revenues;
- The right to set salary levels and to grant bonuses to inventors.

These policies assume an internationally open and competitive market, in contrast with more protectionist industrial promotion efforts of the early 1990s (Lardy 2002). However, Document 18 also requires that preferential policies be accorded only to companies that are certified as software enterprises with software products, based on standards set by the Ministry of Information Industries (MII) and the local audits by the Chinese Software Industries Association. The authentication standards measure an enterprise's scale (value of registered capital, annual income and exports) and evaluate its products.

Chinese policymakers and businesses have also been energetic about learning from the international experience, and there is a proliferation of partnerships and joint ventures with foreign companies. This means that the software industry is developing in a far more global environment than earlier industries. Agencies at all levels target software through policies ranging from research funding and procurement to expansion of education and the creation of state-level software parks. One of the biggest unknowns in the development of the software industry remains the extent to which China's entry into the WTO will increase the transparency and predictability of the business environment and the legal system, particularly with regard to the protection of intellectual property rights.

## 3.2 THE CHINESE SOFTWARE MARKET

### Domestic Market

China exports little software but is assisted by a growing domestic market. Software services dominated with 54 per cent of all China's software output in 2000 ($3.9 billion; Table 3.2), followed by software products with 40 per cent ($2.9 billion) and exports with only 6 per cent ($0.4 billion). Application software such as pre-packaged financial services, security systems, electronic publishing or education products (65 per cent of sales) dominate the product market, with smaller shares of supporting software such as application development tools (21 per cent) and system software (14 per cent) (Figure 3.4)

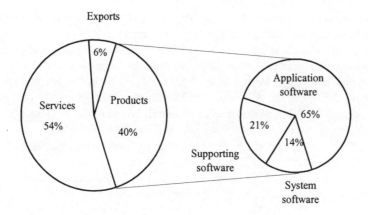

*Source*: created by author from CSIA (2001, p.2).

*Figure 3.4 Chinese software output, 2000*

**Market Players**

International Data Corporation (IDC) estimates that by the end of the year 2000 there were more than 2000 registered software companies in China and another 3000 IT companies involved in the software business (IDC 2001). The latter include computer, consumer electronics and telecommunications companies that develop their own software systems internally. The China Software Industry Association, an industry lobby, has estimated that there are 10 000 software companies in China. This may result from a broader definition of the industry. However the IDC numbers are consistent with the results of a 2001 survey of the industry conducted by the Chinese Ministry of Information Industries, and the State Statistical Bureau.

The domestic industry is extremely fragmented, with thousands of very small enterprises; having fewer than 50 employees, which lack economies of scale or distinctive competencies. These firms typically focus on developing niche applications tailored to unique needs of the domestic market (for example, systems integration or specialised financial software developed for China's unique accounting practices) and adapting products to Chinese language platforms (for example, education software). Only a handful of domestic companies that have gained control of particular product niches have more than 1000 employees or sales revenues over $50 million, including Founder (electronic publishing software), Kingdee (enterprise resource management software), and UFSoft (financial software). In general these products are substantially less expensive and offer more limited functionality than their foreign counterparts.

Foreign corporations, including Microsoft, IBM and Oracle, dominate the software product market in China – accounting for over 65 per cent of packaged software sales – because of their established brands and products. However this market has become increasingly competitive in recent years with new entrants as well as the emergence of new niches. Table 3.3 indicates that in 2000 the top ten firms in the Chinese packaged software market accounted for 28 per cent of total revenues, compared with 1999 when the top ten firms accounted for 35 per cent of the market.

UFSoft and Kingdee are the only domestic software companies ranked in the top ten. This reflects their dominance of the financial software market – the two firms account for about 60 per cent of China's accounting software market – and increasingly the market for enterprise resource management software (Table 3.4). This is due primarily to their privileged knowledge of Chinese financial and managerial practices. They have also benefited from the preferential purchasing practices of Chinese government agencies. By 2002 UFSoft had moved from seventh to fourth rank in total packaged software sales, following only IBM, Microsoft and Oracle.

*Table 3.3  Top ten packaged software vendors: China, 2000*

| Vendor | Revenue ($m) | Share (%) |
| --- | --- | --- |
| IBM | 77.99 | 6.08 |
| Microsoft | 65.07 | 5.07 |
| Oracle | 58.28 | 4.55 |
| Sybase | 30.93 | 2.41 |
| Informix | 26.33 | 2.05 |
| Computer Assoc. | 25.74 | 2.01 |
| UFSoft | 23.30 | 1.82 |
| Novell | 21.49 | 1.68 |
| Lotus | 17.53 | 1.37 |
| Kingdee | 16.25 | 1.27 |
| Others | 919.37 | 71.69 |
| Total | 1282.28 | 100.00 |

*Source*:  IDC (2001).

*Table 3.4  Top ten enterprise resource management vendors: China, 2000*

| Vendor | Revenue ($m) | Share (%) |
| --- | --- | --- |
| UFSoft | 23.3 | 12.9 |
| Kingdee | 16.3 | 9.0 |
| SAP | 14.5 | 8.1 |
| Genersoft | 11.2 | 6.2 |
| New & Grand | 5.7 | 3.2 |
| Anyi | 5.6 | 3.1 |
| Oracle | 5.3 | 2.9 |
| QAD | 4.4 | 2.4 |
| Fourth Shift | 3.3 | 1.8 |
| Symix | 2.6 | 1.4 |
| Others | 87.9 | 48.8 |
| Total | 180.1 | 100.0 |

*Source*:  IDC (2001).

Software services, primarily systems integration, account for more than half of China's total software output. This is at least in part due to the extremely high rates of piracy in the industry (over 90 per cent) that provide a strong disincentive to develop new products; services do not face piracy risk. Table 3.5 lists some of the major players in the software services market. China's leading computer hardware manufacturers such as Legend and Great Wall are active in the IT services market because they see it as a way of expanding beyond their original business. In fact there are very few specialised and dedicated Chinese software providers. US-based software specialist Jessica Ma (2002) reports:

> It is very difficult to be a specialised software producer in China: there is great pressure to become not just a producer of software technology, such as an office automation product, but also to become a service provider and also a systems integrator for the same customer. The customers want software integrated with their product. This makes it very hard to sell stand-alone software. The large companies in China prefer to develop their own software.

As a result, many of the largest software developers in China are diversified IT firms, such as Founder and Legend. Telecommunications equipment manufacturers, Huawei and Zhongxing, for example, are among the largest software producers in China because they develop most of their own software internally.

Chinese entrepreneurs remain pessimistic about the industry's future because of the limited success of domestic firms in the software product market. A manager from a software company that spun out of Peking University is blunt about this:

> I don't think China has its own software industry. My understanding of the definition of a software firm is that: first, the firm has its own software product; second, it has a certain market share. However, most, almost all, of the so-called software firms in China now don't have their own brands. They are just doing low end programming jobs . . . One example of a real software firm is UFSoft. It really has its own brand. However, its success to a large degree is because it is doing accounting software. You know, the accounting system is unique in China, and that's why it's hard for foreign companies to compete with local companies in this field. (personal interview, 2002)

**Immaturity of the Chinese Market**

The Chinese software market, although potentially large, remains immature. Most industry participants agree that few domestic users – government, businesses or individuals – fully appreciate the value of investing in, or paying for, software. This is related as much to organisational immaturity as to resource constraints. In the words of a vice president of Beijing-based software firm:

The biggest problem for the software industry in China today is that the users have not matured enough to use or to understand software. The government and firms still don't have a well-defined governance structure which can tell them when and how to hire or fire employees. How can we expect them to know when they need software? (personal interview, 2002)

Most business or government customers – only recently weaned from the protection of the planned economy – are not sophisticated enough to make balanced independent purchase decisions. In addition, many Chinese enterprises and even local government agencies are still primarily paper-based or hand-labour based, so it makes little sense to talk about higher levels of automation or integration. Even managers who recognise the need to invest in software have great difficulty evaluating investments and the potential returns from investments because Chinese enterprises frequently do not know their actual costs.

In contrast with the Indian software industry, which has grown up serving extremely sophisticated foreign corporations (such as Fortune 100 companies from the USA), the immaturity of the business market makes it difficult for Chinese software firms to develop new products or achieve scale economies. After the government, the largest domestic customers for software in China are the state-owned enterprises. These SOEs, while subject to aggressive restructuring over the past decade, still account for the majority of the software market outside of technology sectors. Yet it is rare for a Chinese SOE to depend on software-derived or software-supported functionality for their competitive advantage. For most; competition is based on price, distribution and relationships. There are, of course, exceptions. There are sophisticated, small and medium-sized Chinese companies with fully integrated Enterprise Resource Planning (ERP) programmes. However most systems in China still do not require highly advanced skill levels. Others fail to see the value of software to their operations. One software consultant reports 'in today's China you can find $30 billion multinationals with virtually no IT functionality besides email and a marketing website'.

The business market in China remains limited also by the general unwillingness of most enterprises to pay for externally developed software. Many large firms prefer to develop software internally because there is little tradition of outsourcing in China. In the 1990s, for example, many Chinese enterprises believed it was better to develop database capabilities internally than to buy a database product. Even those enterprises that do purchase software products or services remain unsophisticated as customers, unsure of what they want and thus unable to provide the feedback that might help domestic producers develop innovative products.

Table 3.5 *Major Chinese software firms, by year founded and ownership*

| Name of firm | Year founded | State-owned enterprise | University spin-off | Private firm | Diversified IT Firm | Public listing |
|---|---|---|---|---|---|---|
| Beijing Legend Software Co., Ltd | 1984 | | | | × | × |
| Peking University Founder Group Co. | 1986 | | × | | × | × |
| Beijing UF Soft Group Corporation Ltd | 1988 | | | × | | × |
| Kingsoft Company Ltd | 1988 | | | × | | × |
| Shenzhen Huawei Technologies Corp | 1988 | | | × | × | |
| China National Computer Software & Technology Service Corporation | 1990 | × | | | | × |
| Sichuan TOP Group Science & Technology Development Co., Ltd | 1992 | | × | | × | × |
| NEUSOFT Group Ltd. | 1993 | | × | | × | × |
| Kingdee International Software Group | 1993 | | | × | | × |
| Shanghai Huateng Software Systems Co.* | 1993 | JV | | | | |
| Beijing Beida Jadebird Company Ltd | 1994 | | × | | | × |
| Shenzhen Zhongxing Telecom Co., Ltd | 1997 | | | | × | × |

*Note:* * Shanghai Huateng is a joint venture between Warburg Pincus and Shanghai Information Investment Inc (a subsidiary of Shanghai Industrial Investment Holdings Co, which is owned by the Shanghai government).

The individual (household) market remains small because Chinese either cannot pay for software at all, or are willing to buy pirated versions. The household market is dominated by pirated or copycat versions of foreign application software products. Desktop software like Microsoft Office is almost entirely pirated. A domestic firm, Kingsoft, has succeeded by developing a local clone of Microsoft Word because its products are supported by government agencies. And Microsoft sells its operating system and application software to computer makers, like Legend and Dell, at a discount, for installations in PCs for sale in China.

## Software Piracy

Extremely high rates of piracy reflect, and reinforce, the immaturity of the Chinese software market. China is ranked second internationally, behind only Vietnam, with a 92 per cent business software piracy rate (Table 3.6). This means that a Chinese company with a new product idea is more likely to have the idea stolen than become a market leader. A recent survey of Chinese software enterprises reports that more than a quarter of respondents consider unauthorised copying, sharing and installation of software to be the most significant barrier to the industry's growth.

Software piracy is especially destructive in the consumer market. Enterprise applications that require large-scale implementation and training are less affected because they are more customised. This helps explain why software services currently occupy a greater share of the market than software products. Pirated software sales in China were estimated at $2.5-5.0 billion in 1999, compared with only $2.1 billion for legitimate software. In other words, a majority of the installed software base in the country is pirated software.

Piracy results, in large part, from the huge discrepancy between software retail prices and low household income. In Beijing, one of China's wealthiest urban areas, average per capita income is RMB19 500 per year. The price of a desktop computer equipped with a Pentium III processor is RMB4000-6000, and a desktop computer with a Pentium IV is RMB6000-8000 or more. Purchasing software packages at the official price soon makes these prohibitively expensive.

The widespread availability of pirated versions of the leading software products means that virtually no individual consumers buy software at the official price. The limited sales revenues of companies like Microsoft suggest that many businesses select pirated alternatives as well (Table 3.7).

Piracy forces domestic firms to compete by cutting price rather than by improving quality or features. A senior executive from Kingsoft reports that: 'Each time we sell an authorised WPS (Word Processing System) copy, there will be 10 pirated copies. If there were only 9 pirated ones, our income would be doubled.' In late 1999 the firm launched an 'Authentic Software Storm' promotion in an effort to reduce piracy: the price of the Kingsoft bilingual and voice-enhanced translation-aid software package was cut by 80 per cent from RMB168 ($20) to RMB28 ($3.33). Of course, this type of price-cutting leaves minimal margins and undermines the ability of firms to invest in research or product development.

*Table 3.6　Business software piracy rates by country, 2000*

| Country | % | Country | % |
|---------|----|---------|----|
| Vietnam | 97 | South Korea | 57 |
| China | 92 | Poland | 54 |
| Indonesia | 88 | Taiwan | 52 |
| Russia | 87 | Italy | 46 |
| Bolivia | 81 | South Africa | 45 |
| Thailand | 79 | France | 40 |
| Greece | 64 | Japan | 38 |
| India | 62 | Germany | 23 |
| Brazil | 59 | UK | 22 |
| Hong Kong | 58 | USA | 21 |

*Source*:　Access Asia: (2001 p.56).

*Table 3.7　Software prices in China*

| | Microsoft official price | Chinese competitor's official price | Street price for pirated version |
|---|---|---|---|
| Operating system | Windows XP 1498 RMB | Red Hat Linux OS 40-50 RMB | 20 RMB |
| Office suite | Office XP 3930 RMB | Kingsoft WPS Office 2000 1400 RMB | 10 RMB |

*Source*:　Center for the Future of China (2002).

The Chinese government has repeatedly announced plans to crack down on software piracy. Most recently in 2000, State Council Document 18 outlined harsh penalties for piracy, including fines of 5-10 times the value of the pirated software, prison sentences and equipment confiscation for manufacturers. In some cases the penalty has included execution. Government officials appear to understand the importance of intellectual property protection, particularly because they want to continue attracting foreign business. However it remains to be seen if these regulations will be enforced adequately. China's membership in the WTO should accelerate progress on formulation and implementation of intellectual property rights protection, but the backwardness of the legal system in China will continue to limit recourse.

## Government as a Market

The government is one of the dominant paying customers of the Chinese software industry. Government ministries, agencies, and institutes at all levels procure software to support the goals of national industrial development as well as to improve their own productivity – and they are frequently urged to procure local rather than foreign-made software. Moreover, resources remain heavily concentrated in the state sector. One Silicon Valley returnee who started an enterprise software company in Beijing puts it bluntly:

> If you want to make big sales in China you have to be political. The telecommunications and finance (banking) sectors make up 50 per cent of the IT budget in China and their structures still reflect the bureaucratic hierarchies of the planned economy. This means you are always dealing with the government. (personal interview, 2002).

Firms with good relations with the government are well positioned to get contracts. Government purchasing often takes the form of large-scale projects such as the central government's 'Golden Projects for Informatisation' Golden Card, Golden Bridge, Golden Customs, and its more recently instituted E-Government programmes. There are also a variety of city-sponsored 'Digital City' or Information Port Programmes that, in the large urban areas, provide huge software development contracts. And a new generation of central government projects is also being developed as China prepares for the 2008 Olympic Games in Beijing: the 'Digital Olympics' project, for example, should provide extensive funding for software companies as well as other IT firms.

While the government is generally seen as a good client in terms of technical competence, ability to communicate, cooperativeness and ability to pay, most Chinese government agencies (like Chinese businesses) are technically unsophisticated and unable to articulate their requirements or specifications clearly. Government procurement can benefit an emerging industry under certain circumstances, but this role is regularly compromised in China by its other, often conflicting, roles. The strong desire among government officials, for either economic or security reasons, to create 'national champions' leads them to invest heavily in domestic software companies, or to rigidly enforce purchasing edicts demanding that all departments and state-owned enterprises purchase Chinese-made components and services.

In 2001, for example, the Beijing municipal government required that all its departments purchase WPS2000, a Chinese-language office software package developed by a domestic firm Kingsoft Co., rather than Microsoft Office 2000 – in spite of widespread agreement on the technical inferiority of the product. (WPS2000 is far less stable than Office and Kingsoft provides virtually no after-sales service or customer support.) In 2002, following the lead of Beijing, the Guangdong provincial government purchased over 4000 packages of WPS2002 software for use in more than 40 departments and bureaux. In some cases, the government attempts to grow domestic competitors by subsidising firms like the Beijing University spin-off Jade Bird, which continues to develop an indigenous database product to compete with Oracle and Sybase, or by providing contracts to start-ups developing Linux software products.

Taking a still more aggressive stance, in early 2003 the State Informatisation Leading Group, an interagency group responsible for IT planning for China's central government, proposed procurement guidelines requiring all central and local governments to buy software from domestic vendors.[9] The guidelines require that all government purchases of foreign-made software gain approval from the Ministry of Finance on a case-by-case basis. These guidelines would severely limit foreign software makers' access to the largest customer in China.[10] The proposal may not be enacted, and even if it is, it may not be well enforced because of the inability of domestic software firms to meet government needs. However it exemplifies the capriciousness of the regulatory environment.

The administrative guidelines set by the Ministry of Information Industries (MII), purportedly to insure standardisation and market regulation, also favour state-owned enterprises and university spin-offs over their private competitors. All applicants for government and major SOE work are required to obtain a Certification of Capability and Quality. This certification also establishes a firm's eligibility for the tax incentives and other promotional measures established for the industry. The standards for this certificate are based on traditional measures of scale such as number of engineers, total net assets, registered capital, and annual revenues, but have little to do with past projects executed, work process or quality. This makes it very difficult for private companies to actually (and honestly) meet the standards.

The few private software firms that have succeeded in China have exploited the government's preference for domestic products, whether for security or nationalistic reasons. UFSoft, Kingsoft and Kingdee all gained an initial advantage by developing low-end copies, or Chinese variants, of Western software (so-called C2C or 'Copy to China'), rather than on the basis of quality, technology or service. Early access to the large and lucrative government market has positioned them well to tap other government and SOE clients, and the government in turn has a growing interest in their survival.

The 'non-governmental' high-tech spin-offs from government research institutes and university computer science departments (such as Founder, TOP and Neusoft) have been heavily favoured in this environment. The founding university or institute, itself government-owned, already has well-established relations with the local governments and state-owned enterprises that help them 'compete for' government contracts. Most universities also own large businesses that require software, from publishing companies to restaurants. And most university spin-offs have little difficulty gaining access to bank financing, something that is not available to private firms. So at the same time that the government is radically restructuring the state-owned companies in traditional industries, it appears to be creating a new generation for the technology sector (see Box 3.3).

---

BOX 3.2: BUILDING ON GOVERNMENT CONNECTIONS: BEIJING UFSOFT GROUP

China's leading producer of accounting and ERP software, UFSoft, was started by Wenjing Wang and Qiqiang Su, both formerly employees of the Finance Department of the Government Office of Administration. It is the only private software company listed on the Chinese stock exchange. During the 1980s Wang oversaw development of the government accounting system and finance-related computer applications for all State Council affiliated institutions. Su was in charge of developing the standardised accounting forms that later provided the template for UFSoft accounting software products. Wang's intimate knowledge of the market for financial software in China combined with Su's technical and product support capabilities enabled them to start UFSoft in Beijing in 1988.

The firm's first CEO, Mr Guo, also had a government background. He reports that his job at the Ministry of Finance gave him both deep knowledge of the status of computer applications in Chinese companies at the time and also invaluable government connections: 'I was in charge of enterprise accounting information, which involved statistical analysis of data from 38 000 state-owned enterprises and 20 000 collectively-owned firms . . . Our government experience helped gain users' trust quickly. We already had relationships with many potentially large customers [for example, governments and state-owned enterprises] and this made it much easier for us to market our products, especially in the early stages.'

UFSoft's marketing strategy reflects knowledge of the government market. According to a former UFSoft marketing manager, the company has adopted the 'top-to-bottom' strategy: it starts marketing a new product by establishing a close relationship with the central government. Adoption by the central government in turn makes it easier to sell to local governments. He reports that: 'About 95 per cent of the central government departments in Beijing now use UFSoft products.' The company has also established about 500-600 agents and 50-60 subsidiary companies throughout China, most of which have focused on building good relationships with the local government. According to him: 'it is much easier to market software to local governments than the central government because usually only one person is in charge. In the central government you have to convince many different people.'

The government still controls the market in several ways. A former CEO elaborates: 'First, a software product must receive evaluation and approval from the Ministry of Finance before it can be marketed in the country. Second, "market entering permission" is required before a product can be sold in local markets. So, for example, only three types of accounting software might be permitted in the Beijing market, even though some fifty financial software products are available in China. A strong relationship with the government helps a lot for entering markets in other provinces and cities.' Not surprisingly, UFSoft has developed China's most extensive and largest software distribution and sales network, with 60 subsidiaries, 60 customer service centres, 500 distributors, and 100 authorised training centres throughout China.

There are many domestic critics of government purchasing as a strategy to develop the domestic industry, both inside and outside of the Chinese bureaucracy. A senior manager of a Peking University spin-off argues that substantial government investments in the development of operating systems and database software have had no public return: 'In the process of investing, a lot of state assets have been visibly or invisibly transferred to these companies, which may produce no return at all.' The central government invested considerably in the development of the Linux operating system, for example, yet the market share remained only 4.1 per cent in 2002. A manager for a venture capital company in Hong Kong concurs: 'China has no comparative advantage in developing Linux. How can Chinese companies compete with Microsoft Windows?' (personal interview, 2002).

The decentralisation of economic policy in China could also undermine the impact of preferential procurement strategies. The growing autonomy of provincial governments to pursue independent development strategies has produced an intense process of inter-regional competition, particularly for technology development. The powerful Shanghai government, for example, continues to use Microsoft products. This does not mean, however, that they oppose preferential purchasing. The success of financial services firm Shanghai Huateng Software Systems Co. appears to be the result of more than a decade of large-scale contracts from China Post and other government agencies.[11]

---

BOX 3.3: GOVERNMENT AS BOTH PRODUCER AND CUSTOMER: CHINA NATIONAL COMPUTER SOFTWARE AND TECHNOLOGY SERVICE CORPORATION

China National Computer Software & Technology Service Corporation (CS&S) is a state-owned enterprise that was established in 1990 as a subsidiary of the China Electronics Corporation (CEC). The company is based in the Zhongguancun Science Park in Beijing and it has more than 30 holding and share-holding companies that specialise in software and information product development, system integration, information service and software development outsourcing. The company's turnover in 2001 was RMB1.33 billion and it had 2020 employees (80 per cent with university degrees), making it one of the largest software enterprises in China.

CS&S has apparently achieved the status of a 'national champion' that fulfils the administrative guidelines established by the government to qualify for the major government software projects. According to the company website: 'CS&S was appointed by China's State Planning and Development Commission as China's North Region Software Base. CS&S is the only software company listed as one of the 520 National Key Enterprises since 1999 and it was the first software company to be classified as a Software Enterprise. CS&S obtained ISO9001 Certification in software development, systems integration, computer training, and software export. CS&S has been ranked among the nation's Top 100 Electronic Information Enterprises for eleven consecutive years and was ranked 62nd in 2002. CS&S was the only systems integrator in China that obtained the National Systems Integration First-Level Qualification in 2000 and passed the national security-related Systems Integration Qualification for systems integration in 2002.' The company website lists 25 major customers; virtually all are large state-owned enterprises.

## Relationship Marketing

The dominance of the government market, as well as the absence of the rule of law, is reflected in the pervasiveness of 'relationship marketing' in China. The importance of connections in obtaining contracts from Chinese enterprises and government institutions is widely recognised. While policymakers are attempting to change this, especially in the newer technology sectors, software producers still spend far more time and energy building reputations and relationships than in the West. A Silicon Valley-based entrepreneur whose company provides content for the mobile Internet in China refers to this as the problem of 'high transaction costs.' He reports:

> For most of us doing business in China today, the biggest challenge is the time that we have to spend going to dinners and banquets, drinking, making friends, and building trust. The hard infrastructure here (like telecommunications and airports) works very well, but the soft infrastructure is still barely developed. If you can't depend on the legal system for remedies, you have to make sure that you trust your business partners, that you speak the same language and know one another well. And since there are no rules, we have to do business on a case-by-case basis, which means building trust case by case.

The Chinese government's inner networks are maze-like in their complexity and there are issues that must be negotiated at municipal and provincial as well as central levels. Establishing and maintaining good government relationships is thus essential to getting anything done in the economy. As a senior researcher at the Beijing IT Industry Promotion Center, puts it: 'The so-called Chinese *guanxi* leads to unfair market competition. No matter what you want to do, there are always lots of realistic (sic) problems facing you, most of which require time-consuming coordination.' (like many Chinese, uses the word 'coordination' to refer to the continuous wining, dining and relationship building that is required to solve the many problems that arise in the closed Chinese environment.) In the absence of transparency, stable regulations and the rule of law, there is no alternative.

Foreign and small firms face particular challenges in this environment. A senior manager from Oracle argues that it is critical for a foreign company trying to compete in China to recruit sales people with great care. The two criteria that Oracle uses in hiring for its sales and marketing team are: (1) the individual's capability, and (2) the quality of his/her network of relationships. A strong relationship network, in his view, depends upon working experience either in related government sectors or for major customers in the target market (which themselves are likely to have strong government ties). Another overseas-Chinese manager suggests that: 'the main task for a marketing vice president in China is to deal with relationships. Marketing depends on *guanxi*.' Virtually every individual we interviewed in the software industry confirmed that sales in China depend on the intensive-intensive process of building and maintaining relationships. A department manager of CASS Information Systems Inc., a small firm spun-off from the Chinese Academy of Sciences, notes that small firms like his that have limited personnel and resources are greatly disadvantaged in this environment.

One indicator of the importance of personal connections in post-reform China is the experience of returnees from the USA. Many of these entrepreneurs, coming from an environment where the quality of the technology and service are key to competition in the software industry, overlook this factor. Having spent more than a decade in the USA most lack the personal connections needed to succeed in the Chinese business environment. In fact it does not seem accidental that the only clear successes among start-ups run by Silicon Valley returnees, UTStarcom and AsiaInfo, are those in which the founders have been able to build on pre-existing personal or family ties in top Chinese business and government circles. For a majority of returnees, however, breaking into the closed relationships of Chinese business remains a major challenge that demands both time and resources.

### Government as Gatekeeper: Microsoft in China

The experience of Microsoft illustrates how the government continues to shape the Chinese software market without directly regulating it. Approximately 60 per cent of computers in China run on Microsoft Windows, but piracy means that the firm's China revenues are less than 5 per cent of what they would be if customers had paid for the software in newly sold computers (IDC). As a result Microsoft has not yet made money in China after more than a decade in the market. The firm's lawyers responded to this situation initially by suing Chinese computer makers as well as corporate users for piracy of its operating systems. However the immaturity of China's legal system meant that they had only limited success in the courts. Instead, Microsoft developed the reputation of a bully, a reputation that was reinforced by the US government's antitrust actions against the firm.

China's state-run newspapers reported in 1999 that several government departments had blacklisted Microsoft and that government officials preferred the Linux operating system to Windows. In 2000 the Ministry of Information Industry subsidised the Chinese Academy of Sciences to commercialise an operating system developed by Red Flag Linux, a Chinese Linux firm. A year later Microsoft lost out to a handful of Chinese Linux firms in bidding for a contract to supply software for the Beijing government. Soon many agencies, from the Chinese Post Office and National Statistics Bureau to the Ministry of Education, had adopted Linux-based systems. Linux controlled only 1.6 per cent of the operating system market in 2001 but its share is expected to double by 2006.

In June 2002 Microsoft abandoned its legal strategy and began instead to invest in building good will with the Chinese government. This underscores the firm's determination to remain a player in China, even at the cost of continuing losses in the short to medium term. In an attempt to relieve concerns that the Windows operating system is not sufficiently secure for government use, Microsoft founder and CEO Bill Gates signed an agreement that gives the Chinese government restricted access to the source code of its operating system. This represents a rare concession from a firm that protects its intellectual property aggressively.

Microsoft also committed $750 million over three years to the development of the Chinese software industry in what amounts to a massive technology transfer scheme.[12] A Memorandum of Understanding (MOU) between Microsoft and China's State Development and Planning Commission (SDPC) states that this investment will be managed by a joint SDPC-Microsoft Cooperation Committee that is chaired by SDPC Minister Zeng Peiyan and Microsoft's Chairman Bill Gates. The MOU involves education and training, research cooperation, strategic investments, and joint ventures with local software companies. As part of this programme, experienced Microsoft employees are now providing software engineering training, promoting basic research in computer science at universities, and establishing joint research labs at Chinese universities. The funds are also underwriting salaries for university faculty and fellowships for dozens of PhD computer science students annually. At the same time, in a high profile announcement, Microsoft became the first foreign corporation admitted as a formal member into the China Software Industry Association, itself a quasi-government organisation.

Microsoft has already established two joint ventures with small local software firms. One is a 50 per cent share of a software services company called Wicresoft – in partnership with Shanghai Alliance Investment – that will develop proprietary software applications for Chinese and foreign customers. Microsoft has already awarded a global outsourcing contract to Wicresoft to provide technical support for Microsoft Windows and Office. The firm hopes to serve other multinationals in China that want to outsource software development. The other joint venture, Censoft, with two publicly listed Chinese IT companies, will develop enterprise and government application software, provide system integration services for government departments and enterprises, and offer software outsourcing, training and consulting services. CENTEK, which holds 51 per cent of the new venture, publicises its 'strong governmental background'. In addition, Microsoft has agreed to open up seven more offices in China by 2005. The payoff for these investments appears to be a growing share of government contracts with agencies like China Telecom, the Public Security Bureau, the Ministry of Inspection and the Port of Ningbo. However the real results may not appear for years (Leonard, 2002; Meredith, 2003).

---

BOX 3.4: TECHNOLOGY-TRANSFER: MICROSOFT'S JOINT
VENTURE WITH CENSOFT CORP. LTD

In 2002, Microsoft announced that it would pay $2.3 million for a 19 per cent stake in the Censoft Corp. Ltd., which has 150 employees in Beijing's Zhongguancun. Most of the company's top employees, including its CEO, have working experience at Microsoft-China and were recommended by the company; most, in fact, are returnees who were educated abroad and have only recently returned to China. These managers brought to Censoft the engineering techniques and the system for large-scale software development they learned at Microsoft – critical managerial know-how that was lacking in the Chinese software industry. The Censoft CEO reports that they also learned a great deal from Microsoft about marketing, building sales in China, demonstrating a product to customers, and launching a product. The benefits for Censoft are clear: the company has won accounts for high-end enterprise applications software and consulting for major Chinese clients such as Huawei and the Bank of China. Their revenue of $20 million in 2003 makes Censoft the thirty-first ranked indigenous software provider in China; and the firm may well become profitable before Microsoft does in China.

This type of partnership is likely to prove a far more effective mechanism for upgrading the Chinese software industry than most government research and procurement programmes. In fact, Microsoft has already invested more than 1200 hours in this intensive-intensive partnership. The gamble for Microsoft, that it will earn more business as a result of this project, appears to be paying off in contracts with government entities. Perhaps more important in the long run, Chinese software developers and customers will become hooked on Microsoft software, which will triumph as a de facto market standard.

## 3.3 SOFTWARE INDUSTRY LABOUR MARKET

**Labour Supply**

The shortage of highly-skilled software professionals is a concern for many software companies in China. The China Software Industry Association reports (CSIA 2003) that there were approximately 330000 professionally trained programmers employed in the industry in 2002, including 180000 technicians. However the supply of university-trained computer and software graduates remains limited. Most Chinese universities do not have software programmes or departments, so software engineers are recruited from computer science and applied mathematics departments. Approximately 37000 students graduate annually from Chinese universities and colleges with computer science degrees; 50 per cent have a software certificate and only about 5 per cent have advanced (master's or doctoral) degrees (Ju 2001).

This compares poorly with the 60000 graduates per year in India, a fact that contributes to the insecurity of Chinese policymakers at India's successful software outsourcing. Some scholars believe that China is short of 'blue collar' programmers who could take on low-end programming jobs. Many industry representatives believe however that high-end talent is the most pressing need for the Chinese software industry. They claim that low-end workers can be recruited from universities and the real shortage is in high-level system architects and designers as well as project managers. University science and engineering programmes in China continue to emphasise the traditional engineering fields rather than computer science. As a result Chinese software firms have even started to recruit workers from India for these positions. Lack of technical capabilities required for systematic analysis and design of software helps to explain the limited presence of Chinese firms in the international software outsourcing business. Chinese workers also typically lack the English language skills needed to communicate with customers and the connections to, or knowledge of, international software markets.

Wages for workers in the software industry are very low by international standards. The data suggest that Chinese software workers earn wages that are half that of their Indian counterparts. There is also a fair amount of regional variation in China. In 2000, the yearly salary for a BA degree-holder in computer science was $7300 in Beijing (North China), $6000 in Shanghai (Southeast China), and $2900 in Xi'an (Western China),[13] see Table 3.8.

There is intense competition for Chinese software developers, in spite of their relatively limited capabilities and work quality. This is reflected in very high turnover rates – as high as 20-30 per cent annually, even in the leading firms. Some people in the industry deem high turnover as the biggest obstacle for further development, especially for small firms.

*Table 3.8  Yearly salaries for computer science degree-holders, 2000 ($)*

|          | BA   | MA     | PhD    |
|----------|------|--------|--------|
| Beijing  | 7300 | 14 500 | 21 000 |
| Shanghai | 6000 | 9000   | n.a.   |
| Xi'an    | 2900 | 4300   | n.a.   |

*Source*:  Global Internet Ventures, China (2001).

This problem is magnified by the preference of Chinese workers for jobs in foreign companies or joint ventures, which pay higher salaries and offer the potential opportunity to go abroad. A study of employment flows in the software industry found that a majority of the employees of Chinese firms – whether owned by the state, collectively or privately – moved to foreign firms or joint ventures or went overseas for additional training rather than moving to other Chinese firms (He 1997). Finally, in spite of labour reforms in the mid-1980s that gave enterprises the right to lay off surplus workers, many Chinese software companies also have difficulty laying off employees because of the need to avoid causing the loss of 'face' in relationships.

**Education and Training**

The Chinese government began to focus attention on software education with the industry's designation as strategic by the 10th Five-Year Plan. The State Department of Education in 2001 authorised the launch of 35 model university-based Software Institutes, with financing from China's banks and domestic as well as foreign companies. The first six software institutes in Beijing are associated with the elite universities such as Peking University, Beijing University of Aeronautics and Astronautics, and Tsinghua University. They admitted approximately 5000 students in 2002. In recognition of the limits of an educational system where memorisation is the dominant method of learning, these institutes are using international textbooks and a corporate management model. They are also free to offer courses and hire faculty based on market demand – unlike China's traditional government-controlled educational institutions.

This is an example of the ability of the Chinese government to redirect resources quickly and on a large scale. Another is the substantial increase during the 1990s in the number of post-graduate degrees granted in science and engineering fields (Figure 3.5). Between 1995 and 2000 the number of science and engineering doctorates granted in China increased by 141 per cent from 518 to 1247. While these degrees were historically oriented toward traditional engineering fields, the field of computer science is gaining faculty and students fast. According to Professor Dehua Ju of East China University of Science and Technology, China has developed a 'talent strategy' in which 'software productivity and quality will be a national priority, with special stress put on such skill upgrading as process improvement, product management, quality assurance, and system analysis and design' (Ju 2001).

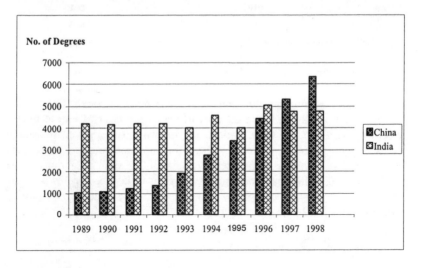

*Source*: NSF(2002)

*Figure 3.5  Science and engineering doctorates granted by domestic universities*

The market for IT training in China reached RMB560 million (about $68 million) in 2001, about a quarter of which ($16 million) is dedicated to software training. In an attempt to build domestic outsourcing capabilities, the government and private firms are developing new software training and English language programmes. Jade Bird, for example, established a core software engineering training programme that attracted more than 12000 trainees in 2001. Foreign corporations and educational institutions are also involved. Carnegie Mellon University has contracts with several large Chinese cities for training courses based on its Software System

## Brain Drain and Brain Circulation

The brain drain is a serious problem for China's software and IT industries. An estimated 30 per cent of the computer science degree-earners from China's most elite universities, such as Tsinghua and Peking University, went abroad to pursue higher degrees in the 1990s. This represented a substantial increase over the preceding decade. Figure 3.6 shows that in the 1980s only 3-5 per cent of China's total postgraduate enrolment left annually to study overseas, but the proportion increased to 10-15 per cent in the following decade. This amounted to an estimated total of 80000 Chinese students studying abroad in 1999 (Guochu and Wenjun 2001).[14]

While accurate data on the number of Chinese students returning after overseas graduation is difficult to find, most sources estimate very limited rates of return, particularly among those studying in the United States (the dominant destination for Chinese postgraduate students). Between 1978 and 1999, for example, one scholar calculates a 14.1 per cent return rate from the USA. Similarly, an NSF study in the late 1990s found that 88 per cent of Chinese with science and technology doctorates from the USA reported that they planned to stay abroad (NSF 1998). The data in the table below, calculated for the OECD, provides the most reliable estimate available.

Chinese provincial and central governments, recognising the severity of the loss of human capital have meanwhile developed a range of programmes that aggressively court talented returnees. The Chinese Academy of Sciences developed the 'Hundred Talent Program', which offers scholars higher salaries than they might earn in the USA as well as generous housing packages, extensive research funding and research teams. (Anecdotal evidence suggests, however, that if these scholars return, they mostly accept positions in multinationals or in local start-ups.)

Chinese policymakers have devoted substantial resources to promoting technical and business exchanges that involve overseas Chinese students. This typically involves events such as conferences, investigation tours, joint research projects and exhibits. Such activities are designed to involve cross-

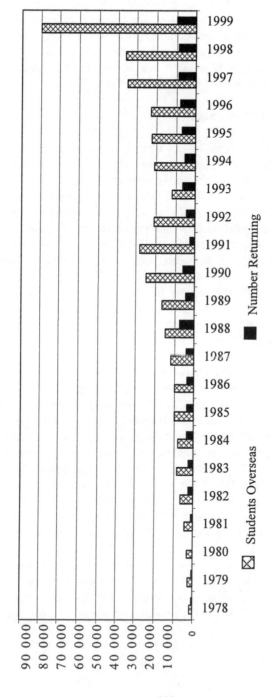

*Source: China Statistics Yearbook,* as reported by Guochu and Wenjur 2001

*Figure 3.6  Chinese students going overseas and returning annually, 1978-1999*

regional exchanges of know-how and information. They also provide opportunities for overseas mainland professionals to build relationships with their domestic counterparts. In some cases a local and central government agency will develop a programme that directly funds such events, in others it will subsidise non-government agencies and the private sector to sponsor such activities. In the late 1990s, Chinese policymakers, academic institutions and technology companies increased their commitment to improving external communications with the overseas Chinese. They sponsored an increasing number of events and programmes in the USA, while also inviting overseas Chinese academics and industry representatives to China to attend conferences and other events. In addition, the Ministry of Education established the 'Chunhui Program' to finance short-term trips to China by overseas Chinese who were trained abroad, to participate in technology-associated activities such as conferences, research projects or other authorised programmes (Dahlman and Aubert 2001).

Government agencies in China also compete to recruit students to return home to start technology enterprises. Representatives of cabinet-level ministries and municipal governments from large cities such as Shanghai and Beijing, as well as more remote Western provinces, pay regular visits to Silicon Valley to encourage Chinese technology professionals to return home. The visiting Chinese officials usually hold dinners or meetings with the Chinese community and use the occasion to publicise the favourable policy and business environment in China. Many municipal governments have established 'Returning Students Venture Parks' within the Development Zones of High and New Technology Enterprise. These parks are exclusively for enterprises run by returnees, and in addition to the infrastructure and financial benefits available in all science parks, they seek to address special needs of returnees such as accelerating bureaucratic processes involved with establishing residency or insuring access to prestigious primary and secondary schools for their children.

It is difficult to determine whether such policies contribute to individual decisions to return. Anecdotal evidence suggests, however, that a growing number of overseas Chinese have returned in recent years – lured by the promise of lucrative market opportunities and pushed by the economic downturn in the USA. Many are accepting jobs at multinationals with China operations; others are returning to start businesses or to work for businesses started by other returnees. It is likely that these returnees will become an important source of technical and managerial skill for the Chinese software industry in the coming decade.

In a survey conducted from May to July 2001 in Silicon Valley (Saxenian et al., 2002), 43 per cent of the highly skilled respondents from Mainland China reported that they would consider returning to live in China in the future. When asked to identify the factors that would influence their decision to return, the great majority (78 per cent) ranked 'professional opportunities' as 'very important' (these factors were ranked between 8 and 10 on a ten point scale with 10 as most important); followed by considerations of 'culture and lifestyle'. They ranked other factors such as favourable government treatment or the experience of barriers to professional advancement in the USA significantly less important (Figure 3.7).

There is ample evidence of 'brain circulation' as well. A small but significant proportion of Chinese technical professionals in Silicon Valley report that they regularly exchange information about jobs and technology with friends and colleagues in China, travel to China for business purposes, advise and help establish business contracts with firms in China, and invest in start-ups based in China. A majority of those who have been involved in starting new companies also report establishing business operations in China, particularly marketing and sales but also hardware design and manufacturing, R&D, and software development and services. These operations are concentrated in the main east coast cities, especially Shanghai, Beijing and Shenzhen/Guangzhou.

The same survey sought to determine the likelihood of returnee entrepreneurship in China. When asked what factors would figure most importantly in their decision to start a business at home, over 50 per cent of Mainland Chinese respondents listed access to the market, the availability of skilled workers, and access to capital as the key factors. Conversely, when asked about problem areas that would deter them from starting a business in China, the factors most frequently mentioned were: (1) government bureaucracy and regulation; (2) an inadequate legal system; and (3) political or economic uncertainty. In short, while the domestic market and skill base will continue to attract entrepreneurs in software and other IT-related fields, the institutional and political environment will likely remain a significant barrier for decades.

## 3.4 OWNERSHIP AND MANAGEMENT

### Ownership in Transition

Transformations in enterprise ownership in China have outpaced those in other elements of the economic infrastructure. The introduction of non-governmental, or collective ownership (university spin-offs), alongside state ownership in the 1980s, was followed in the 1990s by the sanctioning of private ownership of enterprises. However the institutions necessary for a system in which private enterprises compete on equal terms with other

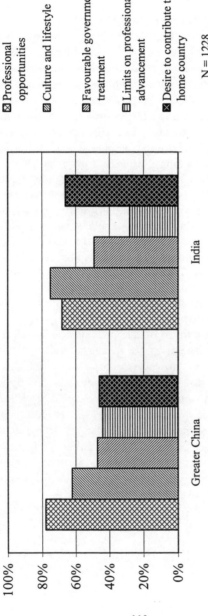

*Source:* Saxenian et al. (2002)

*Figure 3.7 Factors ranked 'very important' in decision to return to live in country of birth*

113

enterprises remain underdeveloped. China's financial markets and regulatory system, in particular, still favour firms that are either government-owned or that are strongly connected to the government through personal and business relationships. The absence of the rule of law leaves little recourse for those who lack such connections.

Currently 30 per cent of the software companies in China are state-owned, 27 per cent are Sino-foreign joint ventures, 20 per cent are collectively owned (university spin-offs), 17 per cent are private, and 6 per cent are foreign-owned. These distinctions are often blurred. State-owned and collectively-owned enterprises both involve substantial government involvement in management as well as finances. Foreign companies often prefer joint ventures with these enterprises precisely because they provide access to the government relationships that are essential to doing business in China. And the private software companies that are most successful in China have succeeded on the basis of strong government relationships.

In 2000, Tsinghua Tongfang Software Co., a spin-off of Tsinghua University, became the first Chinese enterprise to allow employees to buy shares in the company. The company's research employees now own 8 per cent of the RMB50 million ($6.02 million) software company's capital. According to the company's Chairman: 'We want to make it easier to translate research results into products and profits.' This recognition of the importance of researchers' knowledge as intangible assets, and the role of incentives in motivating the workforce, represents an important development in China. There are few models in China for creating an environment that provides incentives to attract and retain skilled employees – something that is critical in the software industry.

The increasingly flexible forms of enterprise ownership in China appear to have provided sufficient incentives for managers and employees to invest their time and resources to grow viable software businesses. It is worth underscoring, however, that ownership patterns do not appear to be a significant constraint on growth because domestic firms are primarily developing low-cost local variants of foreign products, or providing customised services to uncompetitive state markets. However the lack of a reliable legal system, and in particular the failure to protect intellectual property rights, will increasingly undermine efforts by Chinese firms to become technologically innovative because it limits firms' investments in research and new product development.

BOX 3.5 NEUSOFT GROUP: GROWTH BY BUILDING
REPUTATION AND ALLIANCES

Shenyang Neu-Alpine Software Co. Ltd was established in 1993 as a joint
venture between China's Neusoft Co. and Japan's Alpine Electronics to
develop car navigation and audio systems. In 1996 it became the first
specialised software developer in China to be listed on the Shanghai
Stock Exchange. Neusoft Co., a spin-off from the Software Development
Centre of China's North East University, developed the software solutions
for the business and is the largest shareholder (35 per cent) along with
Japan's Alpine Electronics (China), Co. Ltd, which manufactures and
distributes automobile navigation and audio systems (25 per cent).
Neusoft Group Ltd is now the largest publicly listed software company in
China with sales of $134 million and more than 4000 employees in the
year 2000. As with most large Chinese IT companies, there is a complex
set of relationships between the university, the provincial government,
state-owned enterprises and the central government. Professor Jiren Liu
from the Computer Science Department at North East University (NEU)
in Shenyang, Liaoning Province, was the founder of the NEU Software
Center in 1990. He is now the CEO and Chairman of the Board of
Neusoft Group. He is also the Vice President of Northeast University. His
biography notes that he has engaged in 46 national projects, has been
awarded more than 30 other government projects and that he is a Member
of the National People's Party Consultative Committee.

Professor Liu founded the NEU Software Center in 1990 and the State
Planning Commission named it as the first National Engineering Research
Centre for Computer Software in 1993. In the decade following its
founding Neusoft was selected to participate in all of the major national
research programmes in China including the National Torch Project, the
National 863 Plan, the National 9th Five-Year Plan projects, the National
High-tech Industrialisation projects, and so forth. The firm also received
honours, including being named the Software Industry Base for the State
Torch Program, an 'Elite Enterprise' for the national software industry
base, an Achievement Industrialisation base for the State 863 Plan, a
National Trial Enterprise for Technology Innovation and so on.

Neusoft's national reputation improved after China's leading steel
maker and one of its largest SOEs, Shanghai BaoSteel Group Corp., made
a large investment making it a 50 per cent owner in Neusoft Group in
1998. A year later, Zhiang Zemin, General Secretary of the Communist
Party of China (CPC) and President and Chairman of the Central Military

Commission of the CPC made a high profile visit to Neusoft Park and praised its achievements. China's Premier Zhu Rongji in turn visited in 2000 and Hu Jintao, then Vice President and Vice Chairman of the Central Military Commission of the CPC, visited in 2002. According to the company's website, Neusoft's tenth anniversary celebration in Shenyang was attended by 'more than 1600 people, including officials from state, province and city government, as well as representatives of 400 key enterprises in China, representatives of global renown (sic) enterprises as well as Neusoft employees.' Neusoft has built important local alliances: it joined with the Liaoning Science & Technology Venture Capital Co. Ltd to establish the Liaoning Oriental Information Industry Venture Capital Co. in 2000; and it invested in the Neusoft Institute of Information Technology as well as a series of institutes of information technology in other locations including Dalian, Nanhei and Chengdu. Neusoft's most significant domestic partnership, however, may be the cooperation agreement announced in late 2002 with Legend Group, to jointly address the fields of social insurance and medical insurance by combining Legend's line of computer storage products with Neusoft's system integration capabilities in order to provide high-quality customised solutions at low cost.

Neusoft continues to grow its international alliances as well, but its exports remain low ($14 million in 2000). In 2001 the US software company, Computer Associates (CA), invested $65 million to establish a strategic partnership with the Neusoft Group, and took a seat on the Board of Directors. Neusoft also established Neusoft Japan and Neusoft USA in the same year. Neusoft's website also reports strategic partnerships with companies such as Sun, Cisco, Nokia and IBM. The 2002 announcement that Neusoft had formally achieved SEI-CMM (Capability Maturity Model) Level 5, becoming the first Chinese company to be certified CMM5, suggests that it has been using its international connections to improve its software development process and capabilities.

One of Neusoft's most distinctive achievements is the development of a line of innovative digital medical imaging devices, including CAT scanners, X-ray, ultrasound and MRI products. The firm developed capabilities in embedded software during the 1990s and saw an opportunity to link its own imaging software and Intel microprocessors to digital sensors. Neusoft went on to develop and manufacture multipurpose scanners. The firm has had great success selling its products to Chinese hospitals because they are substantially less expensive and also more flexible than the specialised X-ray, MRI, ultrasound and CT scanners made by leading medical electronics companies in the West. Having developed a large-scale market in China, the company is now well positioned to expand into the global market.

*Source*: company websites and interviews (www.neusoft.com/framework/ browse/F10608489B@000/).

## Management Models and Experience

The lack of managerial experience and models for software development is one of the most significant weaknesses of China's software industry. Very few managers have experience in a market economy and most of the software developers in China are young and inexperienced. There are few role models for either group. As a result, there is a proliferation of small software enterprises in China that have had no exposure to process management models or systems integration. A senior manager of a PKU spin-off claims that most things are done haphazardly in Chinese software firms: 'Strictly speaking, there is no real management at all for most firms, especially the small ones' (personal interview, 2002).

It is thus perhaps no surprise that Chinese firms have failed so far to achieve the level of quality and reputation associated with successful outsourcing in India. There is little evidence of the ability to organise large scale, complex software projects involving the development of separate but linked modules by multiple development teams. A 2001 article in *IEEE Software* (Ju 2001) reported that the average yield of a software developer in China was about $25 000 per year, or roughly 13 per cent of that of their Western counterparts. This may be partly related to low labour costs, however it is likely due as well to inadequate management skill and organisation.

The continuing quality gap between Western and Chinese software is one indicator of the immaturity of the industry. Specialists agree that most Chinese software is of poor quality and does not function well: the original source code is rarely maintained, upgrades (when they exist) often do not work as promised, and patches are not available. Chinese firms have also paid very little attention to marketing and customer service. Documentation is recognised in the West, for example, as an essential tool in software development. By recording and explaining their work in detail, software developers can identify and correct problems in a timely way. The documentation process also provides a way to minimise the costs of employee turnover because the documentation belongs to the employer not the programmer. According to a Chinese venture capitalist who splits his time between Beijing and Silicon Valley, software engineers in the United

States typically spend 70 per cent of their working time on documentation, while engineers in Chinese firms devote virtually no attention to the documentation process.

Chinese software firms typically lack the knowledge or resources needed for managing human resources as well. The president of Kingsoft Co., Bojun Qiu, believes that the greatest challenge in running a software company in China is learning how to motivate and retain talented software developers. He says that programmers, unlike sales employees who respond to bonuses or higher salaries, require more than financial incentives and deadlines: 'You cannot be too strict because programming is an innovative job. You cannot force them to finish programming in a certain number of days . . . We are still in the stage of experimentation . . . It is easy for a big international company that adopts some software engineering process to invest in a few hundred people to develop one product. We cannot afford that. We often have to ask one person to do what really requires a whole team' (personal interview, 2002).

Faced with competition from the Indian software industry, Chinese software companies have started to apply for the Carnegie Mellon Capability Maturity Model (CMM) certification. Government agencies are also beginning to provide financial incentives for software companies to engage in these CMM-based evaluations. The Shanghai Software Quality Consortium was established in 2000, for example, to promote software process improvement. In December 2002, Neusoft Co. became the first Chinese enterprise certified CMM Level 5. However most Chinese firms dramatically underestimate the extensive resources and commitment required to achieve these quality management standards and the industry as a whole is likely to remain behind India and the West in the short run. The limited capabilities of Chinese software developers suggest that most firms will have difficulty competing with foreign companies in global software markets, and that the main market opportunity for these enterprises, at least in the near term, will remain systems integration for domestic customers.

## 3.5 SOURCES OF CAPITAL

The immaturity of the Chinese financial system reinforces the advantages of state- and collectively-owned companies in the software industry – and limits the growth of their non-state counterparts. A 1999 survey, conducted by the World Bank's International Finance Corporation, reports that 80 per cent of Chinese private sector companies believe the lack of access to financing has constrained their growth (IFC 2000). The great majority of software enterprises, like all other private enterprises in China, are self-financed because they lack access to bank loans or capital markets. There is a strong bias among bankers in China against lending to private enterprises largely because it is far more risky than investing in state-owned enterprises. According to Central Bank data, in 1999 less than 1 per cent of all working capital loans went to private companies, and these were likely not to go to local private firms, but rather to joint ventures with foreign private companies (Studwell 2002). This problem is particularly acute in software because the banks have virtually no credit analysis capabilities, and in any case prefer to invest in businesses with physical (as opposed to intangible, intellectual) assets.

Software enterprises with close government ties, by contrast, have little trouble gaining access to funding from the state-owned banks that control 65 per cent of the banking sector assets in China. This includes both state-owned enterprises and collectively-owned, university spin-offs like Neusoft, Founder and Legend. It also appears to include the few firms, such as UFSoft and Shanghai Huateng, that have gained the status of 'national champion'. Ironically, this means that in spite of their lack of technical capabilities or commercial track record, state-owned or collectively-owned enterprises have become one of the most important sources of funding for software start-ups in China because of their privileged access to capital, either through venture capital arms (for example, Legend Capital and Neusoft Venture Capital) or through the financing of subsidiaries or spin-offs.

The Chinese stock market in turn, is organised to provide capital for the continued expansion of state-controlled companies. The government approves the list of companies that can raise equity on the public markets, and in 2002 only a handful of over one thousand companies listed on the Shanghai and Shenzhen exchanges were private companies. It took four years of intense lobbying for UFSoft, China's market leader in accounting software, to be publicly listed on Shanghai's main board because of the Chinese regulators' reluctance to approve a privately-owned firm. UFSoft remains the only private enterprise among the 13 software firms listed on the Shanghai and Shenzhen exchanges.

Venture capital (VC) has been an important mechanism for financing new technology ventures in the West, but it is rarely an option for software companies in China. The Chinese central government has aggressively promoted the development of the industry for over a decade, but local and provincial governments have become the key players in the business. The first VC firm in China, 'China New Technology Venture Investment Corp.', was established as a limited corporation in 1985 by the State Science and Technology Council and the Ministry of Finance. The fund was declared bankrupt and closed by the People's Bank of China in 1997. This did not stop local Science and Technology Commissions and Finance Departments from setting up their own VC firms during the 1990s. There has been ongoing study and analysis of the Western experience, and growing sophistication at all levels. The challenge is that the government needs to lead in the creation of VC in order to encourage private investors (who, in China, remain extremely risk–averse); however the very involvement of the government has undermined the incentives needed for true capital venturing.

By 2000 there were 160 domestic VC firms in operation in China with a total of over RMB43 billion under management, along with 50 foreign firms (White et al. 2002). While domestic VC firms are organised differently (by local governments, universities and enterprises) virtually all of the capital in their funds comes from the public sector. However, government financing systematically undermines the financial incentives required to encourage fund managers to make truly high-risk investments, particularly in private enterprises. Nobody loses their job by investing in an SOE – even if it is a bad loan; however a bad investment in a private firm could be very costly. As one Silicon Valley-based entrepreneur who has advised the Chinese government on developing the VC industry notes: 'Venture capital fund managers in China have nothing at stake in the success of their ventures. If they are honest they will take no risk at all; if not, they take advantage of the opportunity to make under-the-table deals with entrepreneurs.' (personal interview, 2002). Another claims that most VC in China is simply a new form of job creation for local governments.

Most of the fund managers in China have no technical or business understanding of the software industry, they lack procedures for objectively evaluating potential projects and ideas, and they have no ability to raise funds outside of the government sector. Moreover, there is little understanding in China of corporate governance. As a result, while the Chinese VC industry has funded many domestic software firms, the funds have typically generated no return at all. As in most of the rest of the world, the dot-com crash has slowed investments considerably and there have been no new VC firms created since 2000.

Growing interest in China from foreign investors has created pressure for reform to improve the environment for equity investments. In 2001 the government issued a notice announcing that foreign companies would be allowed to set up wholly-owned or Sino-foreign cooperative venture capital firms in China.[15] There were also regulatory changes targeted at the VC investments in technology firms including a reduction of minimum levels of capital invested, establishment of a preferential tax regime (10 per cent) for VC investors, and recognition of the limited liability partnership structure that is common to many VC funds in the West.[16] However the failure to specify restrictions on the qualifications for the general partners in a limited liability partnership, means that it is likely that many more venture capital firms in China will fail to earn returns.

International investors remain reluctant to finance start-ups in the Chinese software industry, however, for two reasons: (1) the scarcity of local ventures with viable business plans and technical and managerial talent; and (2) the absence of viable exit strategies, since access to the Chinese stock market is impossible for these firms. Equally important, the RMB is not convertible, so there is no (legal) way to get earnings out of the country. Foreign investments in joint ventures with Chinese enterprises have, since the 1980s, grown as an alternative source of finance for a small number of Chinese software companies. One popular strategy for foreign investors today is to finance IT start-ups that are incorporated abroad, for example, in Silicon Valley, and leverage the technical skill in China for research and product development. This minimises their exposure to the arbitrariness of China's legal and financial institutions, while allowing them to take advantage of its large, very low cost supply of technical talent. In the process they are developing more sophisticated software engineering and development capabilities in China that should contribute to the long-term development of the software industry.

The underlying problem of the Chinese financial system, which affects the entire economy, including software, is the overwhelming burden of the non-performing loans (NPL) that in 2002 accounted for 50 per cent of total banking sector assets.[17] This problem, combined with the lack of sophisticated financial management skills, suggests that it will take at least a decade to reform China's financial system. The development of a healthy financial system will, of course, also require a reliable and well-functioning legal system.

## 3.6 REGIONAL DIFFERENTIATION AND THE SOFTWARE INDUSTRY

The growing disparity in the business environments in different regions of China is a striking aspect of the economic transition. While the country has always been diverse, the decentralisation of government authority and increased administrative autonomy of city and provincial governments has resulted in substantial differences in resources, regulations and performance across China. The uneven geographic distribution of the software industry reflects these differences.

Software firms and employment in China are heavily clustered in the Beijing, Shanghai and Guangdong regions along the eastern coast of China. These three urban areas alone account for 80 per cent of total software sales. It is worth noting, however, that only 16 per cent of the firms are located in

Beijing, but they account for 35 per cent of software sales; conversely, 34 per cent of the firms are located in Shanghai but they account for only 20 per cent of sales. The dominance of Beijing in software likely reflects the concentration of human capital as well as the presence of both city and central governments – and their heavy investments in the development of the IT infrastructure.

The leading research institutes and elite universities in China are located in urban areas on the eastern coast. This contributes to the disproportionate concentration of technical skill and research. Beijing, for example, is the home of 68 universities, 260 research institutes, and one-third of the employees of the Chinese Academy of Science. State funding for R&D goes overwhelmingly to five coastal provinces: Beijing, Shanghai, Jiangsu, Guangdong and Shandong. Even then, it is highly focused. For example, Peking University and Tsinghua University in Beijing alone received about RMB3.6 billion in government research funding, or more than half of the total of RMB6 billion allocated for the promotion of excellence in elite institutions in 2000. Jiaotong University, the top university in Shanghai, doubled the number of graduates between 1995 and 2000 and tripled its total research funding to RMB300 million. Other provinces such as Shanxi, Shandong and Liaoning (home of Neusoft) have successful software firms that are closely linked to local universities and research institutes. The concentration of technical skill, research and university connections in these coastal cities contributes to external economies and a self-reinforcing process of increasing returns, as software firms benefit from the pooling of managerial and technical skill and know-how as well as the benefits of connections to universities or research labs.

In recent years these concentrations have been strengthened by the growing concentration of the market, including high-tech businesses and the urban middle class, along the coast. These regions have become the wealthiest urban centres in China. If they were separate nations they would each have GDP ranking among the top ten in Asia, and ahead of Singapore, Malaysia and the Philippines (Table 3.9).

Chinese policy makers have designated development bases, parks, incubators and zones in their efforts to promote new technology industries. Appendix 1 provides a map of the 53 National High-Tech Industry Development Zones in China. The total R&D investment in these 53 high-tech parks grew dramatically in the 1990s, from RMB15.2 million in 1992 to RMB230.8 million in 1999 (Ministry of Science and Technology 2001). These parks, however, include all businesses that qualify as high technology. The Torch High-Tech Industry Development Plan also developed 14 state-level software parks during the 1990s. By 2002, however, China had a total of 48 software development parks dispersed widely around the country.

In 2001 the Ministry of Information Industry announced a plan to re-centralise resources in the software industry in hopes of enhancing competitiveness. They have identified 10 National Software Industrial Bases located in Beijing, Shanghai, Dalian, Chengdu, Xi'an, Jinan, Hangzhou, Guangzhou, Changsha and Nanjing. These 10 areas will benefit from preferential policies including venture capital funding, support services, and assistance in being listed on the stock exchanges. This represents part of an effort to reinforce the existing concentration of IT-related industries in the urban centres in the eastern and middle regions of China, and should reinforce the already existing concentration of the software industry along the coast.

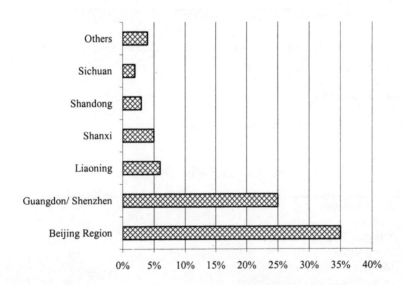

*Source*: CSIA (2001 p. 7).

*Figure 3.8 Share of software firms, by region, 2000*

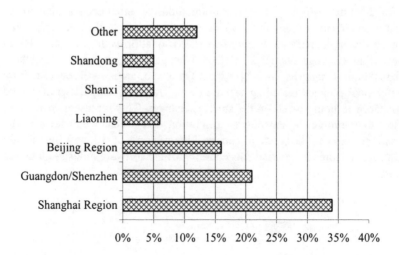

*Source*: CSIA (2001 p. 7).

*Figure 3.9 Share of software sales by region, 2000*

*Table 3.9  GDP ($ bn), south and east Asia, 2001*

| | |
|---|---|
| South Korea | 457 |
| Taiwan | 310 |
| Yangtze Delta (Shanghai) | 234 |
| Hong Kong | 163 |
| Northeast Tristates | 119 |
| Pearl River Delta (Guangzhou) | 116 |
| Beijing Area | 112 |
| Shandong | 104 |
| Singapore | 97 |

*Source*: Ohmae (2002).

# 3.7 THE FUTURE OF THE CHINESE SOFTWARE INDUSTRY

China's software industry is still in its infancy. It lacks technical skills, experience, management know-how, and the capital market, legal protections and transparency that will allow software enterprises to take risks, invest, innovate and become global actors. The goals of the post-1978 reforms – to shift from a planned to a market economy – remain only partially accomplished. Two non-market factors, government and *guanxi*, will continue to affect most aspects of the software business until policymakers address the real challenges facing the software industry, including the need for greater transparency and regulatory consistency, effective financial market regulation, the rule of law and protection of intellectual property rights.

There is also no doubt that China's software industry will continue to grow rapidly. The government's large-scale investments in R&D, education and training, and improvements in the physical infrastructure have already contributed greatly to the economy and will increasingly benefit the software industry, as will China's huge supply of low-cost skill. The state has also been very effective in channelling multinational investments into beneficial relationships with local companies by taking advantage of their desire to gain access to the China market. The level of technology and know-how transfer occurring through joint ventures as well as in the research labs and training programmes set up by foreign firms is already quite high. The Intel China Software Lab, for example, has over 90 engineers engaging in state-of-the-art software for applications including DSP (digital signal processing)/ multimedia products, device drivers, signal integrity technology and so on. There are unique opportunities in developing application software and embedded software for the sophisticated IT hardware manufacturing capabilities that have developed in China over the past decade, including the recent expansion of IC and high-end laptop manufacturing.

Chinese companies are rapidly expanding their foreign connections, in part to enhance their management and process capabilities. The telecommunications equipment company, Huawei, has invested over $60 million in a 3-year-old software development centre in Bangalore, India. The company plans to increase local employment from 600 to 900, with the overwhelming majority being Indian engineers who receive training in China. While Neusoft was the first Chinese company to achieve CMM Level 5, it is likely that many more will follow in the near future. Chinese bookstores in major urban areas are filled with management books, and there is a level of focus and motivation among workers that is easily visible to outsiders. The recession in the USA combined with a high degree of nationalism appears to be triggering an accelerating reverse brain drain of highly educated Chinese engineers from the USA and elsewhere. The success of Legend Computer in dominating the Chinese PC market suggests that domestic firms will be advantaged as well by their local market knowledge and connections.

Visitors to China are regularly impressed by the sophistication of the government officials–many of whom speak fluent English, have travelled extensively abroad, are open to outside views, and are articulate about the challenges facing the corporate and financial sectors. The Chinese Software Industry Association, for example, a government-sponsored approved association of software companies, is engaged in a wide-ranging set of ambitious activities and experiments aimed at accelerating the development of the industry.[18] Visitors who return regularly are also amazed by the pace of change at every level in Chinese society and economy. This makes it very difficult to look into the future with any certainty: China is changing very fast, and also very unevenly, and there are too many political as well as economic factors at play to say much more than there will be continuing change.

**The Impact of Entry into the WTO**

Since entering the World Trade Organisation China has taken steps to liberalise its information technology (IT) sector, including the software industry. This liberalisation is a double-edged sword: on the one hand it has increased the presence of foreign competitors in the Chinese software market, but on the other it should help address some of the constraints on the growth of domestic producers as well. According to the USA-China agreement there are now no restrictions on foreign commercial presence in providing consulting services related to hardware installation. Foreign service providers are also allowed to provide software implementation and data processing services in the form of a joint venture. Starting in January 2001, foreign companies were also allowed to establish joint ventures with the majority share, to provide computer maintenance and repair services.

China's WTO commitments required that after January 2003, wholly foreign-owned enterprises be allowed to enter the Chinese IT market. In addition, foreign personnel, certified engineers or bachelor degree holders with three years' experience will be allowed to provide software services. And China will phase out all software tariffs by the end of 2003 according to the WTO Information Technology Agreement. Foreign suppliers will also be allowed to provide software support services and have more freedom in establishing service centres. This should increase the competitiveness of foreign software vendors in China. However software sold in China must also meet the standards set by the Chinese Platform Standard Committee, which also approves the sale of software in the domestic market. Foreign companies often need to modify their software products in order to meet these local requirements.

Piracy is a major concern of foreign investors in China's software industry. The protection of intellectual property rights has achieved several milestones since 1991, starting with the implementation of the Copyright Law, followed by China's joining the world community in upholding the Berne Convention and the World Copyright Convention. The opening of the Software Registration Centre under the administration of the National Copyright Administration has normalised copyright enforcement in China.

China has also agreed to abide by the WTO's Agreement on Trade-Related Aspects of Intellectual Property Rights to achieve better enforcement of IPR protection. In May 1999, the State Council issued a notice to all government organisations urging them to use only licenced software. Recent reports suggest that the central government plans to begin a nationwide inspection to enhance awareness of protecting copyrighted software in governments. 'Those found using pirated copies will be severely punished', according to Xu Chao, Deputy Director-General of the Department of Intellectual Property Rights under the General Administration of Press and Publication (GAPP). The GAPP, the State Development Planning Commission, the Ministry of Finance and the Ministry of Information Industry have required all government departments to take the lead in using authorised software.

Some who do business in China also report that the true value of the WTO is that it provides an excuse among reformers in the government to undertake far-reaching changes. Others believe that its main value is to provide the perception of China's competitiveness even if there is a tendency among regulators to follow the letter rather than the spirit of their WTO commitments.

## Trends in the Chinese Software Industry

Four distinct – and not necessarily incompatible – trends seem likely to shape the development of the Chinese software industry in coming decades. There is evidence for each of these trends and, while all coexist in China today, they each support different dynamics.

### Government-led development
It seems clear that the government will continue to play a dominant role in the Chinese software industry, both as a customer and as a promoter, investor and regulator. The central government has made several major purchases in recent years in order to support the development of domestic software

products. It will likely continue to make large investments in software research, concentrate these resources in leading companies, and then enforce purchasing fiats demanding that government departments and state-owned enterprises buy Chinese-made components and services. The vision underlying this behaviour is that Chinese software companies will be able to first replicate and then improve upon other people's ideas – much as Japan did with VCR technology in the 1960s and Microsoft did in the 1980s with the user-friendly Macintosh Graphical User Interface and Operating System.

**Software services outsourcing**
Many government officials would like China to follow the model of Indian software outsourcing and leverage its abundant pool of cheap programming talent and growing English language capabilities to provide software services for global corporations. China has already attracted a handful of Indian software companies to locate in urban centres like Shanghai and Beijing. Over time they might induce these companies to make large investments and to outsource their cheaper work to China. This would support the development of management and technical capabilities in the Chinese software industry, while allowing India to focus on higher value-added activities. China's leading telecommunications equipment vendor, Huawei, already has a software centre in Bangalore that employs some 400 Indian programmers. However Indian companies possess what Chinese software firms will continue to lack for a long time to come: excellent English language skills; the ability to conduct business with Western clients in their cultural idiom; an established pipeline of clients; and an internationally acclaimed reputation for trustworthiness, reliability and credibility as a provider of skilled services. Moreover, the existence of a big domestic market means that China will never simply follow India's offshore software-development strategy; but this trend could help China adjust its current completely domestic concentration.

**Foreign investors as partners and mentors**
Foreign information technology companies, attracted by the large local market and the pool of low-cost skilled researchers and programmers, are a fast growing presence in China. Multinationals like Microsoft, Oracle, Adobe, IBM, Lucent and Intel all have software and computing-related R&D centres in China. Many have entered into joint ventures with local Chinese companies as well. These firms work primarily on high-quality, large-scale software projects that are not appropriate for the domestic market. However as they continue to attract the top computer science and programming talent from domestic software firms, and as they accumulate first-hand knowledge of the local market, they could become formidable competitors in the low-

end software market. These joint ventures and R&D centres could also serve as training grounds for the next generation of Chinese software entrepreneurs and managers.

## Brain circulation and industrial upgrading
There are hundreds of thousands of foreign-educated Chinese technical professionals living and working abroad. The global recession in the technology industry, combined with China's continued robust growth, has been responsible for a growing number of overseas Chinese returning to China (or moving to China, in the case of thousands of Taiwanese). These returnees bring with them the skills, knowledge and contacts they have developed in the West. They also often bring a much needed, first-hand understanding of Western business practices, as well as a more finely tuned, quality-oriented mindset. That, coupled with their ability to speak both English and Chinese, along with their understanding of local Chinese business practices, should allow software firms to make themselves attractive candidates for Western outsourcing contracts. The growing brain circulation between Silicon Valley and major metropolitan areas such as Beijing and Shanghai in China suggests the increasing importance of this group of people, as does the growing number of returnees starting software and other technology businesses or setting up business operations in these urban areas.

## NOTES

1. Naughton and Segal (2001: p. 38).
2. Chinese policymakers have even suggested that Microsoft Windows has 'backdoors' that allow either the company or the USA to spy on users (Ibid.).
3. Naugthon and Segal (2001) define techno-nationalism as a policy orientation toward autonomy and independence from other states. The original techno-nationalist states, like Japan and Korea in the 1980s, were willing to bear the economic costs of a strong central-government control alliance with large domestic corporations in order to insure technological and economic independence. They sought to create independent domestic capabilities in critical technologies as well as to develop institutions to diffuse these capabilities throughout the economy. China is pursuing a more laissez-faire variant of techno-nationalism, but remains equally committed to becoming 'masters of our own fate'. (President Zhiang Zemin, 1995).
4. *Guanxi* is loosely translated as 'connection' or 'relationship.' The literature on the subject is extensive, with the main theoretical divide being between those who see the reciprocal obligations and indebtedness that characterise *guanxi* as a cultural phenomenon, distinctive to Chinese society. The alternative view, adopted here, views the client-oriented relations associated with them as a result of the particular institutional structure of Chinese society – but not a fundamentally Chinese phenomenon. See Gold et al. (2002).

5. For more on this view, see Guthrie (1999). Legal scholar Stanley Lubman (2000) cautions, however, that while the Chinese are attempting to formalise a system of regulation and rule of law, business practice still treats such Western concepts as a contract resembling a cage that can be unlocked with appropriate *guanxi*.

6. The '863 Plan' employed approximately 40 000 individuals in over 5200 research projects between 1986 and 2000.

7. This was reflected in the ideological shift made at the 15th Party Congress in 1997, where the legitimacy and contribution of private enterprise were fully acknowledged.

8. Municipalities like Beijing and Shanghai typically add their own incentives to the national policy for the sector. Beijing, for example, offers financial assistance, preferential land prices, and assistance to foreign managerial and technical personnel starting new companies.

9. The proposal applies to all contracts from central and local budgets for E-Government, a multi-billion dollar initiative developed to upgrade the computer and communication networks of several key departments including the tax bureau and customs authority. At least 70 per cent of the initiative's software budget would be earmarked for domestic products. In addition, 50 per cent of most other kinds of government software would have to be purchased from Chinese companies (Pottinger 2003).

10. The proposal apparently exploits a grey area in the WTO restrictions on laws giving domestic companies artificial advantage over foreign competitors (since government procurement contracts are not clearly covered under the WTO).

11. Huateng built the government's first Golden Card Center (for IT banking), the Golden Card National Center in Beijing, and is the market leader in all Golden Card projects. It is also the market leader in the Postal Savings Banks' Green Card National Network, built the first bankcard Internet payment gateway in China, installed 16 bankcard Internet payment gateways for China Post's 'E-Post' project, and provided the solution for China Post's E-Remittance system.

12. This is in addition to the $1 billion the company already spends on business and research in the country (Leonard 2002).

13. This data is similar to that in a 2001 study by a US consulting firm, which reports wages in the software industry in Shenzhen (Guangzhou province) as RMB3000 per month for a junior engineer, RMB6000 per month for a senior engineer, and RMB12 000 per month for a department director. This amounts to average salaries of $4400 per year, $8700 per year, and $17 500 per year respectively. The report estimates that Shenzhen wages are 70-80 per cent of those in Beijing and Shanghai.

14. Guochu and Wenjun (2001) estimate that China has permanently lost 200 000 science and technology workers, which is equivalent to a loss of over RMB40 billion in human capital investment. He calculates the investment by imputing a total investment of RMB200 000 per student.

15. Foreign VC firms are not, however, allowed to invest in securities, futures or other financial markets nor in real estate or other industries that are not open to foreign investment. They are also not allowed to make loans or underwrite or invest with borrowed money (CIEC 2001).

16. Chinese Company Law limits the amount of an enterprise's registered capital that could be granted for the contribution of intangible technology to a maximum of 20 per cent. This limit has been abandoned in practice but not yet in regulations.

(The Chinese government in the late 1990s planned a second board in Shenzhen, modelled after the NASDAQ, for high-risk, high-return companies. However the anticipated opening in 2000 was delayed following the US stock market crash and remains delayed indefinitely.)

17. The total cost of cleaning-up the NPL problem, according to Standard & Poor's, amounts to $700 billion, or about 50 per cent of China's current GDP.

18. These activities include sponsoring symposia that bring together government officials, experts, scholars and representatives of firms and other institutions to discuss shared challenges, such as the availability of capital for start-ups. They also run international software exhibitions, help promote brands and brand names, survey the market, promote international exchanges and cooperation, conduct training, formulate industry standards as well as rules and regulations, and promote software exports. See www.csia.org.cn

**APPENDIX 1  National High-Tech Industry Development Zones in China**

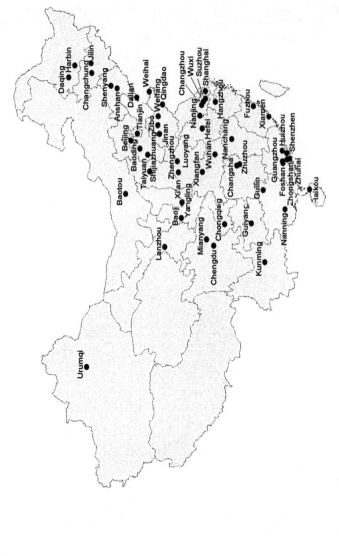

*Source:*  Ministry of Science and Technology (2001).

# 4. Israel

## Susanna Khavul

### SILICON WADI

If the 1990s were about riding the roller-coaster of investments in emerging markets and high technology, then Israel's rise as a centre of innovation and entrepreneurship quintessentially captures this ride. During the 1990s, Israel's rapid growth in entrepreneurial activity and the massive inflow of equity capital led to the co-evolution of the country's real and financial sectors. In July 2000, *Wired* magazine named Israel one of the world's top 'Venture Capitals' and high technology epicentres. This ranking positioned Israel one step behind Silicon Valley, on a par with Boston and Stockholm, and a step ahead of London, Helsinki and Bangalore.

Israel's place in the international technology rankings is all the more noteworthy given how much the country had changed in the decade between 1990 and 2000. At the beginning of the decade, high technology constituted 23 per cent of industrial exports; by the end of the decade high technology's share of exports had jumped 10 per cent. At the beginning of the decade, Israel had two venture capital funds managing $59 million; by the end of the decade, Israel had more than 100 venture capital funds that raised $9.4 billion earmarked for investment in Israeli high-technology companies. At the beginning of the decade, Israel had approximately 500 start-up firms; by the end of the decade, it had more than 2500. At the beginning of the decade, only a handful of Israeli companies were listed on international exchanges; by the end of the decade, more than 150 companies, the majority in high technology, were listed in the USA and Europe.

Israel has undergone an important transformation in its decade of emergence. Five significant economic, social and political trends contributed to the country's rise as a world-class technology centre.

- **Economic liberalisation:** As many other emerging countries have done, Israel liberalised its economy and integrated itself into the global marketplace. For several decades after its establishment, Israel's economy was a mixed market model where the state, large conglomerates with direct links to the state, and powerful labour unions dominated the economy.[1]   In the mid-1980s, Israel faced a massive banking crisis and severe hyperinflation. The deteriorating economic conditions resulted in a substantial flight of skilled labour, primarily to the United States. By the end of the 1980s, Israel had embarked on an economic austerity and stabilisation programme. The liberalisation programme that followed resulted in a freely convertible currency, free flow of foreign capital, partial privatisation of the banking sector, and the introduction of competition into the telecommunications and other key sectors. This dramatic liberalisation of the Israeli economy has facilitated its more complete integration into global markets in capital and trade.

- **Immigration:** With the collapse of the Soviet Union, nearly one million highly-skilled refugees emigrated to Israel. Immigration increased Israel's population by 20 per cent and significantly raised the skill level of its workforce; so much so, that by the end of the decade Israel had the highest number of scientists and engineers, per capita, in the world.

- **National investment in research and development:** During the 1990s, one of the Israeli government's explicit goals was to position the country at the centre of the knowledge economy. To this end, governments, both liberal and conservative, pursued a policy of incentives and outright support for the development of both the financial and technical infrastructure to support a nascent high-technology community. Israel has also invested in military and civilian R&D at a rate that is higher than any other industrialised country. Israel's military and academia have been the source of innovation and training for the country's high-technology sector. Tangible and intangible spillovers from military and academic research, development and training have created an application- and solution-focused technology culture.

- **Foreign investment:** Liberalisation of the economy, an educated and skilled labour force, and continuous investment in R&D made Israel an attractive destination for foreign direct investment and venture capital. In 2000, Israel had more venture capital as a percentage of GDP than any other country, including the United States. Israel had also become a favoured destination for Intel, Microsoft, Cisco, 3Com, Lucent and scores of other international technology giants in search of research and development, investment, and acquisition opportunities. The availability of private venture capital and the presence of multinationals along with the links to the international business and financial sectors that they provided motivated thousands of technology entrepreneurs to start new firms.

- **Prospect of peace:** The prospect of a resolution of the Israeli-Palestinian conflict reduced the perceived political risk for investments in Israel.

Policymakers in other emerging economies often look at the experience of Israel in hopes of reproducing it. Indeed, the Israeli experience illustrates how public policy and private initiative can work in tandem to build a community of entrepreneurs and investors who together can create a dynamic high-technology industry. Certainly, the Israeli experience has important lessons about the power of economic liberalisation and the benefits of immigration, as well as investment in research, development, and education. However, the Israeli experience also suggests that government involvement should be focused and limited; that the volatility in the financial markets can dry up the sources of investment capital; and that human capital and technology are a portable commodity in the global economy.

This chapter examines the emergence and evolution of Israel as a high-technology centre through the lens of its software and information technology sector. Software and information technologies drove global economic growth over the last decade. Software and information technologies now originate from a number of emerging economies including Israel. Israel's share of the global software market is small. At the height of the technology boom, Israel exported approximately $3.7 billion of software products in a global market. Although small in relative terms, Israeli software exports have increased nearly six-fold in a decade. While Israel exported less than half the total value of Indian software sales in 2001, Israel's exports are high value-added products. The industry has average sales per employee of more than $200 000. At the end of 2001, there were approximately 400 software firms of which half a dozen accounted for most of the sales and exports. Israel's software products are concentrated in niche markets, particularly in enterprise software and information security and largely are targeted at business customers. One Israeli software start-up, Mirabilis, did make a substantial contribution to the global consumer market by creating ICQ, the most popular Internet chat program in the world.

Although the growth of the software sector is impressive, Israeli firms have faced a number of important competitive challenges. Israel's domestic market is limited and highly competitive. Israeli software firms have to be export oriented from the start. Israel is not a low-wage country and competition on price is unrealistic. Thus, Israeli firms compete with the most sophisticated and well connected international firms based on the strength of their technologies. Israel is geographically isolated from its target markets in the USA and Europe. To cope with this, many Israeli firms set up dual locations from inception, maintaining research and development in Israel while moving headquarters abroad. The majority of Israeli software firms are also small and poorly capitalised. As a result, many never develop into fully operational companies and become attractive acquisition targets. The solutions Israeli companies adopt to cope with liabilities of newness, smallness, and foreignness present public policy challenges. For example, the potential out-migration of some firms and the stunted growth of others forces Israeli policymakers to ask whether the sector can produce and sustain a critical mass of entrepreneurial firms that develop into medium and large companies.

The downturn in the global economy and political unrest in the Middle East between 2000 and 2003, have put Israel's efforts of the last decade to a severe test. First, the Israeli technology sector was dependent on the inflow of equity capital from abroad and the demand for its products in the USA and Europe. When the global Internet-driven technology boom came to an end in April 2000, the IPO exit option for the venture capitalists, who had invested heavily in the Israel software sector, disappeared. The alternative exit, trade sales, also receded as the value of large multinationals, the would-be acquirers, began to shrink. The venture capital community continued to fund software and Internet start-ups through 2000, but thereafter this source of funding declined. Second, the downturn in the capital markets put downward pressure on corporate purchasing of information technology products and services. This made it more difficult than before for Israeli software firms to sell in the USA and Europe. Finally, the escalation of political conflict in the Middle East and the upsurge of international terrorism has made Israel both a more risky place to invest, and from which to source technology. The size of the political effect is difficult to estimate and will be clear only with time. It is, however, now clear that by integrating with the global economy Israel has opened itself up to growth on the upside and contraction on the downside of the business cycle. To manage the transition out of the current global economic slump, both the government and the private sector have to find strategies to sustain the entrepreneurial dynamism that is the distinct competitive advantage of the Israeli technology industry.

This chapter is organised into three sections. Section 4.1 presents a brief overview of the Israeli software and electronics industry. Section 4.2, the institutional context that has helped an Israeli technology sector to emerge and Section 4.3 discusses the evolution and future direction of the industry. The chapter includes multiple case studies and covers data through 2003. The chapter also looks at the wider lessons that can be learned from the Israeli experience.

## 4.1 EMERGENCE OF ISRAEL'S SOFTWARE INDUSTRY

The global software industry is defined as much by the hundreds of niches that small and medium-sized firms occupy as it is by the global dominance of software powerhouses like Microsoft, Oracle or SAP. The Israeli software sector is a reflection of the global industry. In 2001, the top five Israeli information technology companies, Amdocs, Comverse, Check Point, Mercury Interactive and NDS, had cumulative sales of approximately $4.1 billion. The next ten firms had cumulative sales of approximately $600 million. The vast majority of Israeli software firms are small, young and privately held. By one estimate, there were between 350 and 400 Israeli companies in the information technology and software sectors at the end of 2001 (D&A Directory 2002).

To understand the growth of Israel's software sector, it is important to understand the context of Israel's larger electronics industry. In 2003, electronics and information industries employed approximately 53 500 people of whom 64 per cent were scientists, engineers and technicians. The combined sales of the electronics and information sectors was $13.2 billion, of which $10.8 billion was earned from exports.

As Table 4.1 shows, in 1991, sales and exports were $3.6 billion and $2.3 billion respectively and the industry employed 33 000 people. Of these, 51 per cent were scientists and engineers. In addition to the overall rise in sales and employment, sales per employee had more than doubled from $109 000 to $246 000 from 1991-2003 (Israel Association of Electronics and Information Industries). Between 1991 and 2001, Israeli electronics and information industries reported strong annual growth rates. However, by 2002, global technology markets were in a slump and the political situation in Israel had seriously deteriorated. Between 2000 and 2003, the combined sales revenue of Israeli electronics and information industries decreased by $3.3 billion and 13 300 jobs were lost.

Growth in the software sector mirrored that of the high-technology sector. As Figure 4.1 shows, during the 1990s the software sector also grew at an impressive and steady pace. In 1991, total Israeli software sales were approximately $540 million of which 20 per cent was exported. At the time, software firms employed 5000 people. At the end of 2001, the Israeli software sector had approximately 400 active firms, which employed approximately half of the 35 000 computer professionals in the country.

Over a five-year period in the late 1990s, approximately 15 per cent of the firms funded through various government high-technology assistance programmes were classified as software firms. Israeli software start-ups make up between 10 and 20 per cent of the total number of technology start-ups in Israel. Even after the collapse of the Internet bubble, 22 per cent of venture

*Table 4.1 Israel's electronics and information technologies industries*

| Year | Sales ($m) | Exports ($m) | Exports as percentage of total | Employees | Sales per employee ($ '000) |
|------|-----------|--------------|-------------------------------|-----------|----------------------------|
| 1991 | 3618 | 2283 | 63 | 33 000 | 109 |
| 1992 | 3996 | 2660 | 67 | 34 000 | 117 |
| 1993 | 4610 | 3200 | 69 | 36 500 | 126 |
| 1994 | 5200 | 3750 | 72 | 38 000 | 137 |
| 1995 | 5890 | 4300 | 73 | 40 000 | 147 |
| 1996 | 6500 | 4880 | 75 | 42 000 | 155 |
| 1997 | 7200 | 5700 | 79 | 43 400 | 166 |
| 1998 | 8030 | 6550 | 82 | 44 700 | 180 |
| 1999 | 8580 | 7130 | 83 | 45 800 | 187 |
| 2000 | 15500 | 11 000 | 71 | 66 800 | 232 |
| 2001 | 14 750 | 12 250 | 83 | 62 000 | 238 |
| 2002 | 13 040 | 10 790 | 83 | 54 800 | 238 |
| 2003 | 13 170 | 10 870 | 83 | 53 500 | 246 |

*Notes:*  2000–2003 include software.

*Source:*  Israel Association of Electronics and Information Industries.

*Figure 4.1 Israel's software and information technology industry*

capital firms' investments went to firms developing software. At the height of the technology export boom, software sales reached $3.3 billion and 60 per cent of the product was exported. In 2001, the United States and Europe accounted for approximately 75 per cent of Israeli software sales in equal proportion. Asian markets were a distant third with only 12 per cent of the exports.

For the most part, Israeli software firms are technology niche players. As Table 4.2 shows, at the end of 2001, 133 firms developed Internet-related products, 117 firms developed enterprise software, 60 firms developed information security solutions, and 47 firms offered information storage. In software alone, Israeli firms operate in 92 identifiable technology niches. They develop software for applications in everything from Internet security and e-commerce to home networking and medical devices.

*Table 4.2  Distribution of firms in Israel's high technology sector, 2001*

| Sector | Sub-sector | Number of firms |
|--------|------------|-----------------|
| Software/IT | Enterprise applications | 117 |
| | Internet related | 133 |
| | Information security | 60 |
| | Data storage | 47 |
| Telecomms | Streaming media | 59 |
| | Equipment | 52 |
| | Home networking | 51 |
| | Optical | 40 |
| | Cellular | 164 |
| Medical device | | 172 |
| Life sciences-biotechnology | | 88 |

*Source:*  Calculations by the author, based on data from D&A Directory (2002).

By sales revenue, firms developing software in the enterprise and Internet security sub-sectors were the largest. In terms of the number of firms in 2001, there were two and a half times as many firms in the Internet and enterprise applications sub-sectors than in information security and data storage. Because start-up firms are privately held, financial statements and employee counts are not publicly available. As a result, estimates of revenues and firm size vary widely. In addition, many firms cross a number of technology and application niches, which makes classifying them into sub-sectors problematic.

However, each of the broad areas of concentration can be subdivided further. For example, software firms in enterprise applications develop products and services in four broad areas: 1. Internal operations, such as knowledge management or management tools; 2. Technical operations such as software integration and network management; 3. E-business operations, such as e-commerce, e-content, or web collaboration; 4. Front desk operations, such as analytical tools or call centres. In actual fact, the 117 Israeli firms developing software for enterprise applications cover some 20 niche areas. The story is quite similar for firms in the Internet security sub-sector where there are 60 firms in 19 application areas (D&A Directory 2002). Israeli telecommunications, medical device companies and life-sciences companies also operate in numerous niches. While Israeli software firms are spread across many niches, there are, on average, between three and four Israeli firms occupying any one niche. The structure of the Israeli software industry is such that there are often two or three Israeli firms competing head to head in the same market and for the same clients.

In line with the rest of the technology sector, both in Israel and abroad, by 2002 the sales and exports of Israeli software had decreased. Table 4.3 shows that the only sector of the electronics industry that saw an increase in sales and exports between 2000 and 2002 was defence systems. Software sales fell by nearly half a billion dollars or 14 per cent from their high in 2000.

*Table 4.3  Sales and export by industry group, 2000-2002 ($m)*

| Industry groups | Sales 2000 | Sales 2002 | Exports 2000 | Exports 2002 |
|---|---|---|---|---|
| Communication & telecommunication | 4588 (29.6%) | 3234 (26.0%) | 3432 (31.2%) | 2543 (25.2%) |
| Electronics components | 2589 (16.7%) | 1853 (14.9%) | 2123 (19.3%) | 1796 (17.8%) |
| Industrial and medical systems | 2744 (17.7%) | 2177 (17.5%) | 2178 (19.8%) | 2300 (22.8%) |
| Defence systems | 2325 (15.0%) | 2376 (19.1%) | 1397 (12.7%) | 1554 (15.4%) |
| Software | 3255 (21.0%) | 2799 (22.5%) | 1870 (17.0%) | 1888 (18.8%) |
| Total | 15 501 (100%) | 12 440 (100%) | 11 000 (100%) | 10 080 (100%) |

*Notes*: Numbers rounded.

*Source*: Israel Association of Electronics and Information Industries.

In every high technology subsector, Israel has experienced substantial churning in its population of firms. After the international technology markets crashed, venture capital became more scarce, the political situation in Israel deteriorated, and many technology start-up companies folded. Very limited reliable data is available to allow an estimate of the size of the downturn. However, there is evidence to suggest that between 700 and 1000 high-technology firms closed during the 2000-2002 time period (Yitshaki-Hagai and Khavul 2003). The viability of firms in this sector fluctuates and industry observers estimate that as many as half the software firms still in existence at the end of 2001 are likely to have been closed or sold by the end of 2003.

## Leading Software Sectors

The largest software companies in Israel are mainly developing products and services for enterprise applications and information security. In addition to the Internet sub-sector, enterprise software and information security sub-sectors have seen large concentrations of new firm entry (see Table 4.2 for data in 2001).

### Enterprise software

Modern corporations are complex and dispersed organisations. The efficient management of their internal operations and their customer interfaces has become a prerequisite for superior performance. In addition, the advent and acceptance of electronic commerce has made the seamless integration of corporate front and back office operations the standard of efficiency. Enterprise software tools are the heart of making the modern corporation work. The development and implementation of enterprise software tools has spawned a burgeoning industry. Globally, such giants as SAP and Oracle dominate the enterprise software sector. Three of the largest Israeli software companies – Comverse, Amdocs and Mercury – are formidable competitors in this sector. Their success coupled with the widespread demand for enterprise management tools has pulled many small Israeli software firms into market niches.

Comverse, Amdocs and Mercury were established in the 1980s and in 2001 accounted for approximately $3.4 billion in sales revenues from both inside and outside of Israel. In addition, there were 117 young and small enterprise/software companies operating in Israel. Two-thirds were founded between 1995 and 2001, as e-commerce and telecommunications companies increasingly required enterprise management solutions. Several companies such as Enigma and Ex-Libris that were founded before 1995 had more than one hundred employees and revenues between $20 and $40 million.

However, the average Israeli enterprise software start-up firm had approximately twenty employees and average revenues of less than $2 million.

As is the pattern in other software sub-sectors, Israeli enterprise software companies cluster into niches. In 2001, approximately 60 Israeli enterprise software firms were developing software for internal operations such as knowledge management and sharing, business development and decision support, performance assessment, and financial management. There were 16 firms developing solutions for front desk operations that include analytical tools for customer support and marketing, call centre tools for computerised response and computer and telephone integration. Another 25 firms were developing applications for e-business operations such as web communication, e-publication and content and e-commerce. Finally, a similar number of firms were developing software for technical operations such as software integration and network management. In nearly every niche application, there are multiple Israeli companies with competing products.

With the economic downturn after 2000, many of the enterprise application companies founded in the late 1990s had either been acquired or had closed. However, Comverse, Amdocs and Mercury continue to stand out as Israeli firms that remain international leaders in enterprise software. A number of common threads run through the growth histories of these companies.

First, they are not so much Israeli companies as they are international. While each company has Israeli roots and a substantial presence in Israel, their operations and sales are largely driven by American and European markets. All three are listed on US exchanges and are officially headquartered outside Israel. However, their identities as Israeli companies are continuously reaffirmed. Analysts' reports, company lists, the official NASDAQ website, and the financial press all consistently refer to these companies as Israeli companies. Analysts assess Amdocs, Comverse and Mercury not only in comparison with their industry competitors but also in the context of other Israeli companies on Wall Street. The Israeli business press closely follows the movements in their stock-prices and analyses every press release that is issued and every rumour that surfaces. All three are prominent employers in Israel. As a result, each time they lay-off or hire large numbers of software developers, the news is treated as an indication of the overall health of the Israeli software sector.

Second, similar to their US competitors, Comverse, Amdocs and Mercury have been managed by astute marketers. Being market focused they have taken advantage of opportunities and changes in the market. While technology is the basis of their business, the companies have adapted their products to address market needs. Finally, each company is at the top of its sector and all are quite specialised in what they do. They focus on providing software services primarily to one sector – telecommunications in the case of Comverse and Amdocs, e-solutions implementation for Mercury. They also deliver primarily one type of operation: service delivery for Comverse, front-desks for Amdocs and performance assessment of e-solutions for Mercury. Their management teams are focused and have reacted quickly, reorienting their technologies to promising and value-creating applications.

---

BOX 4.1 MANAGING THE GLOBAL ENTERPRISE [2]

**Comverse Technology**

Comverse Technology was founded in 1984 in New York by Kobi Alexander, an Israeli immigrant to the USA who, after a career in investment banking, invested his life savings in a software and communications start-up. The company has been publicly traded in the USA since 1986. Comverse is a provider of software and systems enabling network-based multimedia-enhanced communications services. Comverse is based in Woodbury, Long Island, New York and has Comverse, Verint System, Inc., Ulticom, Startel and Starcom as subsidiaries. In 1999, Comverse became the first Israel-affiliated company to join the S&P 500 and the NASDAQ 100 indices. In 2002, Comverse had more than 5000 employees in 39 countries. The company has grown through acquisitions of publicly-held competitors and privately-held start-up companies. Through acquisitions, Comverse has expanded its geographic reach and has gained access to technologies that it has incorporated into its own offerings. In the late 1990s, Comverse, in partnership with Soros Fund Management, established a small venture capital operation, ComSor, which invested in start-up companies directly. Comverse has a substantial presence in Israel where it is one of the largest employers of software developers. The ups and downs of Comverse are followed with great interest in the Israeli financial press, both because of its implications for employment and because its stock is widely held. As a large multinational employer, Comverse's relationship with the Israeli government is also important. For example, in January of 2003, after numerous discussions about lay-offs in the previous two years, the Israeli press reported that Comverse had plans to expand its operations in the country and to hire additional employees. As a high-technology company, an investment in R&D would qualify Comverse for tax breaks and government subsidies from the Ministry of Trade and Industry.

---

## Amdocs

With $1.65 billion in sales in 2001, Amdocs is one of the largest Israeli high-technology companies. Amdocs is registered on the island of Guernsey but routinely tops most lists of successful Israeli companies. Amdocs emerged from an older generation of Israeli high-technology firms. Amdocs has its roots in an Israeli software and telecommunications company called Aurec Information that was started in 1982. Aurec Information was a unit of Aurec Group, at the time half-owned by the US telecommunications company Southwestern Bell. In 1984, Aurec Information and Southwestern Bell formed a joint venture, Automated Directory Systems, to market a telephone directory publishing system. A year later, Southwestern Bell acquired 50 per cent of the operation. By 1988 Aurec Information had operations on five continents. In 1995, Amdocs was created as a holding company for these various Aurec businesses. Amdocs offers customer relationship management, billing, and order management systems for communications providers. Amdocs lists as its customers many of the world's leading telecommunications providers. The company's sales have doubled every two years throughout the 1990s. In what was referred to as the largest-ever Israeli IPO, Amdocs became a publicly-traded company on the NASDAQ in 1998. Amdocs has a global presence; its development and support centres span the world from Brazil to the Czech Republic. In 1999-2000, at the height of the Israeli high-tech boom when labour in Israel was particularly scarce, Amdocs was importing Indian software engineers to Cyprus and opened a development centre in Ireland where software engineers are particularly attuned to the needs of the telecommunications industry (Lis 2003). Like Comverse, Amdocs has grown partly through partnerships and acquisitions. However by March 2003, its stock price was valued at one-tenth of its peak three years earlier. Amdocs has seen its fortunes rise and fall with the boom and bust in the telecommunications industry.

## Mercury Interactive

Founded in 1989 and headquartered in Sunnyvale California, Mercury Interactive is a leading provider of enterprise testing, tuning and performance management solutions. Mercury's products and services help companies ensure that their applications support key business objectives both in pre-production and production environments. Organisations worldwide use Mercury's solutions across their information-technology infrastructures in order to minimise hardware and operational expenses, protect revenue streams and enhance their competitive positions. Based on sales revenues of $361 million, Mercury is a distant third to Comverse and Amdocs. In a ranking of Israeli software firms in 2002, Mercury's sales revenue stood between the billions of Comverse and Amdocs and the dozen or so small information-technology firms whose revenues are between $50 and $100 million. Mercury has grown largely organically. In 2001, Mercury made an acquisition that brought complementary products into its portfolio and expanded its customer base by adding 3000 smaller clients. More than twenty Wall Street analysts cover Mercury's stock, and many regard it as a well managed company that has maintained a stable management team over its growth period.

Although they have seized opportunities at the right times, Comverse, Amdocs and Mercury have all suffered from the downturn in the global economy. At the time of writing, Comverse's 2003 sales were estimated to be down by a third. Amdocs has seen its share price drop to one-tenth of what it was at its peak. Mercury, although reporting steady growth, has also seen its value decline. Nevertheless, their position as the largest and most identifiable Israeli software firms makes Comverse, Amdocs and Mercury the standard by which many other Israeli software companies are judged. For example, CEOs of Israeli start-up firms routinely name Mercury (along with Check Point, discussed later) as the Israeli company they most admire. Although they represent an earlier generation of firms, Amdocs, Comverse and Mercury have survived and prospered. CEOs of Israeli start-up firms draw three main lessons from the experience of these firms. First, in order to understand the market and to be close to their customers, it is important to have an international outlook from the start. Second, in order to build sustainable advantage, it is important to gain competencies and stay focused in a specific industry segment. Third, in order to build an international organisation, it is important to manage the relationship between operations in Israel and abroad. For the new generation of Israeli software firms, these three have written the rulebook.

### Information security
Security has become a formidable problem for the global economy. With the expansion of Internet-based commerce and communication, securing corporate and personal assets from fraud and sabotage is a top priority for large and small companies alike. Since the late 1980s, Israeli firms have been developing and selling commercial tools to combat viruses, hackers and intruders interested in penetrating personal computers, networks and broadcast transmissions. While Israeli firms have made the most of the

country's military and academic expertise in the field, they have also used partnerships and acquisition strategies to become formidable international competitors.

The Israeli information security sector is dominated by several older and larger companies that are flanked by dozens of fledgling start-ups. At the beginning of 2002, there were 60 Israeli companies active in the information security field. Most were small with modest sales revenue. More than 80 per cent were under four years old and had an average of 20 employees. For those companies whose sales revenue is available, the average 2001 revenue was around $1 million. However, one company, Check Point, dominates the Israeli information security landscape (see Box 4.2). Check Point, founded in 1994 and trading publicly since 1996, has more than 1000 employees and half a billion dollars in revenues. Check Point's IPO and its world-wide market share of close to 50 per cent in the firewall market have motivated many entrepreneurs to start up new firms. Check Point's success has also spurred venture capital to invest in the sector and has made foreign multinationals take notice of Israeli security expertise.

A number of Israeli information security companies played an important role in the early stages of the global information industry sector. For example, Aladdin, founded in 1985, distributed some of the earliest anti-virus and software protection programs. Memco, founded in 1990 by a team of graduates from Israel's elite central computing unit, first offered consulting services to organisations looking to secure access to their networks. Subsequently, Memco turned their services into products by successfully developing security devices for servers. NDS, a company founded in 1988 by a team of scientists from the Weizmann Institute of Science, developed encryption for satellite and broadcast communications.

There are a number of parallels in the development of these firms. The evolution of information security in Israel owes much to both the military and academia. The founders of Aladdin, Memco and many other Israeli security companies had their formative technical experiences in the elite computing units of the Israeli military. The military, a dispersed organisation that needed to transfer information securely and in real time, was an early innovator in the security field. However, given the classified nature of the military technology, direct commercialisation was not possible. Rather it was the training, ideas and team relationships that were transferred to tackle civilian applications. More prominent transfers to the Israeli information security companies came from academia. In particular, NDS commercialised the encryption algorithms developed by Professor Adi Shamir at the Weizmann Institute of Science. Earlier Professor Shamir, along with colleagues at MIT, co-developed the widely used RSA encryption algorithm (Teubal, et al 2002).

Entrepreneurs starting Israeli companies were initially responsive to a technology push embodied in their skills and ideas. However, successful information security firms such as Aladdin, Memco, Check Point and NDS targeted specific customer needs as a mode of entry into the marketplace. They formed alliances with established companies and looked aggressively to acquire the intellectual property often through the wholesale purchase of other companies. For example, Memco acquired both a US and an Israeli company and formed a strategic alliance with Platinum, a US software company. NDS had a long-standing relationship with Rupert Murdoch's News Corporation to whom it later supplied digital pay-TV platforms. Both Memco and NDS were later themselves acquired by their strategic partners. Each is now only nominally an Israeli company with headquarters abroad and research and development in Israel. For example, NDS is headquartered in the UK and employs 1400 people world-wide of whom 450 are in its research and development centre in Israel. Finally, Aladdin made numerous acquisitions until it merged with a German company.

---

BOX 4.2 MAKING THE MOST OF SECURITY [3]

When system administrators think about Internet security, they most often think Check Point. Check Point is perhaps the best-known Israeli information security company. Gil Shwed, Check Point's CEO, is one of the most recognised software entrepreneurs in Israel and the youngest billionaire on the 2002 Forbes list. The story of how Check Point was founded is often repeated as the quintessential Israeli entrepreneurial beginning. Gil Shwed and his colleagues Marius Nacht and Shlomo Kramer developed their first firewall software product in a hot and cramped Tel Aviv apartment. Shwed had just left the army's top intelligence unit where he was responsible for stringing together the army's many computer networks. It was 1993, the Internet was just emerging and information security was not yet prominent in the minds of developers. Shwed and his colleagues registered their company in Israel and took $400 000 in venture capital from BRM, then an anti-virus software developer located in Jerusalem. For this, their only infusion of venture capital money, Check Point gave away 50 per cent of the equity. To stimulate interest in their product, Check Point hired a venture capitalist based in San Francisco.

Getting customers for an unknown Israeli start-up was not easy. The Internet was only beginning to emerge and many corporations saw the small Israeli company as a liability '...at first Shwed tried to downplay Check Point's Israeli roots, but found ways to use it to his advantage. He started touting the country's impecable security reputation and playing up the executive team's military background. He also set up a small answering service in Boston with a single operator, whom he never met, to answer the phones, giving the appearance of a US office. He opened a Silicon Valley office in 1995'. Check Point's first big sale was to Sun Microsystems, which agreed to bundle the young company's firewall product with its UNIX servers. In 1994, Check Point reached $800 000 in sales.

Today, Check Point provides Internet and network security software products that enable connectivity with security and manageability. The company has a dominant position in those markets. By 2002, Check Point had installed its software in more than a quarter of a million sites and counted as its clients 90 per cent of America's largest 500 firms. In 2002, Check Point's sales were $427 million and net income $255 million. Since 1994, its compound annual growth rate has been 153 per cent. With Check Point's entrepreneurs as role models and Check Point's market success alluring, many other Israeli entrepreneurs have entered the information security sector.

Check Point, the most successful Israeli information security company, captured the entrepreneurial imagination. Numerous smaller Israeli companies were also successful in developing information security solutions and like the industry pioneers many became acquisition targets in the global consolidations of the late 1990s. Scores of others failed outright. There are no clear statistics on how many entrepreneurs, trained in the army or in academia, started with an idea, put together a team, even raised some capital, but never managed to get their companies off the ground. However, even with the downturn in the global economy and the deteriorating business conditions in Israel, at the end of 2001 there were still 60 Israeli start-up firms hoping to repeat the dream.

**Israeli Software Start-up Firms**

Between 1995-2000, Israeli entrepreneurs have started companies at a feverish pace. As in the USA, the motivation for entry is driven by supply and demand in the capital and labour markets. The availability of skills in a given technical area drives the supply of entrepreneurs entering the industry. The ready finance and the global demand for products or services drives the demand for the technology solutions that their start-up firms aim to provide. Opportunities for Israeli technology entrepreneurs have evolved over time. In starting up their firms, technology entrepreneurs have followed the money.

Each new wave in the global technology markets pushed Israeli venture capitalists to invest in companies with capabilities in the appropriate areas. Quite often venture capitalists invested in entrepreneurial teams rather than fully formed companies. Thus, each wave of available finance pulled software entrepreneurs into starting companies.

As Figures 4.2 and 4.3 show, this cohort effect is evident even in the partial picture provided by data from companies that had survived through 2001. Figure 4.2 graphs five technology sectors by founding dates while Figure 4.3 shows the distribution of software firms by sub-sectors. No data is available that captures both the births and deaths of firms in the industry over time. Hence, in interpreting Figures 4.2 and 4.3 it is important to remember that the picture captures both the entry and survival effects. Figure 4.2 suggests that the levels of entry into the software and information technology sector and telecommunications sector saw dramatic peaks between 1997 and 1999. The software and information technology peak precedes the telecommunications peak by approximately one year. After a lag, this pattern tracks the investment in information technology and telecommunications in the global capital markets. Entry into components, capital equipment and life sciences also peaked within the same time frame but much less dramatically. Figure 4.3 breaks down the software and information technology sector into data storage, information security, Internet and enterprise software. The drop in the number of Internet firms started in 2001 is almost as pronounced as the increase in their peak year for start-ups, 1999. The other three software sub-sectors showed continued entry in 2001, albeit at much lower levels than in previous years.

Given that high-technology start-up activity in Israel has increased five-fold in a decade, it is worth asking how Israel compares to other countries in terms of the entrepreneurial orientation of its general population. The Global Entrepreneurship Monitor (Reynolds et al. 2001) uses a structured survey of a cross-section of the adult population towards entrepreneurship. In terms of their total entrepreneurial activity, Israelis do not stand out as particularly active in entrepreneurship. In fact, the research found that the prevalence rate of Israelis starting their own business is at about 7 per cent of the population, which is much the same as other similar sized Western European countries. Nor does it appear that those Israelis who become entrepreneurs are more likely than average Northern Europeans to do so out of necessity. Unlike developing countries, the social security net in Israel is well established. Even with the high rate of firm creation in technology sectors, few Israelis report becoming entrepreneurs because they have identified an opportunity in the market. In many ways, the findings capture a salient piece of the story. Israel is a small country and there is a stylised tendency to represent it as a country-wide 'technology cluster'. Although the high-technology sector in

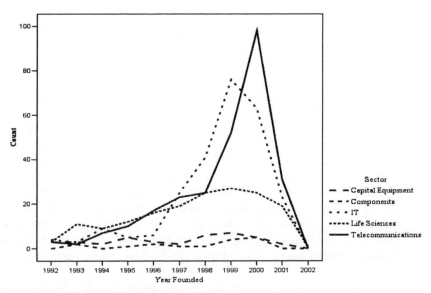

*Source*:   Calculations by the author

*Figure 4.2   Entry of technology firms by sector*

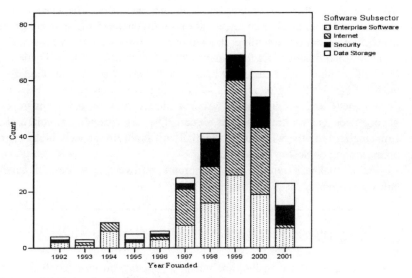

*Source*:   Calculations by the author

*Figure 4.3   Entry of software firms by sub-sector*

Israel is a lead sector in terms of investment, salaries and exports, it does not appear to represent the attitudes and performance of the rest of the economy. For example, during 1998-1999 at the height of the high-tech boom, there were high inflows of resources to high-technology start-ups and wages for software engineers were spiralling. At this time, the rest of the economy was in a mild recession and unemployment had reached an uncomfortable 9 per cent of the labour force.

Just as their counterparts around the world, Israeli companies face the liabilities associated with the newness of their technologies, the dynamics of the market, and the age and size of their firms. After securing financing, the most pressing problem for start-ups is creating demand for their products. In addition, however, Israeli firms also face the liabilities associated with their foreignness. As technology firms, Israeli start-ups know that they have to compete in an international marketplace if they are to grow. As Israeli firms, many also realise that they have to shorten the physical and psychological distance between themselves and their potential customers, many of whom are in the USA.

A profile of the typical Israeli high-technology firm is relevant at this point. Such firms are on average five years old and have eighteen full-time employees (Khavul 2001). They would have been founded by a team of between two and three entrepreneurs of whom 75 per cent are still involved with the firm either as employees or board members. The current top-management team is between three and four individuals. In 70 per cent of the firms, five years after founding, the company is run by a CEO who was one of the original founders. Of the current CEOs, 84 per cent are Israeli nationals and half of them have a technical background. Only 7 per cent of the CEOs have a financial background. These firms are at various stages of product development and product sales. Approximately half of the firms report having sales and additional offices abroad. The statistics paint a picture of a firm smaller but otherwise not substantially different from a technology start-up in London or Boston (Khavul 2001).

Box 4.3 takes as an example Panorama Software, a successful Israeli software company that was started in 1993.

---

BOX 4.3 START-UP LIFE CYCLE [4]

Panorama develops on-line analytical processing business-intelligence tools that provide graphical representation of data in a Microsoft Windows environment. While the majority of Israeli high-technology CEOs are men, Rony Ross is one of the few women to have successfully launched and grown a software company in Israel. Further, she accomplished this without the assistance of government grants or venture capital. In contrast to the mantra that Israel's domestic market is too small to be significant, Ross grew Panorama first by cultivating Israeli customers and then by being the first Israeli CEO to sell her company's technology, but not her company, to Microsoft for a reported $20 million. However, ten years after it was founded, Panorama has raised external financing, hired a North American CEO, and moved its headquarters to Toronto and opened an office in Atlanta.

As a company with a ten-year track record, Panorama both affirms and contradicts commonly accepted notions about Israeli software companies. Rony Ross, Panorama's CEO, with graduate degrees in mathematics, statistics and management, recruited a small development team that consisted of a recent graduate from one of the Israeli military's elite units and three scientists who immigrated to Israel from the former Soviet Union. By building a company that served a broad range of Israeli customers first, Ross was able to develop a software package that was rich in features. Because Israel is geographically compact and Panorama's customers were within easy reach, the company was able to issue version after version of the software and implement every request that customers made. Panorama was also not the first start-up that Ross founded. In starting her first company, Ross had taken government assistance that later complicated the sale of her company to a strategic partner. Panorama neither received grants from the government nor financing from venture capital. Panorama caught the eye of Microsoft, which bought its technology. Panorama's sale foreshadowed the acquisitions boom that swept through Israel in the late 1990s. Finally, like many other Israeli companies trying to grow, Panorama has had to move its headquarters abroad while maintaining a R&D centre in Israel. The story of Panorama aptly captures the emergence and evolution that Israel's software sector has undergone in the last decade.

## Competing Head to Head

The structure of competition in Israel's software industry is worth noting. Israeli firms are active in enterprise software and information security, yet these are broad groupings. A fine-grained analysis suggests that the industry is quite fragmented, with many software application niches that are occupied by about three or four firms. Similar training and experience of Israeli entrepreneurs, or common opportunity search patterns, drove the founding multiple firms that entered the same competitive niches. In addition, portfolio considerations of Israeli venture capitalists and private investors have also played a part in the evolution of the competitive landscape.

Virtual Domination (in Box 4.4) serves as a good example. Orad and Vi[z]rt are two Israeli companies that compete head to head in the international market for virtual studios.

---

BOX 4.4 VIRTUAL DOMINATION [5]

By some estimates two companies, Orad and Vi[z]rt, account for between 50 and 80 percent of all virtual studio sets sold in the world. Both companies were founded in Israel within one year of each other in the mid-1990s. Both companies went public on the NeuerMarkt in Frankfurt within weeks of each other in 1999. As such, Vi[z]rt and Orad serve as interesting examples of two Israeli companies competing head to head in an international market that they dominate.

Virtual studios solve a pressing problem for TV producers: how to have varied studio sets in one studio facility. Virtual studios enable production studios to replace the physical set in the studio with a computer system that generates the 3D background and superimposes it behind the actors according to the camera's position. The great advantage virtual sets offer production studios is enhanced flexibility – changing the set is fast and easy and small studios can appear very large to the viewer at home. With virtual studios, producers can create sets that are physically impossible to build. Although the need had been identified in the 1970s and 1980s, the technology and market for virtual studios matured only in the late 1990s. Israel's entry into the market for virtual studios stems largely from the country's expertise in electro-optics and simulations technology, used particularly in the Israeli air force for training.

In 1993, Dr Miky Tamir, formerly the head of the optics department at Elbit, and Avi Sharir, formerly head of the communication division at Tadiran, founded Orad. The initial funding for Orad came from Ormat, an Israeli conglomerate active in optics, energy and medical devices. Orad was founded around the concept of virtual advertising; however, the use of virtual advertising ran into regulatory problems. The first commercial use of Orad's products was in 1994, when a German television channel ran the soccer World Cup with the assistance of Orad's Digital Replay technology. Then in 1996, the USA-based ABC-News broadcast the US presidential primaries using Orad's virtual studio product CyberSet. Two years after the introduction of virtual sets, the company reached a milestone of 100 installations. On 16 November

1999, a week after Vi[z]rt's IPO, Orad went public on the NeuerMarkt. The IPO valued Orad at $180 million and raised $45.5 million. In 2002, Orad was still part of the Ormat group and is headquartered in Israel with offices in the USA, Germany, the UK, Spain, Hong Kong and Japan.

Orad's main competitor, Vi[z]rt was established in 1994 originally as an Israeli company called RT-Set. RT-Set was a venture of BVR and Pixel Technologies Ltd. RT-Set's parent, BVR, was established to create flight simulation systems and other military training systems. BVR adapted these systems for civilian applications. Many of RT-Set's founding employees had worked in BVR and some of RT-Set's early technology was transferred from BVR. Originally, a strong reliance on real-time technology and experience with 3D graphics led the company to target the development of virtual sets as its main product. While private, the company was funded by a number of Israeli venture capitalists, and on 11 November 1999, a week before Orad, RT-Set went public on the NeuerMarkt. The IPO valued the company at $132 million and raised $48 million. In 2002, the company had offices in Norway, Israel, Austria, the UK and the USA.

RT-Set became Vi[z]rt when it acquired a Norwegian company called Pilot in June of 2000. Pilot was a joint venture between the Norwegian TV2 and the Austrian technical team that had originally developed virtual studio technology for another company, Discrete Logic. RT-Set, fresh from its IPO and with strong capability in virtual studios but not in broadcast graphics, approached Pilot with a merger proposal. When the firms merged, it was Pilot's technology approach that was retained and formed the basis of the new company's offering. Organisationally, the merged company Vi[z]rt had initially retained the Israeli CEO. After a year, Bjarne Berg, a former journalist and the founder of the Norwegian company, took over the management of Vi[z]rt.

The management of the merged company was now geographically dispersed. Vi[z]rt's CEO, CTO and VP of marketing were in Bergen, Norway, but the CFO and the VP of sales remained in Israel. Research and development continued in Israel, Austria and Norway. The Israeli centre continued the development of virtual technology; the Austrian team continued the development of rendering technology used in broadcast graphics; and the Norwegian team continued the development of applications. In addition, each of the company's geographic centres was given regional sales responsibility. Thus, the Israeli team had to sell the product in Asia and Eastern Europe. By the end of 2003, the company's reliance on the virtual studios business represented less than 20 per cent of Vi[z]rt's revenues.

> Technologically, the starting points for Orad and Vi[z]rt were different but the end result in terms of the virtual studios product offering has been nearly the same. In fact, Orad and Vi[z]rt meet in the virtual set market directly. To a lesser extent they compete in broadcast graphics and virtual advertisement. Orad and Vi[z]rt have competed against each other for nearly a decade: early on, as they were developing the technology, and now as they race after the same customers. Reportedly, early in their histories, Orad and RT-Set had discussed the possibility of joining forces, but the discussions stalled. Today, there are no formal connections between the companies but as direct competitors their employees and management keep track of each other vigilantly.

**Summary**

This section has described the rise of Israel as a technology centre between 1990 and 2002. The software sector accounts for about 20 per cent of sales and export revenue in the electronics and information technology sector. Several large firms dominate but approximately 400 smaller companies are active in the sector. The contraction in the global IT market and political instability have caused the number of firms and their revenues to shrink. However, even at a lower level of activity, the Israeli software sector remains dynamic. The rise of the Israeli software sector is closely linked to the role of entrepreneurs who identified opportunities in the global software market and defined their role within it. Israel's rise on the global technology stage can be attributed to a variety of factors in the country's institutional context. The next section discusses these in turn.

## 4.2 INSTITUTIONAL CONTEXT FOR SOFTWARE EMERGENCE

The Israeli software industry emerged in an institutional context where the interplay of public policy and private initiative meant that the process was neither planned nor completely organic. The Israeli government followed a largely sector-neutral support for civilian research and development. In addition to its direct underwriting of R&D in the private sector, the government's support of education and training in academia and the military had positive spillovers for the development of a software industry. The government did take a direct role in creating a venture capital industry in Israel, but it left investment decisions to professional managers rather than bureaucrats. Most importantly, when the job was done, the government relinquished its role. Finally, geopolitical changes also brought to Israel large numbers of skilled immigrants who enriched the country's human capital pool.

**National Investment in Research and Development**

Israeli technology firms have been the beneficiaries of significant public investment in research and development. As a proportion of GDP in the year 2000, Israel has the highest level of investment in civilian research and development of any OECD country (see Table 4.4).

However, in the 1970s and 1980s, the majority of investment in the high-technology industry came from military spending. In the early 1990s, information technology and computing became officially recognized as a distinct sector of the economy. This made the sector eligible for government research and development grants and subsidies. Since 1990, public spending on civilian R&D has reached more than 5000 Israeli firms of which 1500 have been high technology start-up firms (Trajtenberg 2000). In a random-sample survey of Israeli high-technology firms, more than half had received some matching funding from public sources for R&D (Khavul 2001). On a yearly basis over the decade of the 1990s, the Israeli government spend an average of approximately $450 million on civilian R&D, but the total amount of civilian public and private sector R&D in the country is approximately $3 billion. Compared with many international organisations Israel's expenditure is rather modest. For a sense of scale, IBM and Hewlett-Packard spend approximately the same amounts yearly on their corporate research and development (Trajtenberg, 2000).

*Table 4.4   Civilian R&D spending as share of GDP, 2000*

| Country | Civilian R&D spending as share of GDP, 2000 |
|---------|--------------------------------------------|
| Israel  | 4.2 |
| Sweden  | 3.6 |
| Finland | 3.2 |
| USA     | 2.4 |
| UK      | 1.6 |

The Office of the Chief Scientist at the Ministry of Trade and Industry oversees a variety of programmes through which the funds are distributed. There are six separate national programmes and four main international programmes. National programmes support industrial research and development, generic research and development (MAGNET), technological incubation, technology transfer (MAGNETON), assistance to new immigrants (MESER) and assistance to immigrant scientists (BASHAN).

Israeli firms also benefit from a range of bilateral and regional free trade agreements. International programmes include, among others, bilateral funds for cooperative product development with firms in the USA, the UK, South Korea, Singapore and other countries. For the last twenty-five years, Israel and the USA have had a close working relationship that supports private initiative in developing and marketing technology products. In the late 1990s, Israel lobbied and succeeded in becoming a member of the European Commission's Fifth and Sixth Framework Programmes for implementing cooperative research programmes between companies in the EU and those in Israel. Thus, the programmes managed from the Office of the Chief Scientist support research and development locally and target key international markets overseas.

The support for high-technology has been broad-based and not only focused on start-up firms. Of the funding distributed in the last five years, 47 per cent went to medium-sized enterprises, 20 per cent to start-ups, 17 per cent to technology incubators, and 16 per cent to big companies. The Central Bureau of Statistics considers any company with less than 100 employees as small. The Office of the Chief Scientist reports that the money was distributed to the following sectors: 40 per cent to communications, 20 per cent to electronics, 15 per cent to software, 13 per cent to healthcare. For the most part, government support has been sector-neutral and inclusive. The general acceptance rate for grants is approximately 73 per cent across all applications for funding. Some of the funding is distributed as direct grants but most comes in the form of matching funding with various provisions for repayment. For example, the Office of the Chief Scientist administers a very popular matching funds programme that matches up to 50 per cent of the money that a technology firm wants to dedicate to R&D. The programme requires eventual repayment of the funds as a small percentage of the company's revenues.

While most high-technology start-ups have at some point received funding, Israeli entrepreneurs have mixed reactions to government support. A number of programmes have had requirements that force firms to implement future manufacturing in Israel. Over time this has proved a difficult and unpopular provision. Firms lobbied for exemptions to these rules. Firms also argued that in cases where foreign firms were interested in purchasing them, the manufacturing provisions would make them less attractive in the eyes of the potential acquirers. Not surprisingly, they strongly prefer government support that comes with minimal conditions and reporting. However, few turn the money down, especially when other sources of financing dry up.

Other types of government support have come from the Ministry of Finance in the form of reform of the foreign investment laws, dual listing of

Israeli firms on the Tel Aviv stock exchange, and other initiatives to integrate the Israeli economy with the rest of the world.

## Sources of Innovation

### Education

The Israeli software industry has been built on a strong foundation of education. Traditionally, Israel has regarded education and investment in human capital as a vital element in its development policy. Lack of natural resources, limited population and limited territory meant that Israel's long-term competitiveness in international markets would have to come from the skills and innovation of its population.

Prior to the establishment of the State of Israel, Hebrew University (1925), The Technion (1924) and The Weizmann Institute (1934) were the three major centres of university-level learning and research. In the decades after 1948, Bar Ilan University (1955), Tel Aviv University (1956), Ben Gurion University of the Negev (1970) and Haifa University (1971) were established. Over the last twenty years, the percentage of the Jewish population with at least thirteen years of education has risen to 41 per cent from 21 per cent in 1980. Of non-Jewish citizens 21 per cent have thirteen or more years of schooling as compared to 7 per cent twenty years ago (Israel's Central Bureau of Statistics 2000).

The distribution of degrees by subject received from the country's seven top public universities has remained relatively stable over the last twenty years. As in the 1980s, in 2000 approximately 60 per cent of university students received degrees in humanities and social sciences while about 30 per cent of university students received degrees in science, mathematics, and engineering. However, while the traditional universities have not changed significantly, the revolution in overall educational attainment and levels of higher education in the population has come from immigration to Israel and the liberalisation of higher education in Israel (Meltz 2001).

In the late 1970s and the 1980s, the demand for higher education soared. In a series of policy decisions, the state permitted teacher-training colleges, technical and art schools to grant academic first degrees. In addition, the policy changes also permitted the establishment of private colleges and the introduction of foreign competition into the market. Accreditation was tightly controlled by the ministry of education, but the changes brought an explosion in the enrolment of students in non-traditional universities (or 'colleges' as they are called). Figure 4.4 shows this growth. In 1980-1981 the first degrees granted by such colleges represented only 5 per cent of the total; by 2000, such degrees represented 32 per cent. These colleges have been strongly market-demand driven and this is reflected in their course offerings. The bulk of the degrees are given in education, business, social sciences and law. Their prominence in business training is evident and while they are significantly more expensive than the universities, many have excellent reputations with employers. Faculty at these colleges are not expected to do significant research, but have heavy teaching loads and are expected to perform well in the classroom. Their salaries are comparable and, in some cases, higher than in the universities.

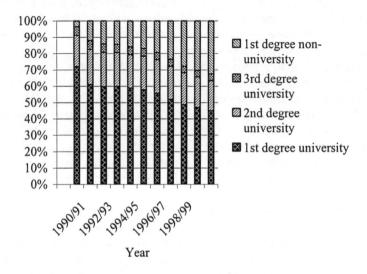

*Sources:* Meltz (2001) and Israel's Central Bureau of Statistics.

*Figure 4.4  Growth in non-university degrees*

Finally, the dismantling of the state monopoly on higher education has also introduced international competition. American and British universities have been particularly active in the market. For example, Metropolitan College, the adult education extension arm of Boston University, for many years ran an active business masters programme in Israel. In recent years, the Open University and Bradford University have also established popular programmes in Israel. In an effort to accommodate working high technology professionals, Tel Aviv University have established a High-Tech School that runs an executive education type of MBA for those working in the technology sector. Financing for the new initiative came partly from the private sector and is run jointly with Northwestern University.

Academic roots have two important effects on the software industry. The first effect is felt through the historically high level of research at universities and through the commercialisation of university inventions. Many of Israel's software companies are based on the inventions of mathematicians and computer scientists from within its universities and research institutes. The second effect is noticeable in the training of workers needed to spur the organisational growth of software companies.

## Military Roots

Israeli software companies can attribute at least part of their origins to either academia or the military. The universities and the military have deep roots in society. Both are national institutions and both have aided innovation. The feedback into the high technology sector from each has been pronounced (Azulai et al. 2002; Dvir and Tishler 2000).

The start of the Israeli high-technology sector was tightly linked to defence requirements of the state. In the first twenty years of Israel's existence, much of the defence technology originated from the country's relationship with France. After the 1967 war, France imposed an arms embargo on Israel. The embargo forced Israel into a policy of self-reliance that stimulated the establishment of a domestic military-industrial complex. Companies such as Israel Aircraft Industries, Tadiran, Elcint, and Rafael became classic defence contractors that competed for research and development money from the state. In later years, when the USA began to grant large subsidies to Israel and Egypt for the development and purchase of largely US-made armaments, the Israeli military defence complex participated in the R&D required to adapt and improve the performance of US materials.

Israeli high technology may have important roots in the defence sector; however, there is little evidence that military technology has been commercialised through traditional defence conversion. For example, a recent study (Azulai et al. 2002) looked specifically at initiatives aimed at stimulating commercialisation and conversion in one of Israel's major defence establishments. Commercialising defence technology through the development of products specifically for civilian use was a stated goal of this organisation. It created an employee incentive programme, established a formal process to screen potential projects, and committed financial and organisational resources to the effort. The authors found that this effort to promote high-technology entrepreneurship failed. The commitment of the firm, and particularly its middle management, to the effort was questionable. Furthermore, it became apparent that the mindset of the employees was locked into defence-related applications. In an atmosphere of general high-technology entrepreneurship that swept the country during the time this programme was in effect, the employees of this defence establishment perceived the transfer of leading-edge technologies to commercial applications as problematic. Few saw the opportunities or were willing to take the initiative.

The impact of the military on Israeli high technology has mainly been though education, training and social capital rather than through traditional defence conversion. Like any top-rate university, the Israeli military is a sophisticated selection machine. The top high-school students are tested and are selected for elite units where they receive technical training and general education. Because nearly everyone in the country has to serve, the intellectual elite of the country is also a vital part of the military. The military runs a number of sophisticated technical training units. For example, TALPIOT is a highly selective programme where men and women receive regular military training but also work towards their university degrees in mathematics, computer science, and physics. Annually, more than 20 000 high school students are recommended for the programme but only thirty-five per year are selected. MAMRAM is the Army's Computer and Data Communications Network Centre. For more than forty years, MAMRAM has been the main computer and software development 'incubator' for the Army. MAMRAM excels at practical training in software design. Its graduates often concurrently earn university degrees and step into high-level jobs in civilian companies upon graduation. Furthermore, the training does not end when the military service is over. MAMRAM has a symbiotic relationship with the software community in Israel. Graduates from MAMRAM return to the unit for reserve duty every year. During their reserve duty they receive additional training, but they also contribute back to MAMRAM by teaching current conscripts and other reservists. Although they train a small proportion of those who serve, elite units such as MAMRAM have strong reputations and appear to contribute significantly to knowledge creation and dissemination in Israel's software community (Yachin 2000; Breznitz 2002). Evidence suggests that the graduates of elite training units are also the elite of the high-tech sector.

## Immigration

Software relies heavily on the skills and knowledge embedded in people. Just as the Israeli technology sector was beginning to emerge, geopolitical changes offered an opportunity that helped the software sector take root. With the fall of the Berlin Wall and tighter restriction on immigration to the United States, Israel became the main destination of many thousands of largely Jewish immigrants. While the majority came from the former Soviet

Union, some immigrants also arrived from South America and South Africa. Between 1989 and 1999, approximately 920 000 refugees entered Israel. Israel's population grew by 20 per cent in the course of a decade. According to official statistics, more than 100 000 of these immigrants were previously trained as scientists and engineers. By the end of the decade, Israel could boast the highest number of scientists and engineers per capita in the world. Such an inflow of human capital proved both an opportunity and a challenge.

Absorption of immigrants became a major government dilemma. While many aspiring immigrant entrants into the software sector were academically accomplished, many others lacked both the training in modern computer systems and a market orientation. For example, many were excellent mathematicians and computer scientists but they only had experience in working with antiquated computers and legacy languages like Fortran. Addressing these gaps required both retraining and adaptation to the new norms of work in a market economy. While for the vast majority of scientists and engineers this adaptation occurred through work, for others, the government implemented a number of support programmes. Such programmes to help immigrants become entrepreneurs were also part of a larger Israeli public policy effort to support science and technology. The Office of the Chief Scientist established programmes such as BASHAN, MATI and Jewish Agency Loan schemes focused on helping immigrants start businesses independently (Lerner et al. 2005). Others, like the government's technology incubator programme, sought to shepherd immigrants with good ideas through the start-up process (Khavul et al. 2000).

In the early 1990s, foreign firms saw Israel with its skilled population of immigrants as a potentially good place to set up subsidiaries. Indeed, the wages for Israeli engineers were 30 per cent to 40 per cent lower than in the USA, but this low-cost advantage did not last long. First, Israel has a relatively high cost of living and a high social and tax burden. Second, despite the large-scale immigration, Israel is a small country with a limited supply of labour. In fact, economists have observed that there has been little evidence that immigration actually put downward pressure on wages in the Israeli economy (Gandal et al. 2002; Friedberg 2000; Friedberg 2001; Beenstock and Fisher 1997). One study (Gandal et al. 2002) has looked at the dynamics of the Israeli labour market in the 1990s. Having analysed both changes in the national output mix and in production technology as potential mechanisms absorbing shocks in labour supply, they concluded that global changes in production technology and specifically skills-based technological change helped Israel sustain its wage structure. In short, the immigration to Israel of highly skilled workers from the former Soviet Union came at a time when the advanced economies – particularly the USA – were undergoing skill-based technical change. This meant that there was little downward pressure on wages in Israel as its skill mix and openness allowed international changes to be transmitted.

By the mid-1990s, immigration began to taper off and immigrants with skills were quickly absorbed into the expanding economy. Wage differentials narrowed dramatically and the cost differential between a top software engineer in Israel and one in Silicon Valley became trivial. Finally, competition from India, the Philippines and China underlined the fact that Israel's future was most certainly not at the low-cost end of the software market. Indeed, a number of Israeli software companies took advantage of low cost Indian programmers and shifted their own development work offshore. By the peak of the Internet bubble, Israel was looking abroad for foreign workers. High-technology firms lobbied the government to issue temporary work visas to engineers from India. For example, Amdocs, a leading Israeli software company, was unable to secure US visas and set up facilities in Cyprus, using imported Indian engineers there instead.

Labour mobility had other important dimensions. For about two decades, and especially in the mid-1980s, Israelis had been emigrating from Israel to the USA and Europe. In Silicon Valley, Israeli engineers have been part of the technology landscape for more than twenty years. Many have risen to executive positions in companies such as 3M and Intel. With Israel's rise as a technology centre, many saw returning to Israel as a viable option. Some convinced their employers to set up R&D facilities in Israel and still others returned to set up high-tech companies of their own. Notably, 'returning Israelis' are a class of immigrant that the government recognises and upon whom it confers rights that favourably impact import duties, taxes, and other benefits. Without a doubt, returning Israelis brought back with them skills and know-how that they acquired abroad.

**Private Sector Investment in Innovation**

Israel's large industrial and military conglomerates financed an earlier generation of high-technology firms. In 1990, there were a number of investment companies financing high-technology in Israel but there was only one venture capital fund. By 2002, Israel had more than 100 active technology venture capital funds, which from 1992 to 2002 raised $9.4 billion in capital (IVA 2003).

Several far-sighted policies of the Israeli government were responsible for the inception and encouragement of the Israeli venture capital industry. In 1992, the Office of Chief Scientist established the Yozma programme and allocated to it $100 million. The programme's main objectives were (i) to encourage international venture capital to enter Israel; (ii) to invest in Israeli high-technology firms; and (iii) to mentor the development of local venture capital talent. Of the $100 million, Yozma invested $80 million into ten funds. International professional venture capital firms raised a matching amount and managed the investments. In 1997, with a self-sustaining venture capital industry, the government sold off its interests in Yozma and the attendant funds.

The Israel Venture Association estimated that of the $9.4 billion raised between 1992 and 2002, Israel's top twenty venture capital funds raised $6.4 billion, nearly 70 per cent of it between 2000 and 2003. At the end of 2002, $5.6 billion had been invested and another $4.1 billion remained available for new and follow-on investments. This investment capital is administered locally but originates from international sources. Many of the major venture funds were connected either through formal alliances or informal partnerships with funds in the US, Canada, the UK and the Far East. Alternatively, their limited partners were foreign institutional investors such as pension funds or large corporations like AT&T or Compaq.

In 2000, the level of domestic venture capital as a proportion of GDP in Israel was higher than in any other country in the world including the USA (Figure 4.5). Just as important, the level of informal investment in business activity was also among the highest in the world (Figure 4.6). Informal investment includes funds provided by private individuals to others who were either setting up or planning to set up businesses (Reynolds et al. 2001). There are more than 1000 Israeli high-technology firms that have received venture capital financing over the years. However, not all their financing came from venture capital. Approximately half came from professional venture capital funds and the other half from corporations, buy-outs or individuals. Thus, the amounts discussed should not be interpreted as the total investment amounts targeted at Israeli high-technology firms.

The 1990s Internet bubble shifted the distribution of funds in favour of Internet related companies. For example, compared with 28 per cent in 1998, investments in software and the Internet accounted for 48 per cent of all venture capital investment in 1999 but subsequently fell to 25 per cent by 2002. The crash in the technology markets had a negative effect on raising capital and on the average amount of financing which firms received. In 2002, Israeli venture capital funds raised $63 million dollars compared with $1.3 billion in the previous year. In fact, a number of funds had to return part of their capital to the limited partners. Finally, while the size of the average investment rose, the number of firms receiving financing fell by nearly 30 per cent. In 2001, 104 funds invested $812 million in 438 companies for an average investment of $1.2 million. In 2002, 91 funds invested $481 million in 298 companies at an average investment of $1.6 million. The amount that Israeli venture capital funds invested per investment is considerably lower

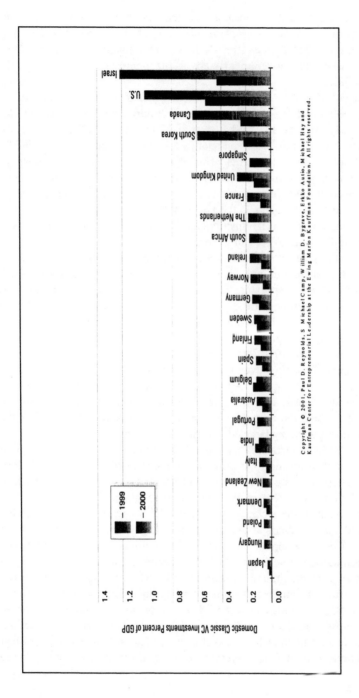

*Figure 4.5  Domestic Venture Capital Investment as a percentage of GDP*

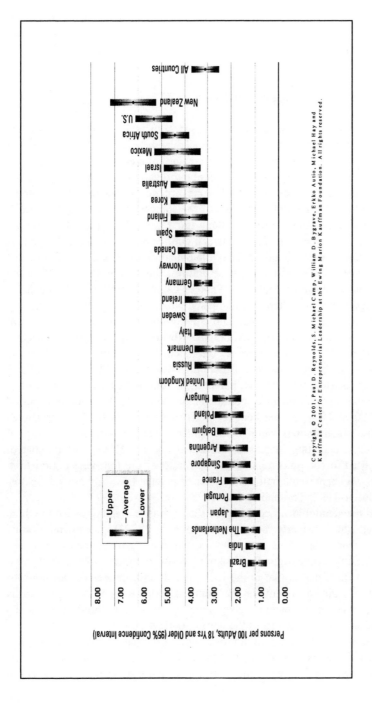

Figure 4.6 *Informal Investment by Country*

than the average US fund would have invested in a company. Although Israeli venture capital was not specifically categorised as 'seed' level financing, in effect, it was. Venture capital funds also came to differentiate themselves based on their stage of financing.

## Appropriating the Fruits of Innovation

Examining patents presents another approach to understanding the sources and potential uses of Israeli innovations (Trajtenberg 2001). Patents are seen as one manifestation of the innovative capacity of a country. Clearly, patents are not a perfect source of information about invention. Many inventions are not appropriate for patenting, and some are never patented for strategic reasons. However, a careful analysis of the sources and ownership of Israeli patents provides some insights about the rate and source of invention. According to Trajtenberg (2001), Israeli entities have received 6304 patents the USA between 1968 and 1997. While patenting by Israelis is a fraction of the patenting by UK and Taiwanese entities, the figures for the 1990s are comparable to those of Finland – another country with an emerging high-technology sector but where one company, Nokia, is a substantial player.

Patenting of computer-related and software-related inventions has grown rapidly over the last ten years. Although software patenting follows different standards in the USA and Europe, the patenting of software algorithms is commonly accepted in each jurisdiction. Since most of Israeli software is externally focused, international patenting is routine and a good indicator of the inventor's commitment to commercialisation. Over the four-year period from 1990 to 1994, 23 per cent (or 452) of all patents filed in the United States by Israeli entities were for computer related sub-sectors. The rate of international patenting increased dramatically in the 1990s. The number of patents filed in computer related sub-sectors over the four-year period from 1990 to 1997 represents half the number of patents filed in these sub-sectors from 1968 to 1997 (Trajtenberg 2001).

From the standpoint of commercialisation, it is interesting to see to whom the intellectual property belongs. Trajtenberg (2001) groups intellectual property owners into four categories: corporations, government, universities and individuals (unassigned). Looking at raw numbers over a thirty-year period, he finds that unlike in the USA, Israeli corporations do not hold the majority of rights to inventions. By contrast, individuals hold a significantly higher proportion of patent rights. Finally, universities hold substantially more patents than in the rest of the world (Table 4.5).

However, Trajtenberg took a closer look at the data for the last ten years and showed that the patenting patterns of Israeli firms have been converging with the norms in the rest of the world. Over the last decade, the number of patents filed yearly by Israelis in the USA has doubled. In terms of domestic talents, the number filed by universities has decreased significantly, while Israeli corporations have increased their patenting significantly. The majority of university patents are in drugs and medicines (36 per cent) and computers and communications (33 per cent). Foreign corporations and Israeli corporations have similar sectoral distributions of patents but foreign corporations are patenting in computers and communications more aggressively than domestic firms.

*Table 4.5  Distribution of patents by assignee type (%)*

| Holder | USA (1963-1993) | All countries (1963-1993) | Israel (1968-1997) |
|---|---|---|---|
| Corporations | 71 | 84 | 43 |
| Individuals | 24 | 15 | 37 |
| Government | 3 | 1 | 6 |
| Universities | 2 | n.a. | 16 |

*Source*:  Trajtenberg (2001).

## Summary

This section focused on the institutional context in which the Israeli software sector emerged. Israel's government has made substantial financial contributions to research and development. The country has also seen an increase in the diversity of higher education offerings – with many aimed at building skills useful in the technology sector. Few countries have benefited from large-scale immigration of highly-skilled immigrants in the way that Israel has. This created a ready labour pool which firms could deploy in developing technology. In addition, private financing of innovation has played a significant part in stimulating entrepreneurship. The inflow of foreign capital, and with it the skill of the venture capital industry, contributed to the professionalisation and evolution of Israel's private equity. The military has been a source of both training and technology. The solution-focused approach the military takes to addressing its own technology needs has migrated into the technology sector and into software development in particular. Research has also shown that Israelis are appropriating the fruits of innovation much more aggressively than a decade ago. The development of high technology and software in Israel depended in some measure on government policy but in large measure on private initiative.

## 4.3  EVOLUTION: GROWTH AND EXIT

The evolution of Israel's software industry has brought growth and opportunities for investors and entrepreneurs to sell and list companies. This section first discusses how Israeli firms use dual location and strategic alliances to expand internationally. It then examines the patterns of acquisitions, listings and failures in the industry.

**Going Global**

Israeli software firms compete in the international market for information technology solutions. Israel's population of 6.5 million provides a limited domestic market. To grow, many Israeli software companies have to internationalise from the start – and they often start with legal incorporation abroad. By one estimate, more than 50 per cent of the companies funded by venture capital are registered abroad, most frequently in the USA (Gordon 2001). A recent survey that randomly sampled Israel technology firms also showed that 50 per cent of the companies, whatever the source of their funding, have offices abroad (Khavul 2001). In choosing their location abroad, 44 per cent reported wanting to be close to the target market, 21 per cent to be close to their strategic partners, 11 per cent to be close to sources of finance, and the remaining 24 per cent to be either close to others in the industry or sources of labour. Consequently, 45 per cent reported that their offices abroad have a marketing function, 23 per cent a distribution function, and the remaining 32 per cent either a headquarters, public relations or R&D function. Firms with offices abroad were also different from those without, in a number of areas. Compared with similarly aged firms without offices abroad, the 'globalisers' had larger top management teams, more managers with international experience, more employees, significantly more outside directors, more rounds of financing from financing sources, and had invested more in R&D. Notably, they also had more top management turnover at all levels.

Maintaining dual identities for Israeli companies is a common operational strategy. Box 4.5, Born to Go Global, illustrates the reasoning behind internationalisation strategies for Business Layers and Interwise, two Israeli enterprise software companies.

BOX 4.5 BORN TO GO GLOBAL [6]

Business Layers is an enterprise software company that develops software to manage the digital credentials for employees. Such credentials guarantee that access to company systems and resources could be granted and withdrawn as needed. The company was founded by three Israeli entrepreneurs, all of whom had extensive experience in the US. Business Layers is both an Israeli and a USA company. The company is Delaware registered and has an Israeli subsidiary. Izhar Shay, one of the company's founders and its current CEO reflects, 'We established both the US and Israeli company in the same week. We did this largely for business reasons. A small company that has to sell enterprise software has to be a US company, in the US market, and respond to its US customers. We also benefit from the more favourable tax structure in the USA. With a view to the future we also considered that if we were to ever go public or be acquired we had better look and smell like a US company.' To be close to the European market, Business Layers established subsidiaries in the UK, France and Germany.

Business Layers does not hide its Israeli identity. In 2002, the company had 115 employees of whom 50 were in Israel. The company has also raised more than $50 million in venture financing. Its Israeli investors are clearly identified alongside more traditional US venture capital funds. The company's backers include several of Israel's most experienced and successful funds and one of its most respected serial entrepreneurs. The biographies of its board members and the top management team unambiguously state their Israeli educational and professional backgrounds. 'We present ourselves as a US company with research and development facilities in Israel. We have a strong Israeli background and we are quite proud of the technology that is developed in Israel,' says Shay.

Maintaining one foot in Israel and another in the USA has other advantages when it comes to enhancing the company's reputation and becoming noticed. 'We are very well connected in the financial and business community in the USA. We know how to attract attention from the right people. The Israeli connection also helps. In Israel we are considered as one of the top 10 enterprise software companies. This echoes across the Ocean. When investment bankers look at Israeli companies or Israeli technologies, our name comes up. Sometimes customer leads come our way to the USA via Israel.' Although from an international perspective, Business Layers, with its estimated revenues of $20 million, would not be considered a large company, in Israel its success is followed closely.

Izhar Shay's views of internationalisation are common even for companies that operated in Israel before relocating. Take Interwise for example. In 1994 Frank Zvi and Hillel Kobrinsky, two Israeli Air Force pilots, left the military with the idea of starting a software company. While in the air force, Zvi and Kobrinsky managed the development of software for planning and control systems. Although the business ideas they considered were not directly related to the technologies they developed for the air force, the skills and approach were similar. Zvi and Kobrinsky recruited a technical team of software developers from their former units in the air force. The e-learning solutions that Interwise developed soon gave way to a broader web communications platform targeted at multinationals.

Since its foundation, Interwise has raised approximately $65 million in three rounds of venture capital financing. Investors in Interwise include not only Israeli funds but also GE Capital and NTT communications of Japan. In 2002, the company had 200 employees of whom 120 were in Israel and 80 were in North America, with representative offices in Europe, Asia and Australia. In contrast to many Israeli high-technology firms registered in the USA, Interwise is an Israeli registered company. In addition, its first customers were domestic; Interwise sold its first systems to Israeli banks. Zvi remarks, 'We started in Israel and sold enough product and to large enough customers to become noticed and prove that our concept works. We then went out and raised our first round of financing and began to sell internationally.'

Shortly after securing the first round of financing, Interwise moved, first its business development and then the main management functions, to offices in Silicon Valley. Proximity to the customers and end users is paramount. In a fluid market and with the company's technology still evolving, he felt that he could not afford to leave the most critical learning to a hired business development or marketing person. 'To understand what your next business step should be, you have to be on the customer's doorstep… I wish I could say I know how to build an international company with the management in Tel Aviv. I would rather have lived in Israel and would rather contribute to its economy than to any other in the world. But, I have not figured it out yet.' Interwise hired US staff when it built offices in the USA. The hiring of US staff rather than moving people from Israel was perceived as less contentious.

The management functions and sales and customer support are distributed across offices outside of Israel while the research and development remain in Israel. Zvi is proud that his is an Israeli company and does not hide it; however, he does concede that most of the time customers are not aware of the connection. 'After all, our employees do not come to the customer and say "we are Israeli". They come to the customer and say "Hello I am Scott McNiel and I work for Interwise".'

As the cases above illustrate, Business Layers was born global; it was registered in Israel and the USA in the same week. Interwise, first registered in Israel, acquired local customers, and then moved its headquarters abroad. Start-ups developing software especially for use in large international corporations face a major problem – getting noticed by the IT purchasing managers. Even well-financed companies with well-known venture capitalists behind them are not immune to quizzical glances from those in a position to purchase their products. Some of the most promising Israeli software companies have had to work hard at establishing legitimacy. To do so they have followed in the footsteps of the industry leaders and have split their operations across continents. They locate sales and marketing close to potential customers and maintain research and development operations in Israel. Government policies have also made it more convenient to register new firms abroad. Israel's corporate tax rate is significantly higher than that of the USA. The merger and acquisitions laws in Israel also make it difficult to look at trade sales as an exit option, especially when payment in shares is ofte the currency. Finally, Israel's volatile political situation means that a US or European corporate identity is a rational hedge against this risk.

The government's R&D funding body acknowledges that dual location is a rational strategy for Israeli companies particularly in hard times. Research and development funds from the Office of the Chief Scientist do not depend on where the management of the company is located or where the company is registered. In May of 2002, the Chief Scientist commented on the apparent relocation of senior management from Israel by saying, 'The entire logic behind the R&D grants is to bring extra returns to the country. Naturally, it would be nice if the managers were also based in Israel, but I have no legal or moral basis to complain if they decide otherwise...After all, there are Israeli companies with overseas subsidiaries whose managers are based here and which benefit from [government] grants' (Yachin 2002). While Israeli companies may be registering abroad and locating their sales and marketing subsidiaries outside Israel, the Bank of Israel has provided further evidence that much of the money they raise actually does stay in Israel. The bank estimated that of the $1.04 billion raised in 2002 by 352 start-ups, $862 million financed Israeli operations while the balance was transferred to support foreign operations, primarily in the USA (Hermoni 2003).

**Forming Strategic Alliances**

To survive, Israeli firms have been aggressive in forming strategic alliances with multinationals across the world. To establish contacts, many firms needed to be noticed by the right people, the industry gurus and evangelists whose recommendations could make or break the company's future. They target leading specialists and recruit them to advisory boards. They also enlist the efforts of the social networks in the greater Israeli and Jewish Diaspora. Box 4.6, Banking on Social Networks, illustrates the importance of international connectedness for building Compugen – one of Israel's leading bioinformatics companies.

---

BOX 4.6 BANKING ON SOCIAL NETWORKS [7]

Compugen applies Israeli software to the science of the human genome. Founded in 1993, Compugen is a bioinformatics and drug discovery company that has developed a computational platform to facilitate genomics and proteomics data modelling and analysis. For example, one of Compugen's products provides molecular biologists and other life scientists with an intuitive and user-friendly online research environment. As is the case with many bioinformatics companies, Compugen started out as a software company selling a product. Over time, Compugen has adopted a hybrid model that provides services using its software in conjunction with traditional wet-lab biology to identify genes and drug targets.

The company went public on the NASDAQ and is now dual-listed on the Tel Aviv Stock Exchange. Compugen is the first biotechnology company to be listed on the Tel Aviv Stock Exchange. In 2002, Compugen had approximately $11 million in sales revenue, and its market capitalisation hovered around $50 million. Compugen generates revenue from the sale of its software as well as licensing and joint development agreements with large pharmaceutical companies such as Pfizer, Novartis, and Abbott. At the time of its IPO in August of 2000, Compugen employed approximately 132 employees of whom 110 were in Israel and the balance in New Jersey and Silicon Valley in the USA.

For Israel, the advent of bioinformatics was an opportunity whose time had to come. Bioinformatics represents a novel convergence of information and computing technologies with the biological sciences. Bioinformatics tools help researchers capture, analyse, visualise and share their findings. In Israel, Compugen, IDGene and other

---

bioinformatics companies could build on the country's scientific expertise in the life sciences and its skills in software development.

While hundreds of Israeli start-ups in wireless, the Internet and optics raised millions of dollars in venture capital investments during the 1990s, start-ups in the life-sciences all but languished. Few Israeli venture capitalists had the patience or the expertise to invest. For government, commercialising the country's biological expertise became a national priority only in the late 1990s. At the end of 2002, the Ministry of Trade and Industry estimated that 160 biotechnology start-up firms operated in Israel. Together, they employed 4000 people and had combined revenues of more than $800 million. The ministry also estimated that 25 new biotechnology companies are started in Israel each year. However, the ability of such companies to survive depended on the ability of their management to secure development and marketing agreements within the international scientific and pharmaceutical community.

Indeed, the origins of Compugen and its successful growth are rooted in the international experience of its founders and the connections of its investors. While participating in the Human Genome Project at Institut Pasteur in Paris in the early 1990s, Dr Mintz, an Israeli biologist, observed that she and her colleagues were producing large volumes of data that computers could not process quickly. She enlisted her husband, Eli Mintz, the future CEO of Compugen, and his two friends from the army's elite TALPIOT programme, to improve the speed with which such data could be analysed. They developed a computer that could analyse biological data one thousand times faster than the next best alternative. Compugen's computers were popular with pharmaceutical companies and were regarded as the gold standard, which even the US Patent Office used. The company secured early investment from a US-based venture fund, generated revenues from the sale of computers and the software, but shortly after ran into problems. While Compugen's computers were popular and powerful, the market for them appeared limited at the time. Thirty pharmaceutical companies bought one each and at quite a low price. It was at this time that the team thought to improve on the algorithms and sell an upgraded version. However, they discovered that, in fact, they could not make any further improvements to the original algorithm because it was 'built on a naïve first premise'. They had to start from scratch and take a different approach – one that would combine software with the value added of scientific discovery.

At that time, Compugen's current chairman, Martin Gerstel, had just retired to Jerusalem. Gerstel had been the founder and former CEO of

ALZA Corporation, an earlier medical start-up in Israel, which in 2001 was sold to Johnson & Johnson for $13 billion. Far from retiring, Gerstel met Compugen's team, at the behest of its US investors. Gerstel saw an opportunity in Compugen and tapped into his network of pharmaceutical contacts. The company opened sales and marketing offices in the USA, and raised additional financing from Israeli and international investors.

**Selling Out**

Since 1993, 225 Israeli technology firms have been acquired either by other Israeli firms or by foreign corporations. However, few acquisitions had as large an impact on the entrepreneurial psyche in Israel as the sale of Mirabilis, and its chat program ICQ, to AOL for $407 million (see Box 4.7, AOL's Hungry Eyeballs). The acquisition of Mirabilis ignited in the venture capital community a fierce race for the next 'home run' – a quick exit with a high return. The acquisition came at a time when the global economy was being redefined into the 'New Economy'. The mood in Israel reflected this apparent change as perceptibly as it did in San Francisco, Boston or London. Many aspiring Israeli entrepreneurs flooded venture capitalists with promises of winning Internet ideas and unbridled enthusiasm. Venture capitalists, flushed with recently-raised billions of dollars, were under pressure from their investors to show Mirabilis-like returns. They competed with each other for deals, chased entrepreneurs, set up incubators and accelerators to shorten the time to market and time to exit.

The day that Mirabilis announced that AOL had agreed to acquire it for $407 million a bumper-sticker circulated in the Israeli venture capital community. It said 'I too was asked to invest.' The point was made. Many were asked but, initially, few investors saw ICQ as a business opportunity. Mirabilis was a product of its time and it made no secret of its Internet strategy – to aggregate as many 'eyeballs' as possible and to sell the business to a large company with the infrastructure to turn all those eyeballs into revenue. AOL did just that; its first advertising deal for ICQ was worth $100 million (Karny 1999). However, ICQ was more than just a technology or a marketing acquisition for AOL. In the words of AOL's senior management, 'an important addition to AOL's management culture, a sort of spice. The Israeli guys don't always accept our culture, and that is a positive process from our point of view' (Dagoni 1999). Having embraced Israeli technology through its acquisition of ICQ, AOL followed with other attempts (Karny 1999).

BOX 4.7 AOL'S HUNGRY EYEBALLS [8]

In Israel, 1998 was referred to as the *Annus Mirabilis*. The sale of Mirabilis to AOL for $407 million drew the dot.com boom into Israel. This acquisition of an Israeli Internet start-up with no revenues is popularly regarded as the defining moment for many would-be Israeli entrepreneurs. Mirabilis created ICQ (I Seek You) a free instant-messaging software program that quickly swept the globe. Within three weeks of the program's launch in 1996, 30 000 people had signed up; after six months, one million; by the time AOL purchased Mirabilis 30 000 users a year were joining. By June of 2000, as AOL and Time Warner were preparing to merge, the US Federal Trade Commission announced it was examining AOL's dominance of instant messaging. The acquisition of ICQ meant that within a year AOL controlled 90 per cent of the instant messaging business, estimated at 100 million users.

To develop the first version of the software, the founders of Mirabilis had reportedly borrowed $100 000 from one of their fathers, Yossi Vardi in 1996. Yossi Vardi is a prominent Israeli businessman. The elder Vardi is well regarded and has many links the high-tech and financial community in Israel and the USA. In many ways, Mirabilis owes its place as the classic Internet 'built to sell' company, initially to Yossi Vardi's deep pockets, and, finally, to his business and financial network. In receipt of the seed financing, the ICQ trio moved to San Jose, California where Internet connections were cheaper than in Israel. They lived and worked out of a small apartment and rented server space from another Israeli company in Silicon Valley. A year later, the US office was moved to New York City where it has remained for several years. The Israeli research, development and customer support operation grew to 100 employees.

The sale of Mirabilis made millionaires out of its founders and the few who invested in the company. It also benefited the Israeli taxpayer; the Israeli treasury received $140 million in tax revenue. ICQ continues to operate in Israel although with reduced staff. A year after the merger, ICQ received a $7 million grant from the Office of Chief Scientist for future R&D, which the company would carry out in Israel. As a technology company with a centre in Israel, ICQ/AOL was certainly eligible, but observers note that the grant looked like an attempt to secure jobs at a time when AOL was in trouble. However, over time, as AOL-TimeWarner's financial problems multiplied, ICQ was forced to reduce its staff by one third in 2001 and another third in

2003 (Alfassy 2001). By the middle of 2001, Israeli venture capitalists, like their counterparts all over the world, were writing off many investments in Internet start-ups. The majority of Israeli Internet firms were neither grounded in technology nor close enough to the market to understand its needs.

It is easy to dismiss the ICQ sale as an Internet bubble phenomenon, and in practical terms it was one company that had no revenues and sold for hundreds of millions of dollars. Mirabilis's success signalled that becoming an acquisition target is a viable and lucrative exit option. Of the 225 sales mentioned above, 200 took place after that of Mirabilis. Companies were started with the express idea that they were for sale. However, as the technology boom of the late 1990s drew to a close, the Israeli press and policymakers became obsessed with a search for the Israeli version of Nokia. That is, a local technology company that becomes a multinational giant. The comparisons between Finland and Israel, both small countries far from the main North American markets, and certainly the example of Nokia, with its long history and only a recent technology focus, obfuscate the issue. The real question is how can Israeli software companies grow and develop into fully-fledged organisations rather than remain local R&D shops. A related question is how can Israel reap some of the added value that its software and information technologies deliver. The consequences of acquisition became an even more significant issue when the global economy deteriorated and many of the acquired firms were scaled down or closed altogether, with previously lucrative technology jobs eliminated in the process.

The reality of small, or even medium-sized, Israeli companies is that they are generally unable to deliver the complete solution customers require. Their competitive edge is innovative technology and unique solutions particularly for the corporate environment. The example of ICQ, with its focus on the consumer market, is an exception. As the previous discussion of going global showed, entrepreneurs find it difficult to grow companies far from their main customer bases in the USA and Europe. Moreover, in competitive environments, speed to market is of the essence and small organisations can lose out as they gear-up their infrastructure. For companies with breakthrough innovations to be adopted, it takes the buy-in of many stakeholders in the industry. Finally, software markets worldwide are consolidating. As a result, small and medium-sized software companies, whether they are from Israel or Silicon Valley, are being acquired. Thus, some people ask what is wrong if Israeli firms are acquired (Kalish 1999)? If the money that the investors, entrepreneurs and the state receive can be recirculated in the economy, that should spur the next cycle of innovation.

## Going Public

Between 1995 and 2002, there have been 168 Israeli share offerings on exchanges in the USA and Europe. As Table 4.6 shows, in total, Israeli companies raised more than $14 billion in the public markets over a seven-year period. The average offering brought $83.8 million of capital to the firm. Firms financed with venture capital accounted for 56 per cent of the offerings but only 38 per cent of the capital raised. In the late 1990s, public markets receptive to IPOs accelerated the pace of investment in Israeli software and information technology companies. For many venture capitalists and entrepreneurs alike, the IPO was a preferred way to realise the value of their investments.

The choice of listing internationally, instead of domestically on the Tel Aviv Stock Exchange (TASE), was a rational decision that allowed firms access to larger sums of capital; however, it was also a socially reinforced choice. The TASE is a small exchange. In 2000, 665 firms with a total capitalisation of $65.3 billion were listed on the TASE. The monthly turnover velocity averaged under 30 per cent. To compare, 531 companies with a total capitalisation of $100 billion were listed on the Taiwanese stock exchange. The monthly turnover velocity averaged 207 per cent (Khavul 2002). The Taiwanese stock exchange is larger and more dynamic and a higher proportion of Taiwanese technology firms go public at home (Rock 2002). For growth-oriented Israeli technology firms, the TASE exchange was not an attractive place to make a public offering. Until 1999, the option to dual list on the TASE did not exist. When the option was finally introduced, 17 companies elected to follow it (interview with Chief Economist of the Tel Aviv Stock Exchange 2002). But size was not the only issue. Listing on international exchanges became the preferred option also because the TASE could not confer the same level of legitimacy upon a firm as an exchange in the USA or Europe. Once a few firms listed abroad, that became the gold standard. In no small part, US and European investment banks with direct links to venture capital firms in Israel also steered firms towards international IPOs. Finally, with a view to the future, firms that wanted to list abroad also incorporated abroad (see Born to Go Global, Box 4.8).

Whether an IPO was the best option for all the companies that pursued them is a matter of some debate in Israel, as it is in the USA and Europe. As with the previous case, AOL's Hungry Eyeballs, which looked at

*Table 4.6  Capital raised in European and US public offerings of Israel companies. 1995–2002*

| Year | All offerings | | Venture capital backed | | |
|---|---|---|---|---|---|
| | Number of offerings | Capital raised ($m) | Number of offerings | Capital raised ($m) | % of capital VC backed |
| 1995 | 14 | 719 | 8 | 245 | 34 |
| 1996 | 32 | 959 | 17 | 638 | 67 |
| 1997 | 23 | 798 | 10 | 635 | 80 |
| 1998 | 19 | 993 | 8 | 220 | 22 |
| 1999 | 32 | 3821 | 20 | 1382 | 36 |
| 2000 | 40 | 5001 | 28 | 2065 | 41 |
| 2001 | 6 | 1259 | 3 | 201 | 16 |
| 2002 | 2 | 522 | 0 | 0 | 0 |
| Total | 168 | 14 072 | 94 | 5386 | 38 |

*Source:* IVA Yearbook (2003)

acquisitions, the answer depends on whose interests the IPOs served. The circumstances around the IPO of Commtouch, a much-observed and widely-held Israeli software company, bring out these issues directly.

---

BOX 4.8 THE GOLDEN TOUCH [9]

Commtouch, an Israeli company focusing on e-mail and the development of messaging application software, is an interesting counterpoint to Mirabilis's build-to-sell strategy for exit (see AOL's Hungry Eyeballs, Box 4.7). Commtouch chose an IPO on the NASDAQ in its attempt to grow beyond its Israeli boundaries. When it went public Commtouch had been operating for eight years, had a subsidiary in Silicon Valley, and an impressive set of financial and strategic investors. Commtouch appeared to have been blessed by Microsoft's golden hand. Microsoft made a $20 million investment in Commtouch and signed a strategic agreement with the company. Over and above Microsoft's ownership stake in the company, Commtouch had also secured a similar sized investment from Paul Allen, one of the Microsoft's early founders and a visionary in high technology. A number of leading Israeli venture capital firms had also invested. The company had a publicity star in its president, Isabel Maxwell, who had rapidly founded the company that brought to the Internet the search engine Magellan that it later sold to Excite. Commtouch's pedigree, for a debut as an international company, was apparently impeccable.

Commtouch, an Israeli registered company, listed on the NASDAQ in July of 1999 as a foreign private issuer. The company raised $48 million at a valuation of $270 million. The timing of Commtouch's IPO was just right. The company's software provided e-mail and messaging solutions to service providers such as application service providers, Internet service providers, wireless carriers, data centres, system integrators and information technology consultants. It provided services to more than 30 million mailboxes worldwide. Commtouch also used its shares to acquire an American company with complementary technology. The tax consequences of re-registering were deemed prohibitive. Further, Commtouch considered but did not list (nor dual list when it became available) on the Tel Aviv Stock Exchange because 'the cost of managing an Israeli listing when you have an American CFO is enormous.' The plight of Commtouch was keenly followed in the Israeli high-tech community and in the business press. By March 2000, Commtouch's share price reached $66.50, when the company had 450 employees in Silicon Valley and Israel. By October of 2002,

Commtouch had imploded. It had burned through an estimated $73 million in cash, was trading at $0.08 and had seven employees left in Silicon Valley. Commtouch's NASDAQ listing was transferred from the main board to NASDAQ's small cap area. It also became the subject of a class action lawsuit when it began to restate its sales projections and financial results.

Commtouch certainly achieved many of the milestones commonly recommended to Israeli high-technology start-ups. The company's software won industry awards (*PC* magazine Awards Editor's Choice to Commtouch Software's Pronto 1996), it had prestigious seed investors, and the most sought-after strategic partners. It leveraged Israel's technology skills to develop its software products and positioned sales and marketing close to the customers in Silicon Valley. Between 1999 and 2000, the revenues at Commtouch increased five-fold and stood at close to $20 million. However, with its IPO, Commtouch became an Internet era company. 'That was the time that if you wanted to have growth, you needed to have media', reflected Gideon Mantel. The growth in Commtouch's expenses, in particular on marketing and administration, were unsustainable. In 2001, Commtouch reported a net loss of $60 million (Commtouch Form 20-F to the Securities and Exchange Commission). With the dot.com collapse, Commtouch's customer base largely evaporated and the company was forced to contract in full public view. Gideon Mantel, the company's CEO, argues that the company reacted swiftly to the changes in the market, 'With the market crash 50 per cent of our customers disappeared within three to six months. Within six weeks of making the decision to take action, we reduced our staffing from nearly 500 to 150 employees. However, when you are a public company every move you make is scrutinized.' The market expectations of Commtouch's success were high, and sustainable growth never materialised. In retrospect, Mantel suggested that the IPO was right for its time, but the IPO was not the right choice for the company in the long run.

Since 2002, Commtouch has exited its main messaging solutions business, sold the acquired company back to its original owners and has tried to redefine itself as a provider of solutions to combat e-mail SPAM. In an effort to start over, Commtouch has put together a new advisory board that includes a professor of management from MIT, the founder and the chief technical officers of a software communications company, and the former vice president of sales for Check Point (*Business Wire* 2002). The company has also received a $1 million grant from the Office of the Chief Scientist to support future R&D and convertible debt financing from a consortium of investors. Commtouch's CEO Gideon Mantel sums up the situation, 'I'm always trying to beat the odds. I did it when we went public, and now I'm trying to do it to salvage the company' (Shwartz 2002).

## Surviving Economic Downturns

In the 1990s, the pattern of initial public offerings, mergers, acquisitions and failures of Israeli high-technology firms followed in lockstep the rise and fall of international technology markets. The NASDAQ, the most watched technology index in the world, was the market reference point for the growth of Israeli firms. Israel was hailed as a 'Silicon Valley on the Med', and its firms became full participants in the technology boom of the 1990s. Many firms were financed by venture capitalists who eventually needed to exit from their investments either through public offerings or trade sales. Hundreds of Israeli firms opened offices in the USA, Europe and Asia in order to be closer to their potential or existing customers and closer to additional sources of financing. When AOL, Microsoft and Oracle went on acquisition sprees, Israeli firms were attractive both for their intellectual property and for their comparatively modest valuations. As the technology-driven bubble burst, start-ups all over the world began to fail and fewer entrepreneurs contemplated entry. In 1999, an estimated 450 new high-technology companies were started. By 2001, this number had dropped by an estimated two-thirds. As Table 4.7 shows, between the last quarter of 1999 and the second quarter of 2003, 140 software firms failed. This represents 16.6 per cent of all firms that failed during this period.[10]

In Israel, as in the USA and Europe, the downturn in the global economy brought about a shake-out of firms across industries. Software firms were hit particularly hard because corporate investment in information technology contracted rapidly. Analysts suggest that whereas in the late 1990s corporations aggressively acquired software, today they are looking for clear returns from information technology, just as from any other investment.

Israeli firms have had to cope with the downturn in the economy and a considerable deterioration with the political situation. The common operational strategy of maintaining dual identities, internationalising early and staying close to the customer has paid off for many firms. Box 4.9, Ahead of the Curve, shows how Business Layers has made the most of adversity.

*Table 4.7  Firm failure from Q4-1999 to Q2-2003*

| Sector | No. of firms | Percentage |
|---|---|---|
| Communications | 148 | 17.6 |
| Software | 140 | 16.6 |
| Internet | 186 | 22.1 |
| Life sciences | 141 | 16.8 |
| Misc tech | 225 | 26.8 |
| Total | 840 | 100 |
| Timing of firm failure | | |
| 1999 Q4 | 7 | 1.0 |
| 2000 | 150 | 17.8 |
| 2001 | 365 | 43.4 |
| 2002 | 301 | 35.8 |
| 2003 Q1-Q2 | 17 | 2.0 |
| Total | 840 | 100 |

*Source*: IVA (2003); calculations by the author.

---

BOX 4.9 AHEAD OF THE CURVE [11]

The downturn in corporate information technology spending and the near collapse in the telecommunications market has also hit hard the more than 100 Israeli enterprise software start-ups. Many companies have had to restructure and have laid off employees both in Israel and abroad. Many of the enterprise software start-up firms still operating in 2002 had to adapt their business models and their operations in order to survive. On 10 September 2001, Business Layers (see Born to Go Global, Box 4.5), announced that it had closed its latest round of financing. Timing for the company appeared to be everything. Months earlier, as the economy began to sag, Business Layers noticed a change in its customers' needs. CEO Izhar Shay describes how Business Layers had to adapt. 'In the heady days of the Internet, e-business and e-everything was the rage. Companies were recruiting and moving people around at fever pitch. They had a desperate need to recruit people and make sure that employees were immediately productive.'

Then the market crashed and the same companies started laying off people. The needs flipped and Business Layers found itself in the de-provisioning business. Companies became obsessed with cost-cutting and security. They needed to make sure that company assets were under lock and key. 'While our technology could support e-provisioning as well as de-provisioning, we had to reposition the company in the minds of our customers and realign the organization from within. We had to position ourselves as a lifecycle company.' As a further hedge on the worsening economic situation in the USA, Business Layers decided that its experience in the USA would be valuable in Europe. The company set up branches in the UK, France and Germany. 'The needs in Europe were broadly similar, but we were ahead of the game in these markets.' Shay believes that for Business Layers, the downturn in the economy prompted the sort of quick redefinition of its business strategy that made the difference not only in its survival but also in its international growth. In December of 2003, Business Layers was acquired.

With every downturn in the Israeli economy or the international financial markets, the Israeli press inevitably asks, 'Can it really be over?' Can the country's romance with technology be finished? Between 2000-2003, there has been some reason to wonder if maybe the high-technology renaissance has run its course. However, this appears highly unlikely because technology expertise in Israel has deep roots in education and training. The financial markets may have slowed the frenzied pace of firm entry and investment, but Israeli firms continue to innovate. Venture capitalists are funding fewer firms, but they argue that the firms have better technologies and more experienced management teams. It is important to remember that Israel now has a substantial cadre of entrepreneurs who have started firms, raised capital, developed products, and in many cases taken those products to market. The learning embedded in this community is valuable human capital. The firms that survive the downturn will likely be more robust than those a generation before.

## 4.4 CONCLUSION

The emergence and evolution of the software industry in Israel has paralleled the country's transformation into an international centre of innovation and entrepreneurship.

At the macro-level, economic liberalisation, national investment in research, development and training along with a massive inflow of human and equity capital during the global economic boom, contributed to Israel's rise. Most recently, on a yearly basis, the Israeli software industry sells nearly $3 billion worth of products to corporate customers located primarily in the USA and Europe. Enterprise applications and information security represent two broad areas where Israeli firms have developed a number of competitive niches. The industry has experienced significant entry and exit of start-up firms but is dominated by a number of older and larger firms that have become significant players in international software markets. The downturn in the global economy and the deteriorating political situation have put the rapid growth in this sector to a severe test over the last decade.

At the micro-level, most Israeli software firms are outwardly oriented and international from the time they are founded. As the boxes 4.1-4.9 illustrate, even young and small firms often maintain dual identities and multiple locations. Such firms focus on growth and locate headquarters close to their main customers and strategic partners while still maintaining research and development facilities in Israel. The venture capital industry, which has raised $9.4 billion over the last decade, has played an active role in funding Israel's software start-ups. Israeli software firms have made attractive acquisition targets for foreign technology powerhouses like Microsoft, Oracle and SAP. The international public markets have also shown considerable appetite for equity in Israeli firms; so much so, that between 1995 and 2002, $14.1 billion was raised.

While seductive, Israel's experience in software and information technology is only partly generalisable to other emerging economies. Israel's software sector competes internationally, based on the strength of the innovative technologies that the country's highly-skilled technical labour force produces. Competing at the high end may be the end goal for some emerging economies, but it is not a niche that is readily open to most. Nevertheless, investment in education and training should be a priority for public policy in countries hoping to build a software and information technology sector. Israel's experience with immigration, which many countries resist, shows how an inflow of skilled workers also can drastically expand the level of human capital in the country. Furthermore, government has an important role to play in supporting basic research and development and promoting entrepreneurship, but that role should be well defined and limited. Finally, while the government can enable, it is entrepreneurs who actually create the innovation and the value added for which Israeli firms are known. Reflecting on the Israeli experience, aspiring software entrepreneurs should consider adopting an international outlook from the start.

## ACKNOWLEDGEMENTS

I thank my colleagues Simon Commander, AnnaLee Saxenian, Ashok Desai, and Alfredo Behrens for stimulating comments on this chapter. I thank Miri Lerner and Shlomo Kalish for their guidance in Israel over the years. In addition, I thank Herve Andre Durand, Jacob Greenblatt, Emily Ng, Roy Wetzberger, and CongCong Zheng for their contributions to this project at different stages.

## NOTES

1. Modern Israel was established as an independent state by a vote of the United Nations in 1948. Israel is a small open economy. The country's territory is 22 145 square kilometres, and it has a population of 6.4 million citizens. Of these 77.8 per cent are Jewish, 15.2 per cent are Muslims, 2.1 per cent are Christians, and 4.8 per cent are of other religious affiliations. In 2000, Israel's GDP was $100 billion, and its GDP per capita was $19 330. In the late 1990s, GDP grew at 4 percent on average and unemployment averaged 8 per cent. In 2000, the penetration of mobile phones in Israel was approximately 65 per cent, and 50 per cent of the population had access to a PC.

2. *Hoover's Online* (www.hoovers.com); Comverse company website (www.comverse.com); *Globes* (2003); Amdocs company website (www.amdocs.com); Lis (2003); Mercury company website (www.mercury.com); *Globes* (May 22, 2001); *D&A Directory* (2002).

3. Goldman (2002).

4. *DM Review* (2003); Nass (2003); Interview with Rony Ross, Chairman of Panorama.

5. Deutsche Boerse; Orad company website (www.orad.co.il); Lehman Brothers (2003); Orad 2002 Annual Report, interview with Bjarne Berg CEO of Vi[z]rt; Vi[z]rt Company web site (www.visrt.com); RT-Set IPO Prospectus; IVA (2003).

6. *Globes* (2002); Business Layers company website (www.businesslayers.com) prior to acquisition; Interwise company website (www.interwise.com); Quotes from interview with Izhar Shay, CEO of Business Layers and interview with Frank Zvi, CEO of Interwise.

7. Compugen company website (www.cgen.com); Tsipori (2000); Jaffe (2003); Blackburn (2001); Interview with Martin Gestel Chairman of Compugen.

8. Sugarman (1998); *Globes* (2000).

9. Quotes from interview with Gideon Mantel CEO of Commtouch; Shwartz (2002); *BusinessWire* (2002).

10. The data presented above are indicative of the relative number of firms that have failed in each sector and their timing. There is no publicly available information on entry and exit of firms in Israel. As a result, it is extremely difficult to accurately reconcile the number of firms founded and the number failing. Direct comparisons between Table 4.2 and Table 4.7

should be made with extreme caution. Table 4.2 is a snapshot of the technology firms active in Israel during 2001; Table 4.7 aggregates firms over a two and one-half-year period during which there is both entry and exit. In addition, Table 4.2 and Table 4.7 are based on different sources, which do not classify firms into sectors in exactly the same way.

11. Quotes from interview with Izhar Shay, CEO of Business Layers.

# 5. Brazil

## Alfredo Behrens

---

### INTRODUCTION

The Brazilian software industry has emerged from the shadows over the last decade. In the 1990s the sector grew rapidly. Annual growth rates exceeded 20 per cent. By 2000-2001 software accounted for over 40 per cent of total IT in Brazil. There has been very rapid growth in the number of software firms and in employment in the software sector although the share of total employment accounted for by the sector remains small. Further, its contribution to GDP still falls below 0.75 per cent. In stark contrast to India, Brazilian software has mostly developed as a domestic industry with a very small export component. Part of this can be attributed to its origins – in particular, earlier policies of protection – as also to subsequent policy choices, but the extent of this focus on the domestic market is yet to be satisfactorily explained. The software sector has also grown alongside a concerted, publicly-led attempt to make Brazil a highly networked economy. Part of this has been through investment in communications infrastructure, part through use of public firms for developing software and part through institutional and legal interventions that have been conducive to wider diffusion of software, including an emphasis on adoption of open source software. This set of initiatives has had some important implications for the demand for software and for IT generally.

### 5.1 ORIGINS OF THE BRAZILIAN SOFTWARE INDUSTRY

The origins of the Brazilian software industry inevitably lead back to the military regime that took over the country in 1964.[1] Until that point, foreign companies led much of the development in Brazilian IT. These companies contributed significantly to IT training, both in-house and through short courses and in shaping university curricula. They were also instrumental in creating a market for specialised labour.

Since the initial diffusion of information technology coincided with a political regime that limited the activities of political parties, much political energy was channelled through professional associations. The nationalist stance of the professional IT associations was welcomed by a military administration sensitive to national security and independence on strategic issues. This otherwise unlikely partnership created the framework for Brazil's IT policy, which was strongly focused on IT hardware.[2] The military's strong emphasis on acquiring know-how in computer manufacture was welcomed by a technological elite who were eager to secure a niche for themselves in Brazilian manufacturing. The economic logic behind this pro-local manufacturing stance was familiar: import substitution, fuelled by political nationalism. The drive to manufacture IT equipment locally garnered a broader support base than just the military and highly-skilled workers – the country's managerial technocracy supported the alliance, while a modernising cadre of entrepreneurs saw a lucrative business opportunity in import substitution.[3] Local operations were initially concentrated on equipment repair, but as they gained familiarity servicing peripheral IT equipment, a local industry developed – initially around the production of video terminals – and this later expanded through a host of tax incentives. This led to bitter disputes in which foreign companies refused to become junior partners in companies to whom they would have to release proprietary technology. At the same time, Brazilian development and funding agencies such as BNDES and FINEP were employed to support local IT manufacture and technology development.

In the 1980s, earlier and broad-based support gave way to an IT policy known as 'market reserve', which meant, in practice, that import licences of IT products were subject to the scrutiny of government officials and to discriminatory import duties or outright banning. As the market reserve policy took shape it acquired a number of features, including:

- Tax breaks favouring domestic production;
- Prohibition of imports of products similar to those produced domestically;
- Restriction of IT product and accessory manufacture to national companies (those with financial and technological decision centres in Brazil);
- High tax burden for imported IT products;
- Export requirements for non-national IT enterprises;
- Mandated investment in Research and Development and manpower training for enterprises.

While the Law of Information, passed in 1984, provided a more stable investment environment, it also explicitly discouraged foreign competition, which led to substantial smuggling and ultimately to relatively low-quality Brazilian IT products.

The market reserve policy did not, however, last into the 1990s. Software, in the form of operating systems, was the centre of a bitter trade dispute in 1987, which paved the way for the abandonment of the policy. Brazil banned Microsoft's MS DOS version 2.0 in October of 1987, alleging the existence of a similar local product, which Microsoft believed to be largely a pirated version of its own.[4] The subsequent threat of American sanctions united disparate groups – such as orange juice, shoe and aircraft exporters – with a share of local manufacturers of IT products in opposition to the government. By May 1988 Brazil had a new Software Law that met most of the interests of foreign software developers. As a consequence of local and foreign opposition, the market reserve policy was abandoned and a new IT law was adopted in 1991.[5]

The new law significantly relaxed discrimination against foreign companies. Although tax incentives for local manufacturing were maintained, they were extended to foreign companies, attracting companies such as Compaq, Acer, IBM and, later, Dell. Instead of being granted on the basis of an index of local manufacture, tax benefits were now granted depending on agreement to Basic Production Processes (PPB), which allowed targeting niches of the productive process. Companies were now required, for instance, to attain ISO 9000 certification in no longer than two years. The government's insistence on adherence to PPB procedures granted local manufacturers a price advantage of up to 35 per cent for legally imported similar PCs.[6] Most importantly, the new law sought to protect the industry while encouraging innovation. Protection now required reciprocity, such as investing at least 5 per cent of gross revenue in research and development activities.

Furthermore, rules regarding government procurement changed and purchasing decisions could be based on quality.[7] The costs of manufacturing IT devices fell, the grey market lost much of its lustre, domestic competition increased, and a consolidation of the market took place. This resulted in fewer, but larger, local IT companies that sought commercial partnerships with foreign manufacturers ranging from joint ventures to distribution channels.[8]

## 5.2 SOFTWARE POLICY AFTER 'MARKET RESERVE'

Software development in Brazil did not begin with the end of the market reserve policy in the late 1980s. Software like Microsiga – the pioneering Brazilian ERP system – had been widely used since the early 1970s. Policymakers had been intent on sponsoring an alternative to MS DOS throughout the early 1980s. But a software policy as such had played second fiddle to the quest of building a national hardware capacity. However, much of the Brazilian software policy was tainted by the same siege mentality that pervaded the shaping of the hardware policy. For instance, at one stage imported software had to be registered with an official agency which required that the coding be revealed. It is not surprising that few foreign software developers agreed to reveal their trade secrets.

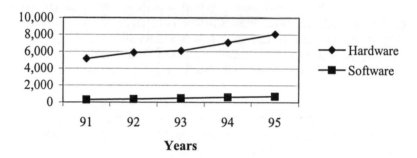

*Source*:   Ministry of Science and Technology data.

*Figure 5.1   IT sales ($ millions), 1991-1995*

In October 1992, the government ceased to protect the Brazilian IT hardware sector. Figure 5.1 shows that the movement away from protection was indeed associated with a significant growth in both hardware and software sales. Faced with the loss of protection, the domestic industry began to consolidate and merge with large foreign players and this in turn resulted in layoffs for a substantial number of qualified employees. As software development offered an employment alternative, as well as export growth potential, more emphasis was placed on funding for the domestic software industry.

This resulted in the creation of Softex,[9] a programme created within the CNPq, Brazil's Council for Scientific Research. Softex was the first (1993) of three pillars of an IT development initiative; the other two were ProTeM and the National Research Network (RNP – precursor of the Internet in Brazil), both of which began in 1994. However, Softex's role as an export promotion body was soon widened. By the mid-1990s Softex had begun establishing offices abroad, but poor results led to a policy reversal, and they were closed. In 1996, Softex ceased to work within the auspices of the CNPq – it was privatised and legally became Sociedade Softex, now a private contractor of CPNq, to be led by a council representing Brazil's IT community.[10] For all its strategic shortcomings, Softex secured a niche for itself as the clearing-house for information about software development and publishing in Brazil. Having dropped its export orientation, Softex nonetheless reached close to 900 members by 2003. Under its aegis, several commendable initiatives have prospered, including a Brazilian software online catalogue in four languages.

## 5.3 CHARACTERISTICS OF THE SOFTWARE INDUSTRY

By 1995, total software sales in Brazil stood at around $700 million and total employment in the sector was around 5000. By end-2003 the Brazilian packaged software market had grown to around $2 billion with a predominantly domestic market focus. Packaged software accounted for around 15 per cent of total IT sales, with IT services accounting for a further 36 per cent. As such, software accounted for only 0.1 per cent of the formal labour force.[11] For those employed in the sector, average earnings were relatively high at $330 per annum – 60 per cent more than the mean for Brazilians employed in the formal sector.[12]

Despite its small size, software development is an elite sector by Brazilian standards in terms of the qualification of its manpower. The level of schooling in software companies is substantially higher than the national average. Over 80 per cent of the labour force of software companies had at least a complete secondary education (11 full years of schooling), while fewer than 40 per cent of the Brazilian labour force had a comparable level of schooling. The share of labour with at least a university degree is more than double the comparable average share for Brazil (see Table 5.1).

*Table 5.1   Personnel in software companies, by schooling level*

|                                    | Software (%) | Brazil (%) |
| ---------------------------------- | ------------ | ---------- |
| Under 4 years                      | 1.0          | 9.5        |
| Full 4 years and under 8 years     | 4.1          | 24.7       |
| Full 8 years and under 11 years    | 11.6         | 26.5       |
| Full 11 years                      | 36.6         | 25.2       |
| Incomplete university studies      | 19.1         | 3.8        |
| BA and above                       | 27.6         | 10.4       |
| Total                              | 100.0        | 100.0      |

*Source*:   RAIS database (2001).

*Table 5.2   Distribution of staff by company size*

| Number of staff | Formally employed | | Cumulative |
| --------------- | ----- | ---- | ---------- |
|                 | Total | %    | %          |
| Under 5         | 5543  | 12.1 | 14.6       |
| 5 to 9          | 4421  | 9.7  | 21.8       |
| 10 to 19        | 5308  | 11.6 | 33.4       |
| 20 to 49        | 8008  | 17.5 | 50.8       |
| 50 to 99        | 4736  | 10.3 | 61 ?       |
| 100 to 249      | 4532  | 9.9  | 71.1       |
| 250 to 499      | 2294  | 5.0  | 76.1       |
| 500 to 999      | 3837  | 8.4  | 84.5       |
| 1000 +          | 7110  | 15.5 |            |

*Source*:   RAIS database (2001).

The sector is populated by small firms – a third of the labour force is employed by companies with fewer than 20 staff, half by companies with under 50 staff; and three-quarters by companies with under 500 staff (see Table 5.2). The labour force is mostly very young. Almost two-thirds of the labour force is under 30 years of age and almost 90 per cent of it is under 40 years of age. Female workers make up 37 per cent of the labour force of software companies and are relatively homogeneously distributed in terms of schooling. There remains a striking absence of foreign workers in the industry. This dearth of foreigners suggests that the sector has been weakly linked to the global software industry, and thus to potential demand abroad for Brazilian software services.

## 5.4 BRAZILIAN SOFTWARE: A PROFILE

The last publicly available software census effort was carried out in 2000-2001 and encompassed all Softex members. Membership of Softex tends to be limited to companies active in software development, publishing or distributing, as well as those developing software for their own use, and may not be comprehensive in its inclusion of companies with fewer than six employees. As such, it cannot be taken as an entirely accurate indicator of the breadth of Brazilian IT activities. Nonetheless, Softex does have data on 699 companies with a total employment of around 67 000 people.[13] This dataset provides a broad picture of the software industry in Brazil.

*Table 5.3  Distribution of companies by staff*

| **Rank** | No. of staff | No. of companies | % |
|----------|--------------|------------------|-----|
| Micro | 1 to 5 | 123 | 17.9 |
| | 6 to 9 | 123 | 17.9 |
| Small | 10 to 49 | 287 | 41.7 |
| Medium | 50 to 99 | 67 | 9.7 |
| Large | 100 to 500 | 68 | 9.9 |
| | over 500 | 21 | 3.0 |
| Total | | 689 | 100.0 |

*Source*:  Software census Softex (2001).

Two-thirds of all 699 companies came into existence after 1991, at about the time the hardware sector lost much of its protection. The software sector is thus relatively new, and it is not surprising that over three-quarters of Softex members are still quite small, being staffed by fewer than 50 people (see Table 5.3). Almost 60 per cent of all companies develop packaged software or develop software for third parties. Significantly, only 12 per cent claimed packaged software development to be their only activity. This lack of specialisation holds for all areas of software development in Brazil. For example, although 10 per cent of companies develop software that will be embodied in hardware devices, the share drops to 1.7 per cent when the same companies are asked whether that was their only software development activity. One-third of the companies claimed to develop software for their own use, but only 2.8 per cent declared that to be their only software development activity (see Table 5.4). [14] While some software developers seem to be organised for meeting software demand by other sectors (57 per cent), only 5 per cent develop software exclusively for third parties. Something similar seems to be the case for the Internet-oriented software developers: less than 3 per cent make their living exclusively from developing software for the Internet.

*Table 5.4  Type of role in software-related activities*

| Type of activity | No. of replies | % of replies |
|---|---|---|
| Packages | 413 | 59.10 |
| Customised | 400 | 57.20 |
| Embodied | 71 | 10.20 |
| Develops software – Internet related | 289 | 41.30 |
| Develops software – own use | 233 | 33.30 |
| Publishes or distributes third-party software | 117 | 16.70 |
| Neither develops nor distributes software | 60 | 8.60 |
| Total number of replies | 1583 | |

*Source*:   Software census Softex (2001).

The lack of specialisation amongst Brazilian software companies has had implications for participation in export markets. Without a clearly defined area of expertise, it is hard for a software company to develop products that it would be capable of servicing abroad, were they exported.

Software sales in 2001 of the 30 largest software-developing companies active in Brazil amounted to $2.1 billion.[15] Most estimates suggest that $200 million a year has probably been the ceiling for all software exports in 2001. In that case, total software exports for 2001 still amounted to less than 10 per cent of the total domestic sales for the top 30 software companies. Exports as a share of all domestic software sales are likely to have been closer to 5 per cent. In short, Brazilian software remains a domestic-oriented industry in a rapidly internationalising economy.

In the context of the domestic market, there has been a clear tendency for greater penetration by foreign firms, not least because software needs to blend with the software solutions used worldwide by foreign investors in Brazil. One estimate – by the Brazilian Association of Software Developers (ASSESPRO) – suggests that the market share of Brazilian companies in the sales of the largest 50 companies dropped by half between 1995 and 2000.

*Table 5.5  Software houses included in Brazil's 200 largest IT companies*

| Company ($'000) | Sales ($ '000) | Research investment in Brazil ($ '000) | R&D as share of sales | Sales per employee ($ '000) | Country of world headquaters |
|---|---|---|---|---|---|
| Microsoft | 438 600 | n.a. | n.a. | 1566 | American |
| Broadvision | 413 916 | n.a. | 12.5 | 180 | American |
| Computer Ass. | 260 000 | n.a. | n.a. | 722 | American |
| Oracle | 227 156 | n.a. | n.a. | 284 | American |
| Consist | 138 136 | n.a. | n.a. | 230 | American |
| SAP Brazil | 127 903 | n.a. | n.a. | 284 | German |
| Datamec | 105 214 | n.a. | n.a. | 126 | Brazilian |
| Integris | 57 309 | n.a. | n.a. | 168 | French |
| DBA | 53 772 | 1450 | 2.7 | 50 | Brazilian |
| Datasul | 43 803 | 4257 | n.a. | 320 | Brazilian |
| Sybase Brazil | 27 801 | n.a. | n.a. | 352 | American |
| Peoplesoft | 26 712 | n.a. | n.a. | 119 | American |
| Everysystems | 25 346 | n.a. | n.a. | 72 | Brazilian |
| JD Edwards | 25 000 | n.a. | n.a. | 231 | American |
| Novell | 22 800 | n.a. | n.a. | 415 | American |
| RM Sistemas | 21 580 | 2942 | 13.6 | 57 | Braziilan |
| Informix | 18 674 | n.a. | ``n.a. | 311 | American |
| Symantec DO | 17 500 | n.a. | n.a. | 625 | American |
| Sterling Comm. | 15 073 | n.a. | n.a. | 457 | American |
| Network Assoc. | 14 381 | n.a. | n.a. | 436 | American |
| Modulo ATT/PS | 13 364 | 3518 | 26.3 | 51 | Brazilian |
| Informatica | 12 901 | 1028 | n.a. | 72 | Brazilian |
| Progress | 10 120 | n.a. | n.a. | 215 | American |
| Procenge | 7460 | 155 | 2.1 | 52 | Brazilian |
| Thru Put Do Brzl | 7001 | n.a. | n.a. | 184 | American |
| PL Alcoran Inf. | 6770 | 225 | 3.3 | 31 | Brazilian |
| Sispro | 5894 | 313 | 5.3 | 27 | Brazilian |
| BRQ | 5662 | n.a. | n.a. | 19 | Brazilian |
| I2 Technologies | 5600 | n.a. | n.a. | 311 | American |
| Cetil Sistemas | 5364 | 452 | 8.4 | 21 | Brazilian |
| Total | 2 104 780 | | | | |

Another estimate – by Info Exame – indicated that 18 foreign software developers accounted for 87 per cent of domestic sales by the top 30 companies in 2000 (see Table 5.5), with a dozen Brazilian companies accounting for the rest. Further, average sales per employee among foreign-owned software developers approached $400 000, as against $70 000 for their Brazilian counterparts. Only four foreign companies posted sales per employee below the overall sample average of $197 000, while only one Brazilian company posted sales per employee above the sample average.[16]

## 5.5 BRAZIL: A NETWORKED ECONOMY

Brazil is one of the four most networked economies in Latin America, according to the Harvard Networked Economy Index (see Table 5.6).[17] Network readiness is measured according to the availability of telecommunications infrastructure, connectivity to the global economy, the accessibility and affordability of the network to the domestic users, and the degree to which the network itself is adequately maintained. As such, Brazil ranks thirty-eighth in a world ranking of network readiness, but only fifty-fourth in public access to the Internet. This is partly due to the high average cost of dial-up and broadband access. Taking income differences into account to reflect the relative effort of each country in achieving network preparedness,[18] Brazil rose to the top of the Latin American ranking in 2001.

*Table 5.6   Comparative drive towards networked economy, 2001*

|            | Harvard's NEI (2001) | Country's Drive Index |
|------------|:--------------------:|:---------------------:|
| Argentina  | 3.71                 | 0.5                   |
| Brazil     | 4.01                 | 1.3                   |
| Chile      | 3.80                 | 0.8                   |
| Mexico     | 3.57                 | 0.6                   |
| Uruguay    | 3.67                 | 0.7                   |

*Note*:   Harvard's NEI was divided by the World Bank's 2001 estimate for each country's income per capita in thousand dollar units.

A key feature has been that the Brazilian government has also been intent on deepening PC penetration and Internet connectivity, with a target of reaching 13 000 schools and over 7 million students by 2003. The public postoffice system promotes Internet kiosks at over 5 000 selected point-of-use sites and the government is planning to offer every Brazilian an e-mail address. These initiatives are supported by NGOs, which offer access points and training in low-income neighbourhoods. Private for-profit initiatives offering Internet kiosks at convenience stores and bakeries provide further accessibility.

Increasing accessibility is not the only government target. Brazil is the Latin American leader in e-government and twentieth in the world ranking. The government provides most federal services to the public over the Internet, and the federal government has engaged in e-procurement, opening government purchases to small and medium-sized companies. State governments are rapidly following suit.

This publicly-sponsored drive towards a highly networked Brazilian economy exists despite a low penetration of PCs per household (10.6 per cent of Brazilian households have a PC). PCs, and even Internet access, remain unaffordable to a large part of the population.

While 50 per cent of upper income households have PCs, they are present in only 4.8 per cent of the lower income households. Moreover, 20 hours of monthly Internet access in Brazil, as a share of income per capita, comes at nearly eight times the cost in the USA and over twice the comparable cost in Argentina and Uruguay.[19] Nonetheless, there is enough Internet 'piggy-backing' to suggest that Internet use exceeds 10 million.

Despite this low PC penetration and high cost of Internet access, e-commerce has flourished in Brazil. The International Data Corporation estimates that e-commerce in Brazil had reached $5.3 billion in 2001 on a rising trend.

E-commerce involves more than just taking orders electronically and has required major streamlining of managerial procedures. As such, e-commerce is a valuable indicator of overall software use, since the requisite streamlining relies on use of enterprise resource planning software. In 2001 the 100 most active e-transaction providers of Brazil recorded close to $23 billion in sales, almost twice as much as in 2000.

Business to business e-transactions accounted for $4.5 billion in 2001, almost $2 billion by Ford alone (see Table 5.7). Intel sales are entirely executed over the Internet, a feat still to be achieved by its American headquarters. Business to consumer transactions are, however, less established (see Table 5.8). Automotive sales accounted for almost $490 million in 2001, while about $120 million were e-purchases by individual customers. E-commerce requires a substantial physical infrastructure to work (both digital and organisational), and the lack of adequate expertise is also a big constraint to the faster development of B2C e-commerce in a country as large as Brazil. Nonetheless, Brazilian software developers and technicians have significantly contributed to achieving an impressive growth of e-sales.

Brazilian banking automation also enabled a quick transition to e-banking in the mid-1990s. This was in part a response to the loss of float revenue stemming from lower inflation rates. The low value of average Brazilian transactions also put pressure on banks to reduce operational costs by promoting e-transactions. The results have been an impressive growth in e-banking, nearly two-thirds of which was accounted for by the three largest Brazilian banks – Banco do Brasil, Bradesco and Itaú.

*Table 5.7   B2B largest nine operators, 2001*

|                      | Activity             | $ millions |
|----------------------|----------------------|-----------:|
| Ford                 | Cars                 | 1,921      |
| Mercado Eletrônico   | e-marketplace        | 833        |
| Intel                | Computers            | 688        |
| Genexis              | e-marketplace        | 500        |
| Cisco                | Computing            | 499        |
| Porto Seguro         | Insurance prepaid    | 325        |
| Grupo VR             | Restaurant           | 250        |
| Itau Seguros         | Insurance            | 202        |
| Ticket Servicos      | Services             | 201        |
| Nine largest         |                      | 5419       |

*Source*:   Info Exame, May 2002, pp 69-70.

*Table 5.8   B2C largest ten operators, 2001*

|                   |            | $ millions |
|-------------------|------------|-----------:|
| General Motors    | Automotive | 435        |
| Mercado Livre     | Auctions   | 78         |
| Carsale           | Automotive | 38         |
| Americanas.com    | Retail     | 30         |
| Submarino         | Retail     | 30         |
| Itautec Philco    | Computers  | 21         |
| Magazine Luiza    | Retail     | 20         |
| Lokau.com         | Auctions   | 19         |
| Ford              | Automotive | 16         |
| Ponto Frio        | Retail     | 16         |
| Ten largest       |            | 703        |

*Source*:   Info Exame, May (2002: 68).

## 5.6 UNDERSTANDING BRAZIL'S EXPORT PERFORMANCE

Thus far, the domestic market, as illustrated by the achievements in e-government and e-business, has provided substantial opportunities for Brazilian companies, despite the increasing encroachment of international software companies into the domestic market.

The official response to Brazil's failure to export was guided by Softex. Picking likely international winners in 1992 would have been a daunting task, even with such a small number of companies. Yet, at its inception, Softex indicated a target of $2 billion in software exports by 2000. The actual figure for all software exports was only $100 million! What went wrong? In retrospect, the problem stemmed from the fact that Softex was not client-led. Rather Softex put its efforts behind pushing what was available. Much of what was available was in turn developed either in imitation of foreign software or developed to address local business problems.

If Softex's efforts had been based more around Brazil's strengths – fast, low-cost competence in software coding – the effort might have been less of a failure. But Softex authorities assumed that the foreign market would readily accept what Brazil was offering its domestic market. When this did not happen, Softex assumed the resistance was due to lack of information. As a result, Brazil began to invest public funds in software branding.

By 1997, Softex had spent nearly $3 million taking 117 Brazilian software developers to nine international fairs. This was a significant effort, given that Softex's budget to support all of its 14 nuclei or incubators in Brazil during the period 1993-1995 stood at just over $2 million.[20]

This network of incubators was Softex's primary focus, and their market orientation is a reflection on Softex's own lack of attention to client need. Certainly, the focus should have been strong, as incubators are supposed to take ideas that cater to the market. One telling indicator to the contrary is that, compared with the responses of head-hunters to questions about their main areas of focus for IT personnel, incubators supported by Softex were developing services for less than half of the areas indicated.[21]

The relative absence – or weakness – of focus on clients has been reflected more widely in the Brazilian software industry. Yet, as Box 5.1 and Box 5.2 suggest – there are examples of Brazilian firms being able to forge strong market-driven strategies.

BOX 5.1 CODE ASSOCIATES

With tight deadlines, for a fixed price, and with a two-year free maintenance guarantee, the Code Associates Solution Centre offers software development in São Paulo. Code Associates have made this sales stance their competitive edge after learning from experience that customers may not know how to define the software solution they want or need.

Code Associates expends considerable effort training clients both to specify their demands and to learn the constraints under which developers work out solutions to the clients' problems. This client-led and cost-conscious approach to software development led Code Associates to focus on careful budgeting and quality process controls based on CMM2 and ISO 9001 procedures. This attitude is at the core of their ability to offer a fixed price, to observe a deadline, and to offer a quality guarantee.

Code Associates believes that their offer is a strong incentive for potential clients to link up with them despite the fact that they are a relatively small firm. Code Associates, at its peak, employed 125 programmers. Code Associates has also partnered with the computing department of a prestigious local university both to secure competent manpower, and to ensure that they remain abreast of technological innovations.

Code Associates is one example of a company making its business model out of strong client orientation. The company offers, not only to deliver for a fixed fee and by an agreed deadline, but also to stand behind its product by offering free adjustments if necessary. Yet, translating their domestic success into an international one has proven difficult. Code Associates has associated with an international consulting group, but has not managed to secure any strategic partners.

BOX 5.2 MICROSIGA AND DATASUL

The two largest Brazilian software houses active in ERP have been Microsiga and Datasul. Microsiga, has a network of franchises and develops software solutions on demand. Its main product is an ERP for small and medium-sized companies. The Microsiga Institute also aims to support software developers in upgrading ideas to a marketable stage. Through its institute, Microsiga learns of new needs and new talents, and, by supplying them with its systems, extends its reach into new markets.

The Microsiga Institute's Latin American Developer project, supported by Microsiga's many partners, helps to bring to fruition the ideas of Latin American start-ups. Relatively large start-ups (under $1 million in sales) submit their ideas to Microsiga's institute in exchange for help in developing them. Microsiga has sustained a network of value added resellers (VARs) in several Latin American countries and Puerto Rico. These VARs find the clients, and Microsiga develops solutions for them in Brazil.

Datasul – a company with an annual turnover of over $50 million a year – has tried to shift into export markets but as yet exports account for no more than 5 per cent of revenues. Microsiga grew around Ernesto Haberkorn, who initiated SIGA software (1969) which sought to integrate administrative and financial costs in a one-stop managerial software. With the advent of microcomputers in 1983, Microsiga grew to account for almost 50 per cent of the Brazilian market in small and medium-sized companies willing to pay for a home-grown ERP software. Since 1998 Microsiga also offers solutions for departments of larger companies. Microsiga has also made inroads into automating commercial ventures. As such, this has led to rapid growth in sales – over 40 per cent per annum – and in employment, now over 800 employees. Much of this expansion has been achieved through franchising. Microsiga has opened 35 regional offices. In 1998 it opened its first representative office abroad, in Argentina.

---

Datasul and Microsiga's strategies for gaining access to foreign markets clearly require a certain scale and as such are not available to the smaller domestic players. But although smaller companies without as clear a client orientation as Datasul and Microsiga may have difficulty competing internationally, some may have a distinct product that, although developed for the domestic market, fills a niche, or has advanced qualities capable of attracting the interest of foreign clients.

One such example is Modulo, a company that has a strong base in Brazil providing security for large computer networks – including the computerisation of the Brazilian elections. Modulo has opened offices in the USA and had sales of around $1 million in 2002. It also aims to expand in other Latin American markets. Similarly a number of other Brazilian companies have been successful in attracting foreign clients through niche strategies. Eversystems offers software products to foreign banks; Epsoft, has sold voice recognition services to Japanese banks, and Sira Informatica has been selling environmental and agricultural software in China. Another company – Cyclades – has migrated to Silicon Valley, so that the Brazil market accounts for only 25 per cent of its communication hardware sales. Automatos also moved to California, but undertakes its Management Service Provider software development in Brazil, where it keeps 95 per cent of its staff. Automatos's non-Brazilian market now accounts for around half its revenues. All of these companies had an established record of niche home sales before they moved abroad.

## 5. 7  BUSINESS ENVIRONMENT AND IMPACT ON SOFTWARE INDUSTRY

Brazil ranks as the tenth largest industrial economy in the world. Its manufacturing industry sits atop a substantial telecommunications network and other infrastructure. Brazilian software developers thus have a significant testing ground for software designed to raise productivity. Nonetheless, the most pressing industry needs may have to do more with Brazil's business environment than with industrial processes. While technology may be similar in Brazil and abroad, the business environment certainly is not, and software developed to solve Brazilian problems may not be attractive abroad.

The business environment has had an impact in a variety of ways (see Box 5.3 on Loja Fácil). Piracy has continued to be a major problem impeding investment in software products. Further, funding options have been effectively limited. Although Brazil has an array of business lines of credit, some effectively subsidised and rationed and offered by official development banks such as BNDES, gaining access to these funding sources is often sufficiently complex to rule it out for the smaller software houses. Further, software entrepreneurs, with little collateral, have also been shut out of commercial bank loans.

---

BOX 5.3 LOJA FÁCIL

Loja Fácil is a software product catering for the management of small shops with approximately 600 sq feet of floor selling space. The software controls sales, revenues and some inventory operations. It is cheap and it works. It has 2000 clients, mostly in São Paulo shopping centres. The product sells for under $200 or is licensed at $32 per month. Ninety per cent of Loja Fácil customers choose the latter, which grants effective technical support. The product could easily sell in other Brazilian states, were it not for the tax-evasion law in some states, which holds the software developer accomplice to the crime if the software is misused with the purpose of evading taxes. According to the entrepreneur who developed and markets the software, the fines are too steep and the judicial procedures too complex to run the risk of being an accomplice to a crime it cannot fully prevent from happening. This is one way that the business environment can halt the modernisation of a small enterprise and dissuade an entrepreneurial software developer from investing further in making its software cover a greater geographical area.

However, the peculiarities of the Brazilian business environment have not always been a disadvantage for local companies. Three decades marked by episodes of high inflation induced domestic banks to deal with interest bearing current accounts, to adapt to an uncertain macroeconomic and regulatory environment as well as provide banking services appropriate to a high inflation context.[22] This led them to design robust and flexible banking automation software.[23] For example, retaining customers during a period of high inflation in the early 1980s required interest bearing current accounts, a practice not allowed by banking regulations at the time. So commercial banks found a way out: they would borrow from clients overnight, and lend those funds out in the secondary market for government bonds. Such operations required efficient software as these transactions, being commonly small and numerous, could not be handled quickly enough by bank clerks. For this and other reasons, the Brazilian financial system became highly automated, and, as bank staff grew familiar with technology, a technologically advanced elite grew within the banks. As a result, Brazilian banks were able to convert early and smoothly to Internet banking. As banks grew through consolidation, the Internet helped them reduce operating costs. By 2001, ten Brazilian banks performed Internet-based transactions amounting to nearly $15 billion, a quarter of which was undertaken by the largest bank, Banco do Brasil. Bradesco and Itaú, accounted for a further 36 per cent, while the leading foreign bank, HSBC, accounted for 10 per cent.

Besides shaping the relationship of banks with their customers, the technical solutions adopted by these banks has helped to shape the relationship between the banks themselves as well as with clearing houses and the Central Bank. The outcome of these closer relationships has been the Brazilian Payments System, a system by which banking transactions get cleared in real time across the country, and which became effective in July 2002. This has required fully linking almost 17 000 branches, almost 7000 points of customer services, and the whole network of ATMs.[24]

Brazil's business environment thus led to a flexibility in Brazilian banking software that could be potentially attractive in foreign markets. Indeed the two largest private Brazilian banks – Bradesco and Itaú – have developed strong in-house software development facilities. But while both of these banks own the software and have not lacked the financial resources to market it abroad, neither have done so.

In the case of Bradesco and Itaú, their software houses have been captive. They have the software development capability, but it is institutionally tied to banks that due to their market positions have remained highly profitable and appear not to have viewed marketing their software as part of their core business.

Yields in the private banking sector have remained consistently high. Net returns have averaged over 23 per cent on their own capital and yield profits well over $550 million a year. In-house software developers have been discouraged from trying to expand sales abroad. The banks' vertical integration has stifled the commercial aggressiveness of their captive software houses.

## 5.8 HUMAN CAPITAL AND AVAILABILITY OF SKILLS

For all its flaws, the market reserve policy did provide an incentive for developing local IT capacity. Over time this has been complemented by major public investment in IT. One consequence has been that IT-related education has burgeoned. By 1999 there were over 14 000 students graduating with IT degrees, over three times the number graduating in 1991.[25] Post-secondary non-university degrees have also provided a minimum of IT skills that companies can build on with in-house training. These come in three categories: The 'Basic IT' and 'IT Technologist' courses require between 2000 and 3000 hours of training, and there is also a 'Technologist' course, which involves 1000 hours of technical courses. Most schools offer the Technologist diploma during the last two years of secondary education, but all three courses are available as post-secondary education. Figure 5.2 suggests that by the end of the 1990s the supply of such education may have outstripped demand as indicated by the diminishing ratio of applications to entries.

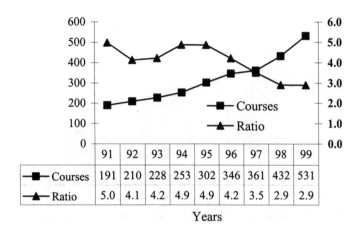

| | 91 | 92 | 93 | 94 | 95 | 96 | 97 | 98 | 99 |
|---|---|---|---|---|---|---|---|---|---|
| —■— Courses | 191 | 210 | 228 | 253 | 302 | 346 | 361 | 432 | 531 |
| —▲— Ratio | 5.0 | 4.1 | 4.2 | 4.9 | 4.9 | 4.2 | 3.5 | 2.9 | 2.9 |

Years

*Figure 5.2 Number of IT courses offered and ratio of candidates per opening*

The picture is less positive at the post-graduate level,[26] relatively few post-graduates are produced by the Brazilian educational system. One implication of this is the relative absence of high-end software personnel, such as conceptualisers. It is the conceptualisers who provide the interface between the problem and the coders, helping to define the problem, structure it in modules, and translate it to an algorithm that the coders can work on. Moreover, the relative lack of highly trained local IT personnel cannot readily be supplemented by Brazilians studying abroad. The number of Brazilian students of Science and Engineering in the USA has remained small.[27] Indeed, while over two thirds of graduate students from India and China study science and engineering, only 30 per cent of a much smaller cohort of Brazilians do the same (see Figure 5.3). A rough estimate suggests that between 10 and 15 per cent of Brazilian PhDs abroad study computer science or related subjects. Finally, the relatively low exposure in foreign training has the wider consequence of further limiting access to international experience and markets.

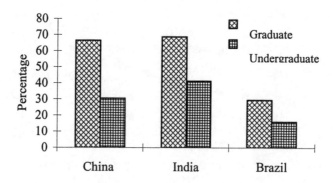

*Figure 5.3   Percentage of science and engineering degrees by country of birth*

What have been the labour market outcomes in the IT sector? One key indicator is the evolution of monthly wages, denominated in US dollars, for the IT sector in São Paulo. Figure 5.4 provides this information for seven IT professional categories between 1994 and 2001. Data related to the last week of June and December for each year and are compiled by the Folha de S. Paulo drawing on responses by 160 companies. The categories reported include a director/manager level position, one technical IT support position, and three degrees of seniority (junior, full and senior) for two different levels of specialisation within the rank and file of IT: systems analysts and programmers.

The data show that the dollar earnings of all categories of IT professionals increased during much of the period, not least as a consequence of an overvalued exchange rate. They subsequently lost ground as that policy was reversed. This wage path is true for all categories except for the entry-level positions. Wage differences across skill groups increased over the reference period. For example, the gap between managerial level IT professionals and junior programmers was significantly larger at the end of the period. Further, wages for other professional services, such as lawyers, appreciated more than those of junior software personnel (see Figure 5.5). Given the evolution of IT wages, particularly for new entrants, this has been reflected in declining enrolments in IT courses.

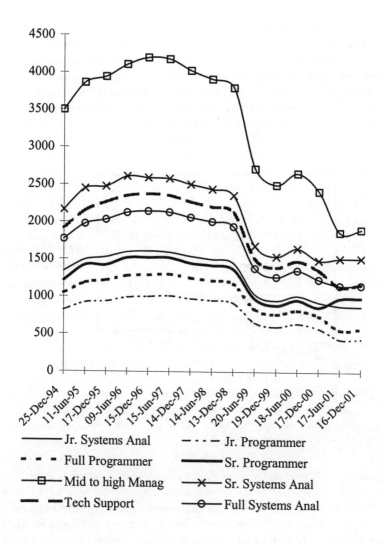

*Figure 5.4 Monthly wage (US$) for selected IT labour categories in metropolitan São Paulo*

## 5.9 FUNDING OF SOFTWARE PROJECTS

Throughout the first half of the 1990s funding opportunities for Brazilian companies – particularly smaller ones - were limited. Loans from financial institutions were generally not available to software firms with little collateral. Further, Brazil has had little tradition of venture capitalism and even less experience with angel investors, beyond immediate family members.[28] In this restrictive financial environment, it has been difficult for fledgling companies to fund themselves unless they were working for a client willing to incur some of the development costs.

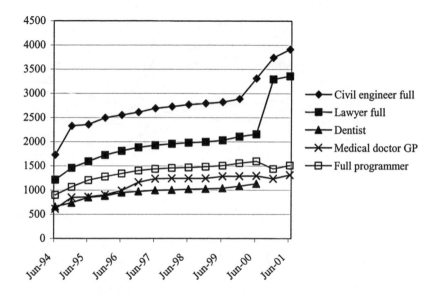

*Figure 5.5  Wage structure over time, current monthly wages in Reals*

There is some evidence that in the second half of the 1990s access to a variety of sources of finance grew quite significantly. A sample of 50 firms found that nearly a third had access to venture capital, business angels or special funds geared towards product development. Interestingly, 40 per cent reported receiving funds from government.[29] In this period, the Brazilian government has attempted to provide a greater flow of public resources for the sector. This has involved use of three instruments: grants, loans and equity investment. These were channelled through three institutions: CNPQ, FINEP and BNDES. The first, CNPQ has been closely linked to the

Brazilian scientific community and has supported academic research through grants and scholarships. FINEP has been Brazil's main agency for funding technology. Uniquely, its mandate allows it to support all phases of an innovative process, including its commercial distribution. BNDES – Brazil's Economic and Social Development Bank – has traditionally funded large enterprises and infrastructure. More recently it has also funded privatisation programmes and has expanded its investments in social areas. BNDESPAR is BNDES' equity funding agency

In the case of the CNPQ, grants did not go directly to the companies. They were first given to the Softex nuclei to fund their operating costs and the services provided to the software developers. The funds were then reallocated to the individual companies. CNPQ funding was planned for the first three years of operation of each Softex nucleus, and increased over this period (Table 5.9). Over the first three years, the total disbursed by CNPQ was $13.9 million. During the period from 1993-1995, the companies received nearly 90 per cent of funding. The average funding for each company was a little more than $20 000 over three years. In general these were small companies, over half of them having turnover of $100 000 to $1 million per annum.

*Table 5.9 Distribution (%) of CNPq funds between software developers and their Softex host nucleus, 1993-1995*

| Year of operation | Developers | Nuclei | USD$ Total |
|---|---|---|---|
| First | 81.1 | 18.9 | 2 196 803 |
| Second | 86.8 | 13.2 | 4 366 627 |
| Third | 91.9 | 8.1 | 7 294 907 |
| Average | 88.6 | 11.4 | 4 619 446 |

*Source*: Based on Funcex data p.93-94.

In the case of FINEP, in 1997 it offered around $23 million in a Softex programme called Call for National Software (CNS). The CNPq pledged a further $5.5 million with which the selected companies could repay at the subsidised interest rate to FINEP. No real collateral was required, there was a 12-month grace period, and the principal was to be repaid in two years. For the first time Brazilian software was being offered substantial risk capital.[30] As a result, 350 companies expressed interest in CNS of which 185 pursued the matter further. Ultimately, 40 software developers were selected; $24 million was allocated by FINEP and CNPq with an average disbursement of $450 000 – a substantial increase over funding hitherto provided by Softex. Interestingly, two-thirds had never taken part in Softex activities. This was a group of more mature companies with higher average turnover and employment.

As there was no collateral requirement, FINEP required a credit insurance fund, which Softex was unable to provide. Eventually, Brazil's small and medium-sized enterprise support organisation (SEBRAE) was brought in to provide the necessary funding. This added a new constraint for the project: SEBRAE would not collaborate with companies with over 100 employees, and it required 8 per cent of all disbursements to be set aside for the credit insurance fund. Furthermore, SEBRAE would only accept 90 per cent of this risk. These conditions meant that 15 per cent of the pre-selected companies had to be left out. The experience with funding was, however, very mixed. Many firms lacked commercial acumen and ability to deploy resources effectively. In terms of exports, a year after inception, SNC applicants were exporting only 33 US cents on each dollar invested and they never attained the ratio of 6:1 envisaged by Softex over a five-year period. FINEP subsequently adopted a policy of funding those who wanted software developed for them, rather than the developers themselves.[31]

A further attempt at motivating export-oriented software development was made in 1998 by BNDES. An alternative fund – PROSOFT – was established with an endowment of $25 million. The aim was to fund up to 85 per cent of the needs of software projects for companies with clear export goals. BNDES's PROSOFT operations fell under the scope of small and medium-sized enterprises and were limited to companies with yearly sales under $15 million. The grace period could be as much as two years, with six years for the repayment of the principal.[32] The loans could not exceed $2 million, or be less than $150 000 – in reality, no loan was under $600 000. The funding was operated through Softex. By November 2001 there were 17 approved operations with a total disbursement of $12 million.

Finally, earlier difficulties had led FINEP to look for other ways to support Brazilian software. In July 2000, FINEP became one of the founding members of the Brazilian Association for Venture Capital, which had mobilised over $2 billion by the end of 2000 and invested nearly $750 million. However, only 1 per cent – just under $8 million – had gone to the software sector.[33] Telecommunications received 34 per cent, new media 20 per cent, and e-commerce, 8 per cent of the investments. By mid-2002, 39 of the 69 members of the Brazilian Association for Venture Capital were private equity funds and venture capital funds. fifteen of these were aimed at sponsoring the type of risk investment suitable for technology companies. One recent initiative has been the launch of SPTec, a $10 million venture capital fund aimed at technology companies in the state of São Paulo.

In conclusion, publicly-sponsored funding for Brazilian software development has had decidedly mixed consequences. Softex's initial efforts through CNPq amounted to some $5 million a year, a figure that increased twentyfold when FINEP agreed to participate in the CNS programme in 1997. Softex talked BNDES into the business, but only 17 projects met the operational guidelines for the $20 million that BNDES had earmarked. A venture capital market brokered by FINEP started with $2 billion in the year 2000, but they only risked $8 million in software ventures. Thus, for almost a decade, third-party investment in Brazilian software development has hovered at around $10 million per year. Despite an increase in the number of projects, and an increasing participation by the private sector, funding for Brazilian software has remained quite limited.

## 5.10 THE PROBLEM OF PIRACY

As a share of all pirated products sold in Brazil, software piracy has remained relatively small, accounting for around 2 per cent of total software sales. Nonetheless, for a software developer the issue is of paramount importance, as it is widely believed that a very significant share of software products in use in Brazil are pirated copies of a paid-for original. Thus, the Brazilian software developer contends not only with other competitors but also with its own pirated product, sold for a little above the cost of reproducing a CD. The government's efforts to curb piracy have been limited and it has been left to the industry associations to promote legal action against piracy.[34] Software developers have also responded by producing software that requires toll-access to databases or keys, and even by the release of flawed software that requires additional and charged assistance to correct.

In addition to fighting piracy, some software companies also have to contend with a form of 'dumping' by competitors. The term is used to describe the practice of circulating software at a price that reflects the cost of making it available to a target market, but does not include the costs of development and marketing. The case of LNQ (see Box 5.4) is illustrative of the consequences that software companies can suffer from piracy and unfair pricing.

---

BOX 5.4 THE CASE OF LNQ

LNQ originally had a mainframe and CADCAM selling background. By the mid-1990s, the PC and associated lower-priced software were making a dent in LNQ's market. Seeing that its future lay in lower-cost software designed for PCs, they identified a niche for themselves in the Brazilian CAD market in the form of architectural design software. To that end,

LNQ established cooperation with an Argentine software developer and created a division to distribute the software at $1000 a copy. This link brought the Argentine developer closer to clients in one of Latin America's largest and fastest growing markets. The arrangement also allowed LNQ to develop conceptualising capabilities that were then passed on to the Argentine developer in exchange for informal discounts on purchases of the software. By 1995 this software accounted for 10 per cent of LNQ's sales. But despite this promising start, LNQ's profits were hard hit both by piracy and by competition from another firm, AutoCAD. Piracy gave Brazilian consumers access to LNQ architectural software for under $20 a copy. However35 AutoCAD, which was developed by Autodesk, sold to mid-sized to large companies for $4000 a copy. Illicit Software piracy by smaller companies or individuals36 helped to ensure AutoCAD became the professional standard in Brazil. In response, by 1998 LNQ had begun to discount their software, initially down to $500, and shortly thereafter to $300 a copy. But even at lower rates LNQ continued to lose market share. LNQ then responded with a new strategy: reducing the price of their software to nil and seeking revenue through associated services sold through e-marketplaces, created by the company for architects, contractors and suppliers. For example, the software allowed architects to plan a house and list the requirements of all inputs. The building contractors and suppliers would then bid for the quotes asked by the architects through LNQ's site. LNQ's revenue would come from advertising on the site and from cuts in the sales made by suppliers and contractors.

LNQ invested up to $1 million to develop the site and create a network of associated suppliers. JP Morgan and local investment banks initially showed an interest in the project, but this evaporated after the technology crash of 2000. Local investment banks, also reduced their exposure to LNQ, and the project floundered. The combined challenge of piracy and the pricing strategy adopted by their main competitor had a seriously adverse impact.

## 5.11 CONCLUSION

This chapter has highlighted a significant – and perhaps surprising – underperformance by Brazil in the software sector. As such, this surprise is both a testimony to Brazil's domestic prowess in the field – such as in e-commerce, robotics or bank automation – and an indictment of Brazil's software export policy. Brazil's strength in domestic software might have been expected to lead to greater export exposure.

Why, then, has Brazil's international success failed to live up to its domestic promise? During much of the 1990s the domestic currency was substantially overvalued. The role of macroeconomic policy in drawing the largely domestic orientation of the Brazilian software industry also needs to be emphasised. More recently, post-2000, substantial depreciation of the currency has occurred and this could be helpful to a greater export orientation. This chapter has also argued that one important feature has been a lack of openness. Brazilian software developers have failed to familiarise themselves with foreign quality standards by studying abroad. Nor have Brazilians had the opportunity to learn such traits by working with expatriates in Brazil, as there are practically no foreigners formally employed in the Brazilian software industry. Limited proficiency in foreign languages, few connections abroad and little international travel have reinforced the sense of relative isolation. Entrepreneurs' lack of familiarity with foreign business circles has ultimately contributed to the failure of many software developers to focus effectively on meeting the needs of potential clients.

A related issue is the use of foreign labour. Remarkably few foreigners have been employed in the software sector. This appears in retrospect to be mainly a disadvantage. So far the brunt of official policy has been to send Brazilians out to scout, mostly at fairs. However, additional efforts could be diverted to motivating foreigners with appropriate skills to work in Brazil. That there was no effort even to think about the implications of such a policy is mostly the result of a siege mentality that has persisted.

This siege mentality can be traced back to the military dictatorship era. The strong and autarkic nature of official software policy in Brazil stemmed from an ideological preference. This resisted foreign cooperation and hampered Brazilian involvement in world markets. This stance has also affected the way software developers have been trained and incubated, not least their effective segregation from non-technologists. Breaking this pattern will be crucial for the healthy growth of the sector, both domestically and internationally.

Brazilian software developers have proven highly skilled in providing software solutions and networking the economy, but they have mostly failed at selling, even domestically where Brazilian firms have been losing market share. One facet of the problem lies in the lack of business skills among technologists. Merging or establishing strategic alliances with companies from other economies could help break the managerial deadlock and contribute to greater Brazilian software participation in international markets. These alliances may be hard to structure, but this policy could have been pursued at the very least by encouraging internships for Brazilian software developers in companies abroad.

Brazilian banks have been at the forefront of banking automation in the developing world and some of their software has even been a world leader – such as the open architecture software on which their Internet banking is based, and the associated security measures. Yet the banks' software houses have been deprived of the sales force to encourage management to reap the benefits of their software abroad. The technology managers in software houses are not even required to pay attention to the market, as their software companies are sized to the demand of their holding banks. At present, there is no incentive for banks to subcontract other software houses to try and take advantage of international opportunities. Software houses submerged in banking conglomerates are likely to remain stifled and ultimately lose competitiveness as a result. Unless these software houses are separated from their financial conglomerates there is little future for them.

Finally, a much overlooked area of Brazilian IT proficiency, which could be exported, is the knowledge of how to network a mid to low-income economy. Brazil has introduced a surprising level of networking for a developing country, and has excelled, despite income limitations, in making government, the private sector and NGOs have access to the Internet. E-commerce has flourished, despite regulatory setbacks. Other countries might welcome such knowledge and expertise, but there have been no signs of Brazilian consulting companies packaging this knowledge and making it available.

NOTES
1. Government policy has explicitly invited local manufacturing of computers since the 1950s. For a comprehensive review of players and intentions in the framing and development of the Brazilian IT policy see Jorge Ruben Biton, Tapia,: 'A trajetória da política de informática brasileira (1977-1991) atores, instituições e estratégias', PhD dissertation, University of Campinas, November 1993.
2. Schwartzman characterizes this phase as one of 'bureaucratic insulation' in which science policy decisions were made with little observation of formal peer review processes. S. Schwartzman, 'High Technology vs Self Reliance: Brazil enters the computer age' MIT Symposium on 'The Computer Question in Brazil', Cambridge, Mass. 18 April 1985.
3. The eccentric alliance of military, IT pioneers and managerial technocracy yielded a surprisingly innovative cadre of public employees. In the case of Telebrás, the former holding of state-owned telecommunication companies, the company recruited from the best management schools as well as in the top IT-oriented schools.
4. Data on software sales for this period is scant. Tapia (op. cit. p. 228), believes that software sales in Brazil in 1987 amounted to $624 million

and that 90 per cent of them were imports, leaving $62 million for local developers.

5. Law 8.248/91.
6. Local manufacturing was exempted, until 1999, of 15 per cent tax on industrialised products.
7. A bitter complaint reflected in 'Export IT, Brazil, an update', US Department of Commerce, July 2002, p. 5.
8. Decree No. 1.070/94.
9. Brazilian Society for the Promotion and Export of Software, Softex for the Brazilian acronym of Software Sociedade Brasileira para Promoção e Exportação de Software, created in 1992 and operational in 1993.
10. The list of the IT society represented in the Council of Softex includes CNPq, FINEP, ASSESSPRO (Brazilian software developers), ABES (mostly foreign software developers), SUCESU (veteran society of computer users), ABINEE (representing electro-electronic industry, including heavy industry), BNDES (national development bank), SEBRAE (technical support provider for small and medium enterprises) APEX (agency for export promotion) and SBC (Brazilian Computing Society).
11. The Brazilian Ministry of Labour and Employment, through the RAIS database, collects annual data on formally employed staff by all companies in the whole spectrum of economic activity, including 5.5 million companies. Those focused on software development and related consulting comprised 16 067 companies in 2001.
12. This wage rate is, however, a poor indicator of the hourly wage for an IT worker because the IT sector is more prone to hire staff under less formal agreements than old economy industries.
13. The Softex 2001 census is based on the reports of 699 companies of the 877 Softex members. The total employment reported by Softex is about 50per cent higher than the total formal employment figure rendered by official Ministry of Labour (RAIS) statistics, which focuses only on formally employed labour of all software and consulting companies. Preliminary results, on which these comments are based, can be found at: http://www.mct.gov.br/sepin/Dsi/CensoSW/censoSW2001.htm.
14. Many of those that produce software for their own use are large companies with large software developing units, such as banks. Some may also sell software to third parties, perhaps even packaged software but, by and large, they seem to be very different from the rest of Softex's membership.
15. Info Exame, number 185, 2001, actually posts the sales of the 200 largest IT companies, from which 30 software developers were selected for this study.
16. The staff numbers of the foreign companies include only those employed in Brazil. No foreign companies declared research expenses in Brazil. The total number of employees in that sample is 10 711.

17. Readiness for the Networked World, Harvard University's Center for International Development- study for the World Economic Forum. Harvard's NEI Index attempts to portray a community's degree of preparedness to take part in an interconnected world.
18. Harvard's NEI was divided by the World Bank's 2001 estimate for each country's income per capita.
19. Brazilian overall tax rate on telephone services, at 40.2 per cent, is two to three times higher than the tax burden in many neighbouring countries; in Ronaldo R de F. Mourão, 'Por que pagamos tão caro pela telefonia?' *Telebrasil*, June/July 2002: 46.
20. Funcex, p.93.
21. Desenvolvimento Estratégico em Informática. Project evaluation, UNDP, BRA/92/019, September 1999, p. 72.
22. Brazil's Efficient Payment System: A Legacy of High Inflation. Robert Listfield and Fernando Montes-Negret (November 1996) World Bank.
23. For example, the largest private bank – Bradesco – has an online client base third only to Bank of America and Wells Fargo.
24. Automação de serviços financeiros no Brasil, Economia e Tecnologia, 4(5) September 2001.
25. Course names changed over a decade, but BA courses whose graduates are contemplated here as undergraduate courses in IT are: Systems Analysis, Data Processing Management, Computer Science, Computing, Informatics, Data Processing, Computer Networks, Wireless Computing, Digital Technology and Telecommunications.
26. Jose Carlos Maldonado: Pos-Graduacão em Ciência de Computação no Brasil, Situação Atual. XXIst SBC conference, Fortaleza, CA, Brazil, 2001
27. National Science Foundation data for 1997/98, provided by Annalee Saxenian. Of the 9057 PhDs in Science and Engineering awarded to foreign students in the USA. in 2000, 126 went to Brazilians, 2358 went to Chinese nationals (People's Republic) and 821 to Indians.
28. Timid risk investment experiences began through BNDE initiatives in the early 1970s, but they were focused on industries within the import substitution model. During the 1980s Companhias de Participacão were the preferred risk-investment modality, but they were not focused on emerging technologies. Only the CVM normative instruction 209 of 1994 regulated the private risk-investment framework for investment in small technology-based companies. CVM stands for Commissão de Valores Mobiliários, with oversight attributions over the capital market similar to those of the America Securities Exchange Commission (SEC).
29. See Botelho et al. (2003).
30. Much of the information on FINEP's involvement with software was kindly provided by Paulo Tosta da Silva in a stimulating interview and subsequent e-mails during May 2002.
31. Desenvolvimento Estratégico em Informática, UNDP evaluation report, September 1999, BRA/92?019, p.82.
32. The guarantees for the loans were the shares of the companies, meaning that the beneficiaries had to transform themselves into a corporation and have their balance sheets audited, which would cost them about $6000 a year. Much of the

information on BNDES' PROSOFT was kindly provided by Carlos Castello Branco in an interview on 9 November 2001 and in many subsequent e-mails.

33. Of these, 78 per cent were late or expansion-building investments. Early phase investments accounted for 7 per cent. Ninety-eight per cent of the investments were made in the state of São Paolo

34. The Business Software Alliance sponsored 418 court actions against Brazilian users of pirated software in 2001. http:www.bas.org/brasil/press/newsreleases/ 2202-01-31.890.phtml, accessed on 4 March 2003.

35. According to FGV 13th survey (CIA/EASP) March 2002, AutoCAD then held 80% of the technical drawing market in Brazil. This survey draws data on over 2000 companies amongst which are 60 per cent of the largest in the country.

36. A Google search on 15 October 2002, for reporting on court sanctions regarding piracy of AutoCAD rendered only five non-independent cases.

# Bibliography

Access Asia Limited (2001), 'Computer software in China: a market analysis', Shanghai, China.

Acemoglu, D., P. Aghion and F. Zilibotti (2002), 'Distance to frontier, selection and economic growth', mimeo University College, London.

Alfassy, Y. (2001), 'ICQ fires 35 of 100 employees' Globes: Israel's Business Arena, 6 August, (www.globes.co.il)

Azulai, I., M. Lerner and A. Tishler (2002), 'Converting military technology through corporate entrepreneurship', *Research Policy*, **31**, 419-35.

Arora, A. and S. Athreye (2002), 'The software industry and India's economic development', *Information Economics and Policy*, **14**, 253-73.

Arora, A., V. Arunachalam, J. Asundi and R. Fernandes (2001), 'The Indian software services industry', *Research Policy*, **30**, 1267-87.

Arora, Ashish, V.S. Arunachalam, Jai Asundi and Ronald Fernandes (2000), 'The Indian software industry', mimeo, Carnegie Mellon University, Pittsburg.

Arora, A., J. Asundi, and R. Fernandes (2000), 'Supply and demand for software developers in India, mimeo, Carnegie Mellon, Pittsburgh.

Arora, A. and J. Asundi (1999), 'Quality certification and the economics of contract software: a study of the Indian software industry', NBER Working Paper 7260, Cambridge, Mass, July.

Banerji, A. and E. Duflo (1999), 'Indian software and the limits of contracting', *Quarterly Journal of Economics*, **115**(3), pp.989-1017.

Beenstock, M. and J. Fisher (1997), 'The macroeconomic effect of immigration: Israel in the 1990s', *Welwirtschaftliches Archiv*, **133**, 330-58.

Behrens, A. (2003), 'Brazilian software: the quest for an export strategy', mimeo, FECAP and London Business School, April.

Beijing Software Industry Promotion Center (2001), *Report of Beijing Software*.

Beine, M., F. Docquier and H. Rapoport (2001), 'Brain drain and economic growth: theory and evidence', *Journal of Development Economics*, **64**(1), 275-89.

Blackburn, N. (2001), 'The evolution of Compugen' The Jerusalem Post, 1 November, (www.jpost.co.il).

Bresnahan, T., A. Gambardella, and A. Saxenian (2001), 'Old economy inputs for new economy outcomes: cluster formation in the new silicon valleys', *Industrial and Corporate Change*, **10** (4), December, 833-60.

Breznitz, D. (2002) 'The military as a public space – The role of the IDF in the Israeli software innovation system,' mimeo, STE-WP-13-2002.

Brizendine, Thomas (2002), 'Software integration in China', *The China Business Review*, March-April, 26-31.

Business Wire (2002), 'Enterprise security, communication and entrepreneurial leaders join new Commtouch advisory board', 13 February, (www.businesswire.com).

CDAC (2003), Centre for Development of Advanced Computing. Param Padma, Poona, http://www.cdacindia.com/html/parampma.asp.

Center for the Future of China (2002), 'The future of China's software industry' *2002: China Five-Year Forecast*, Beijing/San Francisco.

China National Computer Software and Technology Service Corporation (CS&S) (2001), *Profile of CS&S*, http://www.css.com.cn/enhome/php.

CIEC (China International Economic Consultants Co.) (2001), 'Foreign venture capital granted access to Chinese market', *CIEC Economic Brief,* **169**, 17 September.

CMIE (Centre for Monitoring Indian Economy) (2003),. Prowess database (digital), Bombay.

Commander, S., M. Kangasniemi, and A. Winters (2004), 'The brain drain: curse or boon?', in R. Baldwin and L.A. Winters (eds), *Challenges to Globalization*, NBER and Chicago University Press.

Commander, S., M. Kangasniemi, and A. Winters (2003), 'A beneficial brain drain: the software industry', mimeo, London Business School and University of Sussex, May,.

Commtouch Form 20-F to the Securities and Exchange Commission (www.sec.gov).

CSIA (China Software Industry Association) (2001), *2000 Annual Report of China Software Industry*, Beijing.

CSIA (China Software Industry Association) (2003), *Introduction of China Software Industry Association*, www.csia.org/cn/chinese_en/about/about.htm, March.

D&A Directory (2002), Source: Israel Association of Electronics Industries, 2000-2002 include software Israel Association of Electronic Industries.

D&A Directory (multiple years 2000-2002), published by D&A Hi-Tech Information Ltd. Tel Aviv.

Dagoni, R. (1999), 'AOL deputy chair: Mirabilis acquisition improves our management culture' Globes: Israel's Business Arena, 29 September, (www.globes.co.il).

Dahlman, Carl J. and Jean-Eric Aubert (2001), *China and the Knowledge Economy: Seizing the 21st Century*, WBI Development Studies, Washington, DC: The World Bank

Davidson, R. (2000). 'FTC to look into AOL's ICQ-based control of instant messaging market', Globes: Israel's Business Arena, 15 June, (www.globes.co.il).

Desai, A. (2003), The dynamics of the Indian information technology industry, mimeo, London Business School, April.

DM Review (2003). 'Panorama moves into North American market' (www.dmreview.com).

Dvir, D. and A. Tishler (2000), 'The changing role of the defense industry in Israel's industrial and technological development', *Defense Analysis*, **16**(1) 33-52.

EFY Enterprises (2002), *IT directory 2001-02*, Delhi.

Evans, Peter (1992), 'Indian informatics in the eighties: the changing character of state involvement', *World Development*, **20**(1), 1-18.

Feldman, M. and A. Abuganim (2003), 'Development of the Israel high-tech sector 1995-1999: labour force and wages', (www.bankisrael.gov.il).

Friedberg, R. (2000), 'You can't take it with you? Immigrant assimilation and the profitability of human capital', *Journal of Labor Economics*, **18**, 21-251.

Friedberg, R. (2001), 'The impact of immigration on the Israeli labor market', *Quarterly Journal of Economics*, **116**, 1373-408.

Gandal, N., G. H. Hanson and M.J. Slaughter (2002), 'Technology, trade, and adjustment to immigration in Israel', *European Economic Review*, **48**, 403-28.

Gerschenkron, A. (1962), *Economic Backwardness in Historical Perspective*, Cambridge, Mass.:Harvard University Press.

Global Internet Ventures (2001), 'China overview of China's software industry' Internal document, Beijing, China.

Globes, (2002), 'NTT communications invests $1million in Interwise', 29 January, Globes: Israel's Business Arena, (www.globes.co.il).

Globes, (2001), 'Mercury interactive buys freshwater software for $147 million in cash', Globes: Israel's Business Arena, 22 May, (www.globes.co.il).

Gold, Thomas, Doug Guthrie and David Wank (eds) (2002), *Social Connections in China: Institutions, Culture, and the Changing Nature of Guanxi*, Cambridge, UK: Cambridge University Press.

Goldman, L. (March 18, 2002), 'A fortune in firewalls', *Forbes*, **169** (6).

Gordon, B. (2001), 'Start-ups prefer to register abroad', The Jerusalem Post 11 January, (www.jpost.co.il).

Guo, Chengzhong (2001), 'History of China's informatisation', *China Information Almanac*, Beijing.

Guochu, Zhang and Li Wenjun (2001), *International Mobility of China's Resources in Science and Technology and its Impact*, Organisation for Economic Cooperation and Development: COM/DSTI/DEELSA/RD (2001)1.

Guthrie, Doug (1999), *Dragon in a Three-Piece Suit: The Emergence of Capitalism in China*, Princeton, NJ: Princeton University Press.

Hausmann, R. and D. Rodrik (2002), 'Economic development as self-discovery', mimeo, Kennedy School of Government, Harvard University, Cambridge, Mass.

Heeks, R. (1996), *India's Software Industry: State Policy, Liberalisation and Industrial Development*, New Delhi: Sage Publications.

He, Zhongli (1997), 'Personnel Mobility in the Emerging Labour Market in the People's Republic of China', Master's Thesis, Acadia University, Canada.

Hermoni, O. (2003), 'Spending blue and white', The Marker: Haaretz Group 21 March, (www.themarker.com)

Hong Kong Trade Development Council (2001), 'WTO accession', Hong Kong,, http://www.tdctrade.com/alert/ch0103c.htm

Hoover's Online, (www.hoovers.com).

IDC (International Data Corporation) (2001), 'China Software Market Overview, 2000-2005', Beijing, http://www.idc.com.

IFC (International Finance Corporation) (2000), *China's Emerging Private Enterprises: Prospects for the New Century*, Washington, DC: IFC.

IMF (International Monetary Fund) (various years), *International Financial Statistics Yearbooks*, Washington DC.

Indian Software Industry Development (2001), 'International and national perspective'. *Economic and Political Weekly*, **XXXVI**(45), 4278-90.

*Industry Development* (2001), Beijing.

Israel Association of Electronics and Information Industries (www.iaei.org.il).

Israel Association of Software Houses, (www.iash.org.il).

Israel Central Bureau of Statistics, (www.cbs.gov.il)

Israel Venture Association (IVA) Yearbooks (multiple years 1997-2003). Giza Publishers, (www.ivc.co.il).

Jaffe, S. (2003), 'Israeli biotech' *The Scientist*, **17**(2), 40-1.

Ju, Dehua (2001), 'China's Budding Software Industry', *IEEE Software* May/June.

Kagami, M. and M. Tsuji (eds) (2002), *Digital Divide or Digital Jump*, Tokyo: Institute of Developing Economies.

Kalish, S. (1999), 'So what if they buy us?' The Jerusalem Post, 20 January, p.13.

Karny, Y. (1999), 'The biggest winner', Globes: Israel's Business Arena, 15 December, (www.globes.co.il).

Kattuman, P. and A. Bhattacharjee (2002), 'Software in India: Development Implications of Globalisation and the International Division of Labour', in Kagami and Tsuji (eds), *Digital Divide or Digital Jump*, Tokyo: Institute of Developing Economies

Khavul, S. (2001), 'Money and knowledge: sources of seed capital and the performance of high-technology start-ups', UMI reference #3002602 www.umi.com, Doctoral dissertation, Boston University, Boston.

Khavul, S. (2002), 'Liabilities of foreignness and the internationalization of high technology firms', mimeo, presented at Cambridge University Venture Capital and Law Forum, 8 March.

Khavul, S. (2003), 'The Emergence and Evolution of Israel's Software Industry', mimeo, London Business School, April.

Kumar, Nagesh (2001), 'Developing countries in international division of labour in software and service industries: lessons from Indian experience'. Background paper prepared for International Labour Organisation, *World Employment Report*, Geneva.

Lardy, Nicholas R. (2002), *Integrating China into the Global Economy* Washington, DC: Brookings.

Leonard, David (2002), 'Microsoft to invest $750 million in China's software industry', *Info World*, 28 June.

Lerner, M., S. Khavul and R. Hisrich (2005), 'Immigrants from the former Soviet Union as ethnic entrepreneurs in Israel: the long-term survival and performance in business ownership', in L.P.Dana (ed), *Handbook of Ethnic EntrepreneurshipResearch*, Edward Elgar (forthcoming).

Lis, A. (2003), 'Amdocs opens a Dublin develoment centre with Irish government's support', Globes: Israel's Business Arena, 12 Jan, (www.globes.co.il).

Lubman, Stanley, (2000), *Bird in a Cage: Legal Reform in China after Mao*, PaloAlto, CA:Stanford University Press.

Ma, Jessica (2002), 'The China Wave: a reality check', presented at Chinese Internet and Networking Association (CINA), Biltmore Hotel, Santa Clara CA, 23 February.

Meltz, N.M. (2001), 'Academic colleges: transforming higher education in Israel', *Higher Education Policy*, **14**(4), 343-59.

Meng, Q. and M. Li (2002), 'New Economy and ICT development in China', *Information Economics and Policy*, **14**, 275-95.

Meredith, Robyn (2003), 'Microsoft's Long March' *Forbes*, 17 February.

Ministry of Information Technology (1999a), *Information Technology Action Plan. Part I – Software*, New Delhi.

Ministry of Science and Technology of the People's Republic of China (1999b), *Information Technology Action Plan. Part II – New Policy Paradigm for the Hardware Industry*, New Delhi.

Ministry of Science and Technology of the People's Republic of China (1999c), *Information Technology Action Plan. Part III – Long Term National IT Policy*, New Delhi.

Ministry of Science and Technology of the People's Republic of China (2001), *Annual Report on the Development of High-tech Industry Development Zones*, Beijing.

Mishmari, A. (2002), 'The world was wrong, Compugen was right', Globes Israel Business Arena, 13 May, (www.globes.co.il).

Mountford, A. (1997), 'Can a brain drain be good for growth in the source economy?', *Journal of Development Economics*, **53** (2), 287-303.

Naroola, Gurmeet (2001), *The Entrepreneurial Connection*, New Delhi: McGraw Hill.

NASSCOM (2002a), *The IT Industry in India: Strategic Review 2002*, NASSCOM, New Delhi.

NASSCOM (2002b), *Indian IT Software and Services Directory 2002*, New Delhi.

NASSCOM (2003), *The IT Industry in India: Strategic Review 2003*, New Delhi.

NASSCOM (2003b), *Resource Centre: Facts and Figures*, New Delhi, http://www.nasscom.org/artdisplay.asp?cat_id=315

Naughton, Barry and Adam Segal (2001), 'Technology Development in the New Millenium: China in Search of a Workable Model' February 2001 revision of paper presented to meeting on Innovation and Crisis: Asian Technology at the Millenium, Cambridge, MA, 15-16 September 2000.

NSF (National Science Foundation) (1998),, Division of Science Resource Statistics *Statistical Profiles of Foreign Doctoral Students in Science and Engineering: Plans to Stay in the United States,* Arlington, VA, http://www.nsf.gov/sbe/srs/nsf99304/start.htm.

NSF (National Science Foundation) (2002), Division of Science Resources Statistics *Science and Engineering Indicators* Arlington, VA, April, Appendix Table 2-39 http://www.nsf.gov/sbe/srs/seind02/append/c2/at02-39.xls.

OECD (2001), *International Mobility of the Highly Skilled*, Paris.

OECD (2002), *Information Technology Outlook,* Paris.

Ohmae, Kenichi (2002), 'Profits and perils in China', *strategy+business*, **26**, first quarter, Booz Allen Hamilton Inc.

Patibandla, M. and B. Petersen (2002), 'Role of transnational corporations in the evolution of a high-tech industry: the case of India's software industry', *World Development*, **30** (9), 1561-77.

Pottinger, Matt (2003) 'Software firms face setback in China – proposed rules would force regional governments to use domestic vendors' *The Wall Street* Journal, 7 March, p B.5

Reynolds, P.D., S.M.Camp, W.D.Bygrave, E.Autio and M. Hay (2001), Global Entrepreneurship Monitor Executive Report, London Business School and Babson College.

Rock, E. B. (2002), 'Coming to America? Venture capital, corporate indentity and U.S. securities law', mimeo, presented at Cambridge University Venture Capital and Law Forum, 8 March.

Rodrik, D. (1994), Getting interventions right: how South Korea and Taiwan grew rich, NBER Working Paper 4964, Cambridge, Mass.

Rodrik, D. (1996), 'Coordination failures and government policy: A model with applications to East Asia and Eastern Europe', *Journal of International Economics*, **40**, 1-22.

Rodrik, D. (1997), 'The paradoxes of the successful state', *European Economic Review*, **41**, 411-42.

Saxenian, AnnaLee (1999), *Silicon Valley's New Immigrant Entrepreneurs*. Public Policy Institute of California, San Francisco, CA.

Saxenian, A-L. (2001), 'The Silicon Valley connection: transnational networks and regional development in Taiwan, China and India', mimeo, Stanford University.

Saxenian, A.-L. (2003), 'Government and Guanxi: the Chinese software industry in transition', mimeo, University of Berkeley and London Business School, April.

Saxenian, A-L with M. Yasuyuki, and Q. Xiaohong (2002), *Local and Global Networks: Immigrant Professionals in Silicon Valley*, Public Policy Institute of California. San Francisco.

Shleifer, A. and R. Vishny (1998), *The Grabbing Hand: Government Pathologies and their Cure*, Cambridge, Mass:. Harvard University Press.

Shwartz, J. (2002), 'Thousands of tech firms refuse to play the swan song', *USA Today*, 14 October.

SIIA-USITO Trade Mission to China (2002), *Rethinking China's Software Market*, March.

Software Technology Parks of India (2000), *Annual Report 1999-2000*. Delhi, www.stpi.soft.net.

Studwell, Joe (2002), *The China Dream: The Quest for the Last Great Untapped Market on Earth*, New York: Atlantic Monthly Press.

Subject Group on Knowledge-based Industries, Prime Minister's Council on Trade and Industry (2000), 'Recommendations of the task force on knowledge-based industries', Prime Minister's Office, New Delhi, http://www.nic.in/pmcouncils/reports/knowl/

Sugarman, M.L. (1998), 'Annus Mirabilis', The Jerusalem Report, 30-4, 3 August.

Suttmeier, Richard P. and Cong Cao (1999), 'China faces the new industrial revolution: achievement and uncertainty in the search for research and innovation strategies', *Asian Perspective*, **23**(3).

Teubal, M., G. Avnimeleh and A. Gayuego (2002), 'Company growth, acquisition, and access to complementary assets in Israel's data security Sector', mimeo, Hebrew University, Jerusalem.

Trajtenberg, M. (2000), 'R&D policy in Israel: an overview and reassessment', mimeo.

Trajtenberg, M. (2001), 'Innovation in Israel 1968 – 1997: comparative analysis using patent data', *Research Policy*, 363-89.

Tsao, (2001), 'Chinese labor market in the era of information technology, unpublished manuscript, Research Institute of Economy, Trade and Industry, Tokyo, Japan.

UFSoft website, 'About UFSoft', http://www.ufsoft.com.cn/english/about.asp.

United States Information Technology Office (USITO) Translation of State Council Document 181. 'Policies for Encouraging the Development of

Software Industry and Integrated Circuit Industry', http://www.usito.org/ index.pl/semiconductor_regulations.

USCIS (2003), Department of Homeland Security. Office of Management. Office of Immigration Statistics, *Yearbook of Immigration Statistics,* Washington DC, http://uscis.gov/graphics/shared/aboutus/statistics/ ybpage.htm.

US Embassy, Beijing (1996), 'China's science and technology policy for the twenty-first century – a view from the top, November. www.usembassy-china.org.cn/english/sandt/stpol1.htm

US Embassy, Beijing (2002), 'An evaluation of China's science and technology system and its impact on the research community', October, www.usembassy-china.org.cn/sandt/ST-Report.doc

USINS (1997-2002), United States Immigration and Naturalization Service, Bureau of Citizenship and Immigration Services, *Statistical Yearbooks 1996-2001,* Washington DC: http://www.immigration.gov/graphics/ aboutus/statistics/ybpave.htm.

Varma, Yograj (2001), 'Mega spenders: DQ-IDC survey', *Dataquest,* **30** November, 68-73.

Wank, David L. (1999), *Commodifying Communism: Business, Trust, and Politics in a Chinese City,* Cambridge UK: Cambridge University Press.

White, Steven, Jian Gao and Wei Zhang (2002), 'China's venture capital industry: institutional trajectories and system structure', International Conference on Financial Systems, Corporate Investment in Innovation and Venture Capital, Brussels, 7-8 November.

The World Bank (2002), *World Development Indicators,* Washington, DC: IBRD.

Yachin, D. (2000), 'MAMRAM' Globes: Israel's Business Arena, 8 November, (www.globes.co.il).

Yachin, D. (, 2002), 'Vernia: sending managers overseas logical under current circumstances', Globes: Israel's Business Arena, 13 March, (www.globes.co.il).

Yitshaki-Hagai, R. and S. Khavul (2003), 'Learning from firm closure in Israeli high technology: paper summary', In W. B. Bygrave et al., (eds). *Frontiers of Entrepreneurship Research,* p.48.

# Index